Perfectly Good Food

Also by Margaret Li and Irene Li

Double Awesome Chinese Food

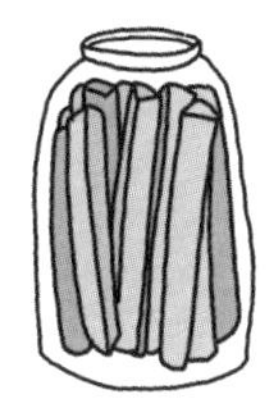

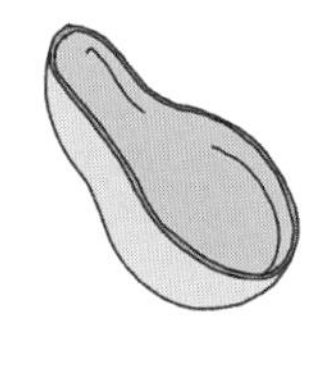

Perfectly Good Food

A Totally Achievable Zero Waste Approach to Home Cooking

Margaret Li AND **Irene Li**

Illustrations BY **Iris Gottlieb**

W. W. NORTON & COMPANY

Celebrating a Century of Independent Publishing

Printed in the United States of America
First Edition

For information about special discounts for bulk purchases, please contact W. W. Norton Special Sales at specialsales@wwnorton.com or 800-233-4830

Manufacturing by Versa Press
Book design by Allison Chi
Production manager: Lauren Abbate

ISBN: 978-0-393-54107-6 (pbk)

W. W. Norton & Company, Inc.
500 Fifth Avenue, New York, N.Y. 10110
www.wwnorton.com

W. W. Norton & Company Ltd.
15 Carlisle Street, London W1D 3BS

1 2 3 4 5 6 7 8 9 0

To Mom, *the OG zero-waster, who we might lovingly tease about rescuing every takeout sauce imaginable, but who has also inspired us with her dedicated food-saving habits and creative combinations, her boundless love of adventure, and her lifelong support of our every project. You are truly one-of-a-kind.* ***To Andy***, *without whom we would not be mei meis and might never have found our way into the industry. And* ***to Dad***, *who passed on a deep love for tinned fish and ordering Chinese food with abandon, we miss you every day.*

Contents

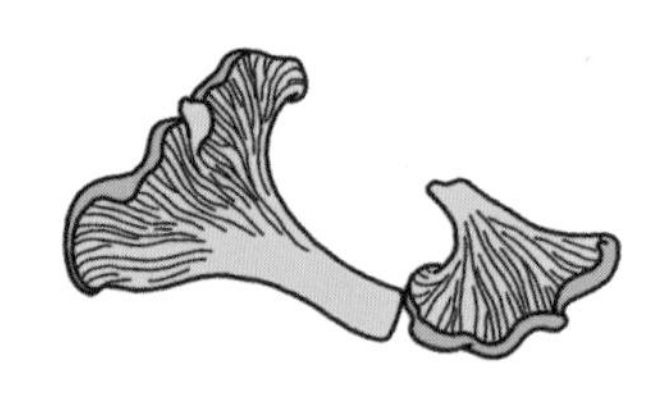

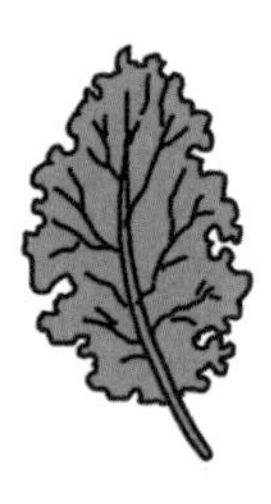

   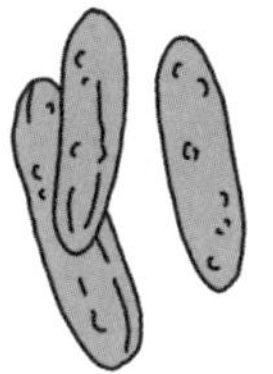 

*Hero Recipes are our favorite catchall recipes, easily adaptable to help you use up any combination of fruits and vegetables in your kitchen.

Getting Started

LET'S
DO
THIS!

You're in the checkout line at the supermarket, unloading your grocery selections onto the conveyor belt, and you've got big plans: tons of fresh herbs and greens, beautiful seasonal vegetables, bulk bags of fruit, a few protein choices, and so on. You survey what's before you and feel proud. You're an accomplished home cook and a savvy shopper, and you've got so much good eating in front of you.

A busy week later, and you're not feeling so accomplished anymore. You open your fridge and stare at the wilted kale and droopy cilantro, an old bag of carrots, and chicken thighs nearing their expiration date. The apples are wrinkled and those nice avocados you splurged on don't look so nice anymore. What to do? The old you would have thrown it all out and ordered pizza, but the new you bought this cookbook.

Together, we're going to cut down on your food waste and save you money. Turn these pages to look up the ingredients you have on hand, and you might soon be eating stir-fried kale with quick-pickled carrots and roast chicken pasta with cilantro-avocado pesto, while the aroma of apple crisp wafts out of your oven. You emerge victorious, every bit as proud as you were at the supermarket.

Everyone who buys or prepares food has found themselves in a similar situation, whether you cook for one person or feed a huge household. In your kitchen, you might have ingredients left over from specific recipes, ingredients you bought with great intentions but don't know how to use, and ingredients that have been ignored in your fridge for so long you're not sure you should eat them. We aim to solve all those problems and more. With ingredients laid out in an organized, easy-to-reference field guide, you can look up any item in your kitchen and find a way to use it up. We're here to help you stop wasting perfectly good food and get dinner on the table more efficiently and cheaply than ever before.

If you're sick of wasting food, you're not the only one. The average American household of four wastes about $30 in food every week. Over the course of a year, that's more than $1500 in the trash.[*] Multiply that by an entire country of homes and businesses, and we're wasting approximately $400 billion growing, processing, packaging, distributing, and selling food that no one is going to eat. That's almost 40 percent of the food produced in the United States going into the trash, and about one-third of food wasted around the globe.[†] At the same time, it's estimated that over 10 percent of American households are food insecure, meaning they don't have reliable access to enough food to be healthy and safe.[‡] How can we be throwing out so much food at the same time people are going hungry?

There's work to be done at every step of the food chain, from farms to supermarkets to restaurants, but a surprising amount of food waste happens at the individual level. Households are the largest source of food waste in most higher-income countries, with homes responsible for about 37 percent of the uneaten food in the United States.[§] You might think, who cares

*Natural Resources Defense Council, Save The Food (https://savethefood.com).

†EPA, From Farm to Kitchen: The Environmental Impacts of U.S. Food Waste (https://www.epa.gov/system/files/documents/2021-11/from-farm-to-kitchen-the-environmental-impacts-of-u.s.-food-waste_508-tagged.pdf).

‡USDA, Economic Research Service, using data from the December 2020 Current Population Survey Food Security Supplement, U.S. Census Bureau (https://www.ers.usda.gov/topics/food-nutrition-assistance/food-security-in-the-u-s/key-statistics-graphics/#foodsecure).

§ReFED (https://refed.org/action-areas/reshape-consumer-environments).

if I buy an entire package of baby spinach and throw it out? But not only is that your money and a meal getting wasted, but also all the resources like water, farmland, and labor that went into producing that spinach. In addition, food waste is the number one material thrown into landfills, where it rots and emits harmful levels of greenhouse gas. It's estimated that if global food waste were a country, it would have the third largest carbon footprint in the world, after only China and the US.* Once you realize how much food waste affects our environment, it's not surprising that climate research group Project Drawdown ranks reduced food waste as the most impactful solution toward addressing climate change.†

Even small shifts in behavior and thinking can help save your food and your money. Reducing food waste isn't an all-or-nothing goal. Maybe this week you'll toss your wilted spinach into an omelet instead of into the trash; maybe next year you'll be composting and making carrot top pesto.

Who are we and why listen to us? We're sisters Margaret—who goes by Mei—and Irene Li, and we've been running restaurants, writing cookbooks, and working toward a more sustainable food system for the past decade. We cofounded an award-winning food truck and restaurant that's now a dumpling company in Boston, so we're used to dealing with food waste on a large scale. Our restaurant, Mei Mei, was certified as a sustainable business and recognized for its efforts to cut down on food waste. In the notoriously difficult restaurant industry, successful businesses track their ingredient costs down to the tenth of a percentage point. If we waste food, we're throwing away money. In addition, we pay for our compost service by the pound, so we're incentivized to keep our food waste to a minimum. From cilantro stems in our curry to yellowed collard greens in our pesto, our cooks strategically use every edible part of a plant or an animal. Plus, we work closely with farmers and producers throughout the local food system, visiting farms and participating in community harvest days. We

*United Nations Environment Programme, 2021 Food Waste Index (https://www.unep.org/resources/report/unep-food-waste-index-report-2021).

†Project Drawdown, Table of Solutions (https://drawdown.org/solutions/table-of-solutions).

see the immense amount of love, care, and effort that goes into producing food. No one wants all that hard work to go to waste.

Our time in professional food service led to our first cookbook, *Double Awesome Chinese Food,* which included suggestions on how to eat sustainably and repurpose leftovers. While writing the book, we got to thinking about how flexible ingredient lists and accommodating recipe instructions can help people use up food they already have rather than rushing out to buy more. The experience inspired us to start Food Waste Feast, an online project to help home cooks stop wasting perfectly good food. Through social media videos and a website full of recipes and ideas, we've taught thousands of people how to save a head of lettuce or make a fridge-cleanout meal.

After years of running Food Waste Feast and a dumpling company, working with food nonprofits, and chatting with home cooks all over the world, we know we're not the only ones who hate throwing out food at home. We find joy and fun in figuring out how to utilize every ingredient in the kitchen. As people who love to cook and also love games, coming up with ways to combine random ingredients into a meal is as gratifying as solving a puzzle—and then we get to eat it! Much tastier than the Sunday crossword. Our hope is that this book will help you find enjoyment and satisfaction in eating well and living well, all the while saving food, saving money, and—little by little—helping to save the planet.

How to Use This Book

RECIPES OF ALL SHAPES AND SIZES: No matter where you are in your food waste journey, we want to help you learn how to use up your ingredients in the easiest and most delicious ways. We've divided the book into Vegetables, Fruits, and Proteins and Dairy, so you can quickly look up a full recipe or an inspiring idea for any ingredient hanging out in your fridge. If you're not looking to make dinner but still want to save something from the trash, each section also includes storage tips and quick projects to extend shelf life and give you new recipe components (goodbye wrinkly old garlic cloves, hellooooo garlic confit). And for moments when it seems you should probably throw something out—when herbs start to dry out, scallions get a bit slimy, or blueberries show a few spots of mold—we'll try to help you determine what's safe to eat, then give you a bunch of suggestions and recipes to get the most out of it. And for the people who manage to cook nearly everything they buy, there are tips for how to use the scraps and bits you might be throwing out, like strawberry tops or kale stems.

THEN A HERO COMES ALONG: The centerpiece of the vegetable and fruit sections of the book is a collection of super flexible Hero Recipes designed to help you rescue food and get dinner on the table with minimal drama and no extra trips to the grocery store. These "greatest hits"—stews, frittatas, bread puddings, pancakes, and more—are the backbone of mealtime in our own kitchens and are meant to be adjustable and adaptable. We love following recipes and making a dish look as perfect as a glossy magazine cover. But we'd argue it's just as much of a victory to design a meal using your own creativity while keeping perfectly good food out of the trash.

LIKE WITH LIKE: Cooking can be more fun off-script. Our ingredient categories are loosely based on texture, flavor profile, and functional role in recipes—aromatics together, dense root veggies together, and so on. This means that in most recipes, you can generally swap one item for another within that chapter, giving you almost infinite flexibility. As you get comfortable with a wider variety of ingredients, you'll develop your own sense for what substitutions work well for you and your pantry and fridge. And most importantly, what you like to eat!

VEGGIES TO THE FRONT: Much of the book consists of vegetables, which sadly get tossed in the trash more often than most of us would like. They're perishable, hard to buy in specific quantities, and sometimes challenging to use up, especially if they're unfamiliar or not very sexy—we're looking at you, CSA box full of kohlrabi! By contrast, home cooks are less likely to throw out meat and seafood, primarily because these ingredients cost more, freeze well, and are typically the feature ingredient in a dish. Environmentally minded cooks are also eating less meat these days, often choosing smaller portions or finding plant-based alternatives. As a result, we focus more on recipes where adding meat is a flexible option, with some extra attention toward using up leftover meat and seafood on page 292.

A Food Waste

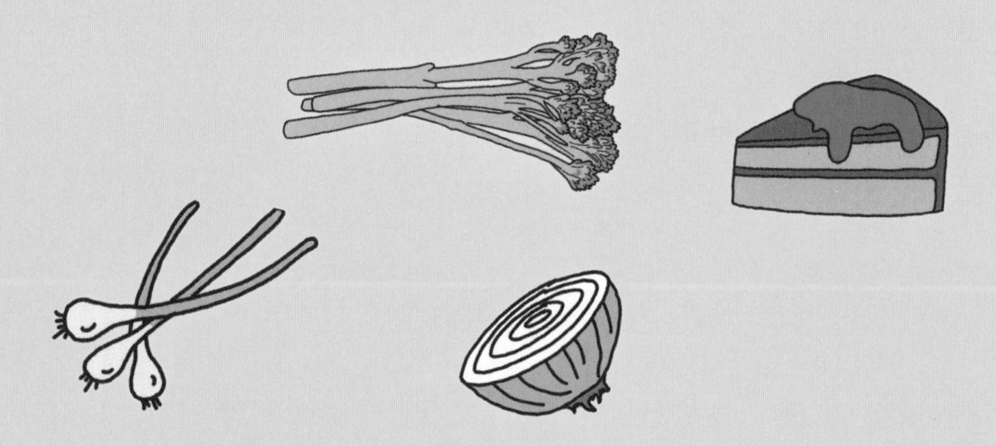

1. **Look for possibilities.** Your vegetables might be wilted or your leftovers might feel tired, but you can transform them into something delicious, we promise.

2. **Free your mind.** Let go of habitual thinking (yes, you can cook cucumber!) and adherence to notions of authenticity (go ahead and put cheese in a dumpling!) and you'll have so much more flexibility in using up your food.

3. **Trust your senses.** Your eyes and nose can generally tell you more about whether an ingredient is good to eat than a best-by date, especially on a pantry item. If your senses tell you it's fine, then it's probably OK to eat (by a healthy, non-immunocompromised adult). If your senses tell you it's gross, then get rid of it.

Feast Manifesto

4. **Make your kitchen work for you.** Arrange your fridge and freezer so you can see things—that way you'll be more likely to remember to eat them. Stock up on shelf-stable and frozen foods (canned beans! puff pastry!); they'll help you round out a meal to use up the fresh items.

5. **Be brave and be creative.** Try new combinations, substitute with what you have, and experiment with new flavors. Make it how you like it and you'll be more likely to eat it, and that's what matters.

6. **It's all good.** We believe in cutting down on food waste, but we also believe in not being too hard on yourself. Yes, the future of our planet is of the utmost importance, but it does not rest solely on your ability to eat all your broccoli leaves.

7. **Small steps are part of the journey.** Zero waste is an idea and an inspiration, not a state of being. Small mindful changes can make a big difference, and all of it adds up to saving more food, more money, and more landfill space.

Zero-Waste Kitchen Strategies

Some of the best ways to reduce food waste aren't recipes but systems or strategies to implement in your home. Don't let the idea of "zero waste" intimidate you—it's a useful concept, not a literal description. Whether you're just starting out or you're already whipping up smoothies and composting your scraps, there are always more ways for each of us to slowly minimize our food waste footprint.

Shop your kitchen first.

Before you go out and buy food, see what you have that needs to be eaten. You can save so much food and money (and time at the supermarket) by glancing at your pantry and refrigerator before heading out. You might get inspired by what you already have in your crisper drawer and how you might incorporate it into a new recipe. Or a quick peek in the freezer might remind you that you already have a frozen version of something you were about to buy fresh. FIFO (first in, first out), the accounting method used for inventory in the restaurant industry, is a good mantra to remember: Use any older ingredients before buying or opening newer versions and you'll cut down on redundant (and then often wasted) food. Whether you've got just a few items around or an already well-stocked fridge, a glance at your existing ingredients can prevent unnecessary purchases—and kick-start your cooking creativity.

Add some organizational systems to your fridge setup, like an Eat-Me-First Box.

We started using an Eat-Me-First Box at home after Irene set up a huge one in the walk-in fridge at our restaurant. It's a simple concept: Start keeping all the things that need to be eaten first in one container and store it close to eye level at the front of the refrigerator. Fill it with any partially used ingredients like the end of a cheese wedge, half-cut onion, or zested lemon, as well as ingredients that need to be used soon like browning apples or tomatoes. Then when you start cooking, you know where to reach first. Over time, you will get into the habit of transferring items to the box every time you rummage through the fridge. And while you're poking around in there, move items like highly perishable vegetables, older leftovers, or best-by-date-approaching meat to the front to remind yourself to eat them soon. Designating specific zones of the fridgc, such as a leftovers shelf or a kids snack area, can also help ensure food doesn't get lost in the back.

Save food with Smoothie and Stock Bags.

Setting up a system of resealable freezer bags for odds and ends will help you cut down on a significant amount of kitchen waste. We keep a Smoothie Bag in the freezer for uneaten fruit slices (if you have kids, you know what we're talking about) and fruit that's getting old but not rotten or moldy—think wrinkly berries, browning bananas (peel them first!), and overly soft peaches. Once it all gets blended up, the wrinkles and bruised spots won't matter. When you're ready to make a smoothie, turn to page 228.

The Kitchen Scrap Stock Bag is a home for chicken carcasses, rib bones, past-their-prime vegetables (like that last limp carrot), and a huge array of vegetable trimmings. Stash a bowl by the side of your cutting board, put scraps in as you prep veggies, then dump it all in the bag when you clean up. Pop the bag in the freezer and keep adding to it; once it's full, it's time to make homemade stock (page 34)!

View expiration dates with an open mind.

Did you know that the expiration dates we commonly see on packaged food (sell by, best by, use by, and best before) aren't based on any standardized system of food safety? Generally, these dates refer to when the manufacturer thinks the product will be "at its best quality," which can be days, if not weeks or even years from when a product is actually unsafe to eat. It's been estimated that nine out of ten Americans are regularly wasting edible food based on these ambiguous dates,* but you can basically ignore them when it comes to shelf-stable pantry goods (with the exception of baby formula). With refrigerated items, use the smell test and look for visible signs of deterioration rather than relying solely on the date on the package (paying special attention to products like raw cheeses or deli meats). If, after relying on your common sense (and other senses!) you still aren't sure what to do, follow our updated version of the old adage: "When [still] in doubt, throw it out."

*Natural Resources Defense Council (https://www.nrdc.org/resources/dating-game-how-confusing-food-date-labels-lead-food-waste-america).

Compost! It's not as hard as you think.

Why is composting food waste a big deal? Ideally, all food would be eaten (by a person or an animal), but if it's not going to be eaten, why does it matter whether it gets composted or thrown into landfill? It's a good question and a much more serious issue than many people realize.

Unfortunately, when food waste or other organic matter breaks down without oxygen (as when it's sealed inside a trash bag in a landfill), it releases methane. Methane is a greenhouse gas that contributes to global warming and can be more than eighty times more powerful than carbon dioxide when it comes to contributing to climate change.*

By contrast, when organic waste is composted under the right conditions, the process releases little to no methane. As Irene learned while becoming a Certified Master Composter, composting food waste produces "black gold"—it saves the nutrients and returns them to the soil to help grow more plants and food. It's basically magic.

Composting can be a challenge, especially for people with little access to outdoor space. If you're outdoorsy or into gardening, composting at home might be a natural fit. Mei considers herself moderately terrible at yard maintenance, so she pays for a compost company to pick up her food scraps every week. These industrial compost services can often take a wider variety of items than a home compost bin, such as meat bones, pizza boxes, and paper towels, allowing you to significantly reduce the amount you send to landfill. Irene lives in a third-floor apartment and is lucky enough to have access to curbside food waste collection. If you don't have local pickup services, other options include bringing your compost to a community garden, public waste facility, or farmers' market, or using an app like ShareWaste to find someone who will take your scraps. Freezing your food scraps can help minimize odors if you're worried about bad smells.

---

*Environmental Defense Fund (https://www.edf.org/climate/methane-crucial-opportunity-climate-fight).

FREEZE ANYTHING STICKY ON A SHEET PAN
(YOUR FINGERS MIGHT STICK TO IT WHEN FROZEN, WATCH OUT!)
LAY FREEZER BAGS FLAT – THE CONTENTS WILL BE THIN ENOUGH TO BREAK OFF JUST A HUNK OF IT
(ONE SLURP OF SOUP)
TOMATO SAUCE JAN
5/20
FREEZE LIQUIDS WITH ROOM TO EXPAND
FROM STUDIO APT
PUREE
TO ONE BEDROOM
SLICE BREAD BEFORE FREEZING
4/20
SLICE AND FREEZE THOSE TOO-MANY BANANAS
COFFEE CUBES: THAW FOR A PRE-BREWED CUP OR ADD TO COFFEE TO MAKE AN ICED CUP THAT ONLY GETS STRONGER THE MORE IT WARMS UP
EVEN CHILLIER THAN CHILLED WHITE WINE
THROW INTO SANGRIA THAT'LL BE SERVED A LITTLE LATER
LABEL
EVERYTHING

FREEZE YOUR FOOD!

Freezing is so important for reducing food waste that it deserves its own section. Your freezer is a magical tool that essentially stops the countdown clock on perishable ingredients. It's useful for many different types of food, from raw fruit to cooked meat, and will keep your food safe for months or even years. Here are a few freezer basics:

- Let cooked food cool at least to room temperature before freezing, or chill in the fridge before transferring to the freezer. An important thermodynamics tip from Irene: The thinner a layer of food, the faster it cools, and metal draws heat away faster than plastic. So spread your piping-hot jam on a sheet pan to cool, and it'll be freezer-ready in no time.
- Freeze leftovers within three or four days. The freezer stops the clock but can't turn it back, so make sure to get food into the freezer while it's still good to eat.
- To thaw frozen food, the best and safest method is transferring it to the refrigerator. However, it can take a day or sometimes more for items to thaw in the fridge, especially large cuts of meat. If you need to thaw something quickly, seal it tightly in a sturdy resealable plastic bag and place in cold water, changing the water every 20 to 30 minutes. Food thawed this way should be cooked right away and cannot be refrozen without cooking first. The microwave oven also defrosts quickly, but very unevenly, so we almost never use it for defrosting. If you defrost in the microwave, cook the food right away afterward. And of course, frozen cooked meals like sauces, soups, and stews can be reheated directly in a pot on the stove.
- Frozen food that has thawed in the fridge can be refrozen safely (even meat!), according to the USDA. Once it has been out of the fridge for 2 hours or so, however, it's best not to refreeze.

- Once something has been in the freezer for an indeterminate amount of time (What *is* that mysterious wrapped item shoved in the back?), whether to eat is more a question of quality than safety. As long as the freezer stays below 0 degrees, items will keep indefinitely, but after a certain point they will degrade in quality.

Speaking of quality, these freezer techniques will keep your food tastier and make preparation easier:

- When you're packaging up items for the freezer, press out as much air as possible. Air in the package allows room for moisture to leave the food and form ice crystals on the outside, also known as freezer burn. Freezer-burned food isn't unsafe, but it doesn't taste as good. Avoid it by making your food as airtight as possible, which may mean repackaging items from their store wrapping. For meat, wrap tightly in plastic wrap or freezer paper, then enclose with a layer of aluminum foil or a plastic bag with the air squeezed out. For fruits and vegetables, use a freezer bag (silicone and heavy-duty plastic are both tough and reusable) and make sure all the air is pushed out. Hard containers can be easier to stack, but they leave your food open to much more air exposure. One important exception to the "no air" rule: Liquids expand when frozen, so always leave extra space within a container, especially glass (we freeze in glass with the lids off, then screw the lids on tightly once the food is frozen).

- For anything remotely sticky, like soft berries or just-folded dumplings, lay them out on a sheet pan or plate to freeze for an hour or so before transferring to a resealable bag. This will help keep the items separate and prevent them from solidifying into a large, unidentifiable mound.

- Prep items so they're easy to use once defrosted. Peel bananas, cut bread into chunks, and puree tomatoes so they can be made directly into sauce or soup.

- Whenever possible, divide into smaller portions so you can thaw only what you need. Divide meat into meal-size portions. Ingredients you use in small quantities, like sauces, can be frozen in ice cube trays or muffin tins and then dumped into a resealable bag. Another option is to freeze sauces or purees in a flattened freezer bag, then break off a piece whenever you need it.
- Label, label, label! Despite best intentions, it's very easy to forget about something in the back of the freezer. You're much more likely to eat it if you know that bag of brown mush is actually that fantastic lentil soup you made last October. Permanent markers and painter's tape are a good, easily removable option to stick directly onto your containers. If you want to get really organized, put a whiteboard or pad of paper on your freezer door with a list of what's inside.
- Freezer burn can also happen with temperature fluctuations and over long periods of time, so try not to open your freezer too often or leave things in too long. Again, this is less a safety issue than a taste issue—as long as the freezer never completely loses power, last year's steak isn't harmful to eat. But the longer it stays in the fridge, the longer it has to degrade. Try for a freezer clean-out dinner every so often—it's faster than take-out and already paid for!
- Most vegetables will store and reheat better when blanched (cooked briefly in boiling water) before freezing. Blanching stops the enzymes that break down food, so blanching before freezing helps maintain color, texture, and nutrients. In addition, blanched vegetables are much easier to use in a dish once thawed—most can go directly into a Hero Recipe.

  Fill a large pot with enough water to cover your vegetables and add salt. Bring to a boil over high heat while you chop your ingredients into roughly equal chunks. If using hearty greens, or another ingredient with different parts like stems and leaves, separate into two piles.

Once the water boils, add your ingredients, staggering if necessary so longer-cooking parts like stems go into the water before leaves. Use a spoon or spatula to make sure everything is submerged and cook until just tender and brightly colored (see the guidelines below). Once cooked, strain in a colander and run under cold water for about 30 seconds or place in an ice bath. Once the vegetables are cool, drain well. For leafy greens, use your hands to press out as much water as possible in the colander or rolled in a clean dish towel. Store in a resealable bag with the air pressed out (more air means more chance of freezer burn) and use in any of the Hero Recipes.

Here is a rough guide to blanching, but keep in mind that the timing will vary depending on the size and shape of your vegetable pieces:

Light leafy greens	30 seconds—1 minute
Hearty greens	Leaves: 1–3 minutes, Stems: 2–4 minutes
Broccoli and friends (cauliflower, Brussels sprouts, etc.)	3–5 minutes
Summer vegetables	Squash and peppers: 2 minutes; Corn and okra: 3–4 minutes
Roots, tubers, and winter squash	3–5 minutes

Stocking Your Kitchen

Putting flexible and creative meals together is all about having the right building blocks. We rely heavily on a few freezer and pantry items to help create food-rescuing dishes quickly and easily. These all keep for a long time in the cupboard or freezer or, in the case of eggs, in the fridge for much longer than you think (we've never once encountered a rotten egg, and our restaurant used to buy more than two thousand eggs each week). As long as you've got a few of these in regular rotation, there will always be a delicious dish within reach.

Refrigerator

EGGS: Eggs are versatile for sweet and savory dishes and cleaning out the fridge with a Sheet Pan Frittata (page 308), quiche, or Baked Eggs (page 104). We always use large eggs, and recommend organic and/or pasture-raised, or the best you can afford.

Fridge or freezer

PUFF PASTRY AND PIE CRUST: If you have pastry in the house, you can have a casual fruit galette (page 241) or dinner party–worthy savory tart (see note on page 72) on the table within the hour.

PIZZA DOUGH: Once risen, pizza dough freezes well and just needs to be thawed before using. Got some food that needs to be used up? Put it on a pizza!

Pantry

COCONUT MILK (IDEALLY UNSWEETENED AND FULL-FAT): Coconut Milk can help you use up almost any vegetable or meat in Cream-of-Anything Soup (page 48), Toss-in-Any-Vegetable Stew (page 55), or Quick Cauliflower and Chicken Curry (page 187), and more.

DRIED PASTA: You can make a simple and satisfying meal with any type of pasta—see our Anything-in-the-Kitchen Pasta (page 68). Enough said.

RICE: Fried rice can be so much more than frozen peas and diced carrots. Toss in new vegetables, stir in any protein, and make the eggs any way you like. Turn to our Fridge-Cleanout Fried Rice (page 62)—time to get creative!

WHOLE GRAINS: If you're looking to change up your pasta game or eat fewer refined flours, look to grains such as farro or quinoa to bulk up stews and soups, or to top with various ingredients for a grain bowl or mix into a Grain Salad (page 162).

CANNED OR DRIED BEANS: Beans are useful for everything from quick party dips (see our Any-Bean Dip on page 306) to an instant protein add-on for pasta or grain bowls to an entire last-minute dinner built around the beans of your choice (Baked Beans with Whatever You Have, page 309).

CANNED TOMATOES: Make instant tomato sauce, stew, soup, and so much more.

STOCK PASTE OR CUBES: Ideally we'd have homemade Kitchen Scrap Stock (page 34) on hand at all times, but sometimes it just isn't in the cards. We love Better Than Bouillon concentrated stock paste for an instant alternative.

Our Favorite Cooking Ingredients

OILS: We store a basic extra-virgin olive oil near the stove for cooking, as well as a neutral oil like canola or grapeseed for dishes requiring higher heat. Then we keep fancier extra-virgin olive oil and toasted sesame oil on hand for drizzling and dressings, stored in the pantry away from heat and light for better preservation.

ACIDS: We always stock a few milder, less expensive vinegars like rice or apple cider vinegar for cooking and pickling, reserving more flavorful options like balsamic or sherry vinegar for last-minute drizzling. Lemons and limes last in the fridge for ages and add brightness to just about any dish (don't forget to use or freeze the zest!).

SWEETENERS: Our sweetener of choice is maple syrup (keep it in the fridge once opened or it can grow mold, as we learned the hard way), and we use it in place of sugar in many sweet and savory dishes. Honey and agave are good alternatives, and we also keep brown and white sugar around for baking, sealed tight in lidded jars to prevent them from becoming rock-hard lumps.

AROMATICS: Garlic and onions (we tend to buy yellow for cooking and red for pickles, but will use whatever is available) are absolute essentials; ginger and scallions come in a close second. To keep the latter two around longer, pop the ginger in the freezer and you can still grate it directly into dishes, and stick scallion roots in a glass of water to regrow on your windowsill.

SEASONINGS: The value of kosher salt to every dish made in our kitchens cannot be overestimated (we use Diamond Crystal brand, which sprinkles nicely and is less salty than Morton, so use about half the salt specified if using Morton). We also adore large flakes of Maldon sea salt for last-minute seasoning at the table. Our other go-to spices include black pepper (freshly ground), chili flakes of some kind, ground turmeric, cumin, and Sichuan peppercorns. Find the ones you like best and buy in small quantities so you can get good-quality, well-sourced products and they don't get neglected in your spice cupboard for more than a year. They won't go *bad* exactly, but the taste can turn flat and musty.

FLAVOR AND TEXTURE BOOSTERS: The more you cook, the more you'll reach for certain ingredients to add depth and spark your taste buds. We're obsessive buyers of items like soy sauce, fish sauce, anchovies, Parmesan, miso, capers, olives, and pickles. Our Chinese heritage means that Shaoxing wine, black vinegar, and chili crisp are essential staples (buy them online or at any Asian market), so you'll find those flavors in a number of recipes. Soy sauce in particular is such a valuable source of umami—we both buy Kikkoman by the jug and decant it into squirt bottles to be kept by the stove (tamari and coconut aminos are good substitutes if you can't have soy sauce for any reason). Curate your own selection of favorites and you can piece together a magnificent meal with whatever needs to be used up.

Useful Kitchen Equipment

No-waste cooking doesn't require any specialized tools or fancy kitchen equipment. But it's worth investing in a few items that help get the job done faster and easier, making you more likely to actually cook and eat the food you've got.

THE BASICS: At the bare minimum, you'll want to have a sharp, good-quality chef's knife and a solid, stable cutting board; a skillet for which you have a lid (or something that can serve as a lid); a glass or metal baking dish; a Dutch oven or other large pot with a lid; and mixing bowls of various sizes. You'll also need cooking spoons, tongs, spatulas, a whisk, and a ladle.

RIMMED BAKING SHEETS: Also known as sheet pans, these kitchen workhorses are useful for everything from roasting veggies to laying out cut fruit for freezing. We particularly love our 9 x 13-inch baking sheet (a quarter sheet pan in restaurant lingo)—its smaller size is ideal for making a Sheet Pan Frittata (page 308) or fitting into an already packed freezer. Silicone baking mats are a good reusable alternative to parchment paper for lining your baking sheets.

CUTTING AND PROCESSING TOOLS: Mandolines, rasp graters (often sold under the brand name Microplane), and box graters are all excellent for general prepping as well as thinly slicing pickles, grating cheese, and mincing garlic and ginger into paste. A food processor isn't an absolute must except for making nut butters, but it will save you quite a lot of tedious knife work when it comes to making sauces, salsas, and more.

A GOOD BLENDER: We own both a high-speed blender and an immersion blender, also known as a stick blender or hand blender. The high-speed one is ideal for mixing up a smoothie (page 228) or a Fresh Tomato Bloody Mary (page 106) or even Banana Ice Cream (page 267). The immersion blender is convenient for blending soups in the pot as well as making quick sauces and dressings in small amounts.

OUR FAVORITE KITCHEN TOOLS

STACKS OF CLEAR CONTAINERS: We use these for storing leftovers, fridge pickles, cooked grains, dressings, and more. Buy reusable glass food storage containers (we like Pyrex) and/or save assorted pickle and jam jars—glass is better for the environment and safer for microwaving leftovers. We also wash and save plastic deli containers and takeout containers; it's a great way to repurpose what would otherwise be a single-use item.

PERMANENT MARKERS AND EASILY REMOVABLE PAINTER'S TAPE: You'll need these or something similar for labeling containers and bags so you don't have to guess what that brown liquid is after 6 months in the freezer. Spiced cider? Beef stock? Now you know!

REUSABLE STORAGE BAGS: Often made of silicone, these are great for freezing food and generally minimizing plastic bag usage, although sturdy zip-top plastic freezer bags are also easy to wash and reuse. Freeze anything wet, like a sauce or paste, with the bag flat so the food freezes in a flat slab. This makes frozen bags easier to stack and store, and also allows you to break off a corner of frozen sauce so you don't have to defrost the whole bag.

BREATHABLE BAGS OR WRAPS: Beeswax paper and reusable produce bags (we love Vejibags) can help extend the life of your produce by allowing fruits and vegetables to maintain the ideal humidity without trapping gas or too much moisture. Certain fruits, such as apples, bananas, and tomatoes, emit a natural gas called ethylene that speeds the ripening process for fruits and vegetables that are sensitive to it (if you've ever heard someone say to put an apple in a bag with an avocado to help it ripen faster, that's why!). Breathable storage options let the gas out and keep produce from spoiling too quickly; storing ethylene-releasing produce separate from ethylene-sensitive produce helps too. And don't forget to take advantage of your refrigerator drawer design—the lower-humidity crisper drawer lets ethylene escape so fruits last longer, while the higher-humidity drawer helps vegetables stay crisp and sprightly instead of dry and droopy.

ICE CUBE TRAYS: These are helpful for freezing small amounts of sauce, chopped herbs in oil, tomato paste, and extra liquids like leftover coffee or the last of a bottle of wine for your next batch of Freewheeling Berry Sangria (page 256). Once the item is frozen, we transfer the cubes to labeled resealable bags. We use silicone trays meant for oversized cocktail cubes; not only are they more flexible than plastic molds, you can bake silicone trays in a 350-degree oven for an hour to remove any residual food flavors.

Vegetabl
getables V
les Veget
getables V
Vegetabl
getables V

Welcome to the **Vegetables** section, a place you can turn to when you find yourself with lots of vegetables and no plans for dinner. Flip directly to a category when you've got something specific to use up—look at **Alliums and Aromatics** for ideas for rescuing wrinkly scallions, or the **Roots, Tubers, and Winter Squash** pages for what to do with the last of the bag of potatoes. And for those times when you have a full crisper drawer and need a way to use up a slew of ingredients, we invite you to peruse the **Hero Recipes**. These mix-and-match recipes, often more of a template than a specific set of instructions, are meant to be adapted based on what *you* have in your kitchen. Start in the front of the Hero Recipes if you're on the hunt for a side dish or a lighter option, flip toward the back for the heartier, dinner-in-one-pan type of meals.

Kitchen Scrap Stock

We love the feeling of making something from what feels like nothing. For free! As in, we used to throw out onion skins, leek ends, and herb stems but now transform them into a highly useful item that might cost upwards of five dollars at the grocery store.

Scrap stock is more of a process than a recipe, given that you'll likely have to build up to it by saving scraps over the course of multiple cooking sessions. Stash a sturdy resealable bag in the freezer and every time you prep vegetables, add scraps like the following:

- **skins and ends of alliums, such as onions, shallots, garlic, scallions, and leeks**
- **corncobs**
- **ends and peels of root vegetables, like carrots, parsnips, potatoes, and beets**
- **ends and leaves or fronds of stalks like celery, fennel, and asparagus**
- **mushroom stems**
- **herb stems**
- **pepper cores**
- **any whole vegetable versions of the above that are wilted but not yet spoiled or moldy (give them a rough chop before you dump them into the bag)**
- **other flavor enhancers: Parmesan rinds or seaweed, such as kombu**

Members of the Brassica family (cabbage, Brussels sprouts, broccoli, cauliflower, etc.) can make your stock bitter, so we compost those, or add them only in moderation. Same goes for too many onion skins.

If you eat meat, save the bones from chicken carcasses or beef roasts (raw or salvaged from the dinner table), or supplement with cheap bones like chicken wings and necks and stash them in the bag alongside your veggie scraps to make meat stock.

(continues)

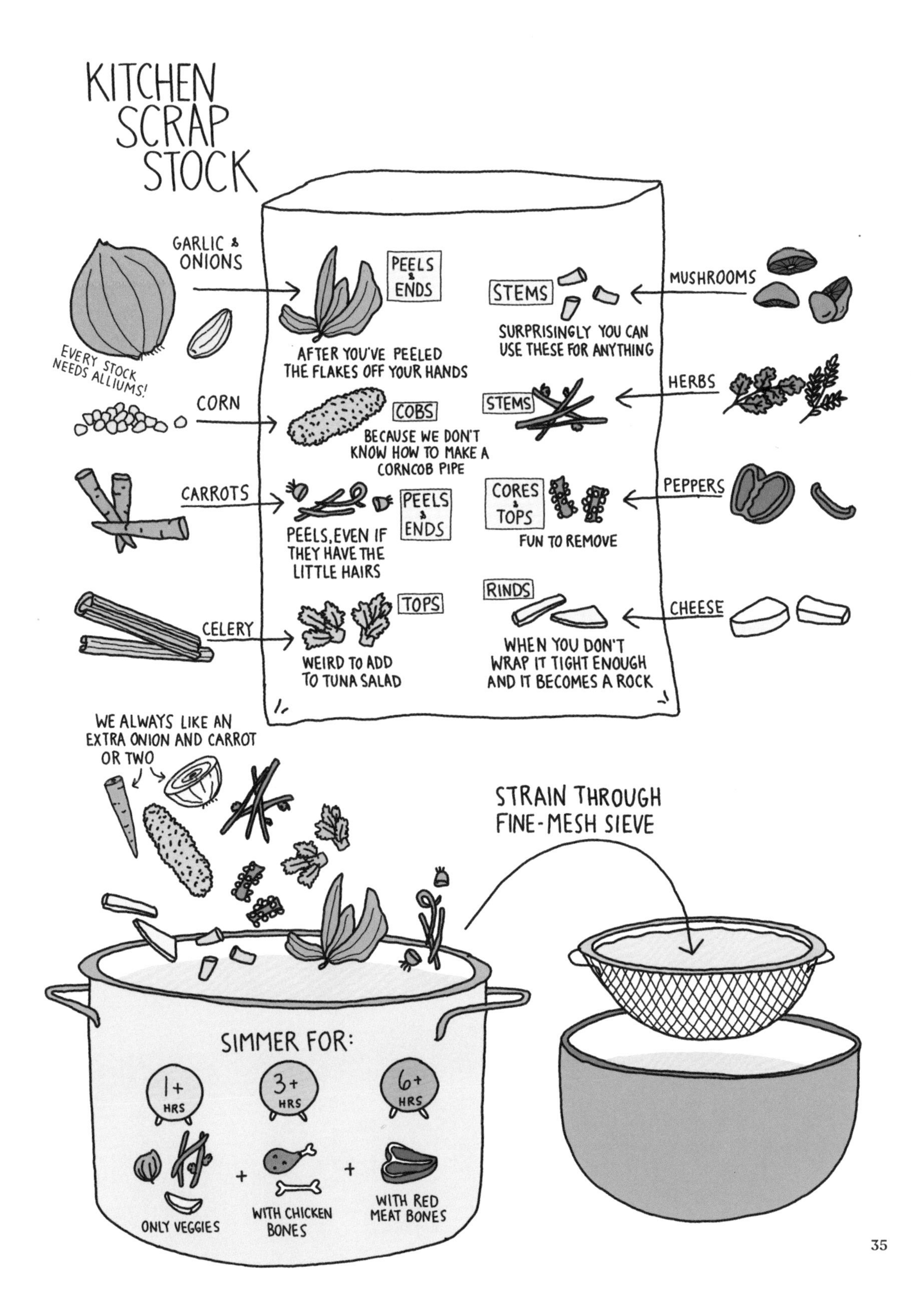
KITCHEN SCRAP STOCK
GARLIC & ONIONS
PEELS & ENDS
AFTER YOU'VE PEELED THE FLAKES OFF YOUR HANDS
EVERY STOCK NEEDS ALLIUMS!
MUSHROOMS
STEMS
SURPRISINGLY YOU CAN USE THESE FOR ANYTHING
CORN
COBS
BECAUSE WE DON'T KNOW HOW TO MAKE A CORNCOB PIPE
HERBS
STEMS
CARROTS
PEELS & ENDS
PEELS, EVEN IF THEY HAVE THE LITTLE HAIRS
PEPPERS
CORES & TOPS
FUN TO REMOVE
CELERY
TOPS
WEIRD TO ADD TO TUNA SALAD
CHEESE
RINDS
WHEN YOU DON'T WRAP IT TIGHT ENOUGH AND IT BECOMES A ROCK
WE ALWAYS LIKE AN EXTRA ONION AND CARROT OR TWO
STRAIN THROUGH FINE-MESH SIEVE
SIMMER FOR:
1+ HRS
3+ HRS
6+ HRS
ONLY VEGGIES
+
WITH CHICKEN BONES
+
WITH RED MEAT BONES

Once you fill your bag, it's time to make stock! We add extra aromatics to deepen and even out the flavor, such as a quartered onion or two (no need to peel), a few smashed garlic cloves, and some carrots or celery stalks. You can take the optional step of roasting your vegetables and/or bones (toss everything in a bit of oil first) at 450 degrees for half an hour or so to deepen the flavor.

Put all your scraps and vegetables in a large pot and add water until everything starts to float. Bring to a boil over high heat, then reduce to a simmer. If you're using meat, skim the surface of any foam. Simmer for 30 to 45 minutes at a minimum, but ideally 2 to 3 hours. If you're using meat bones and want to extract all the collagen and minerals, simmer for at least 3 hours for poultry bones and as long as 6 to 10 hours for pork, beef, or lamb bones (a pressure cooker is a great time-saver when it comes to making stock—check your cooker's instructions for information on timing).

Strain the stock through a fine-mesh sieve or colander lined with cheesecloth or a kitchen towel. Store in an airtight container in the fridge (label and date highly recommended) for about a week. If it's been hanging out for a while and you have no immediate cooking plans, transfer it to the freezer, ideally portioned into small containers so you only have to thaw what you need (and it will defrost much faster).

Pickle It!

When you've got so much produce that you're shoving bags into your fridge like the overhead compartment on a packed airplane, think pickles. When you've got just a few lonely vegetables (or even fruits!) that you've ignored for weeks, think pickles. Now, if you're up for canning and long-term storage, good for you. You'll have beautiful jars of fresh produce in your pantry through a time-honored tradition of preserving and canning. But this recipe is all about quick pickles that can be put together in no time at all and then live in the refrigerator for a month or so, maybe more. Pickled bits add a welcome pop of brightness and acid to just about every meal—sandwiches, tacos, savory pancakes, the list goes on.

There are infinite combinations for pickle brine out there, varying your types of vinegar, spices, herbs, and ratios. We'll give you a starting point, then you can adjust depending on how tangy you like your pickles and what you have in the kitchen. We usually use unseasoned rice vinegar or apple cider vinegar—they're relatively neutral and inexpensive—but you can use what you like, as long as you keep the color and flavor in mind. We start with a very basic brine that we call the 1:1:1:1 ratio.

1 cup hot water
1 cup vinegar, ideally something clear and mild
1 tablespoon kosher salt
1 tablespoon sugar
Vegetables, for pickling

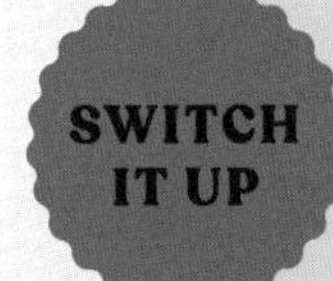

- Experiment with fresh add-ins like smashed garlic cloves; slices of ginger; rosemary, thyme, or dill sprigs; or strips of citrus zest.
- Optional dried add-ins include peppercorns of any kind; mustard, coriander, or caraway seeds; dried chiles or chili flakes; 1 teaspoon ground turmeric or paprika.

(continues)

In a large bowl, mix the hot water, vinegar, salt, and sugar until the salt and sugar dissolve, then taste. If it's too tangy, add more water. If it's not tangy enough, add more vinegar. If you like a sweeter pickle, stir in more sugar. You get the idea.

Cut your vegetables into bite-size pieces (or keep them whole if you think it looks nicer). Hard vegetables like beets and carrots will be easier to eat in thin slices or shreds; soft vegetables like cucumbers and zucchini can be kept in larger pieces or cut into spears, rounds, or chunks. Dump them into a quart container and fill to the top with the brine. (This amount usually works, but it will depend on the size, shape, and amount of what you're pickling, so be flexible. The nice thing about a ratio is that it can easily be scaled up or down depending on how much you have to pickle.) If you're doing multiple vegetables, you can pile them into one container or split them among smaller jars, up to you.

Sometimes we stop here and just keep it simple. Other times we raid the fridge and spice drawer and see what might be good for flavoring. See what you have from our list of optional add-ins or what else looks good in your kitchen.

Let the pickles sit at room temperature until cool, then transfer to the fridge. We try to give them at least a day for the flavors to develop, but we've been known to sneak some after an hour or so in a pickle emergency.

NO-WASTE TIPS

- If you have a small amount of veggies to use up, like a quarter onion or half a carrot, make virtually instantaneous pickles to eat right away. Slice thinly, top with a pinch each of salt and sugar, cover with a tablespoon or two of vinegar, and let sit while you make the rest of your meal.
- You can reuse the existing brine from a store-bought pickle jar! Once you're done with the pickles, briefly boil the brine, then use it to pickle another jar of vegetables.

PICKLING BASICS

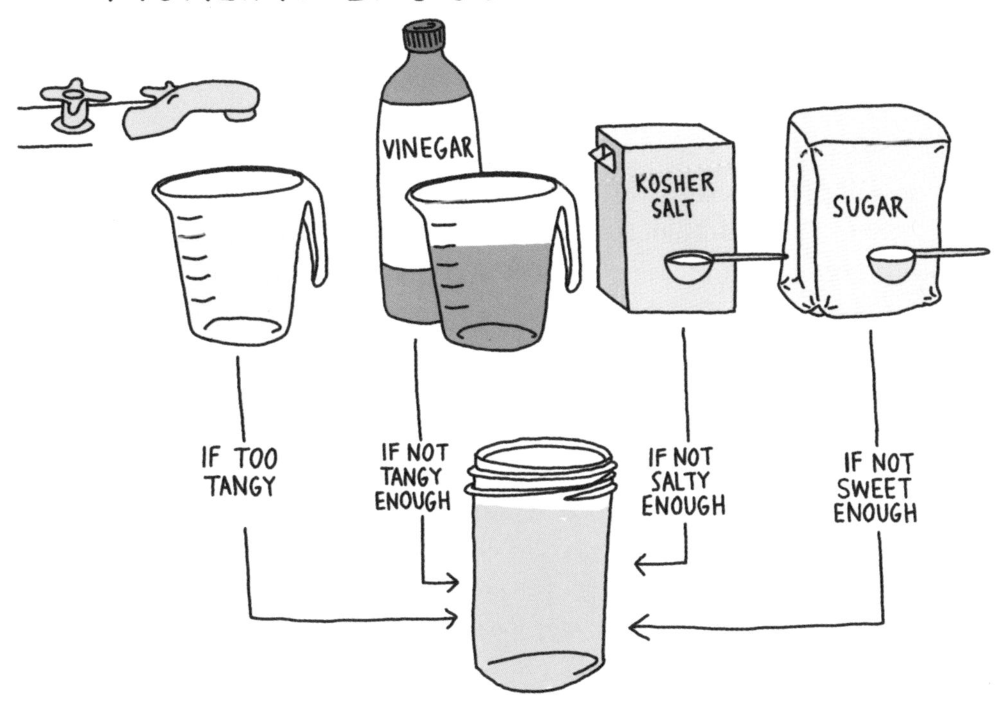

Slow-Poached Vegetables in Olive Oil

Cooking food at a low temperature in fat to preserve it for longer—often called confit—always seemed to us like a fancy thing one does only with duck legs and copious amounts of duck fat. Let's be real—who has either of those items around? However, we've recently been confit-ing every vegetable we can find—asparagus, fennel, squash, you name it—in a warm bath of olive oil. It's very satisfyingly hands-off: After a bit of prep work, you pop your vegetables into a low-heat oven and ignore them for at least an hour. Once cooked, they last for ages in the fridge, topped with a protective layer of solidified olive oil. Pull them out anytime to warm up and toss on a salad, or sear in a pan for a fantastic meal in just a few minutes. And don't let that flavorful oil go to waste; scoop out a spoonful to fry an omelet, sear a steak, or even confit more vegetables. It's the gift that keeps on giving.

Vegetables you want to confit, such as 1 bunch asparagus, 1 head broccoli, 1 butternut squash, or 1 bunch celery (Keep in mind that you can combine veggies of relatively similar tenderness.)

A good amount of extra-virgin olive oil (Exactly how much will depend on the amount of veggies you're trying to confit. Conventional wisdom would have you submerge the vegetables completely in olive oil, but we don't bother. Olive oil is expensive, plus most vegetables will collapse into the oil as they cook so they end up covered eventually. We buy relatively inexpensive olive oil in bulk primarily for this reason—this isn't the time to use your fancy oil.)

Kosher salt and freshly ground black pepper

Not essential, but really very lovely: sliced lemons, garlic cloves still in their skins, anchovies, chili flakes, peppercorns, sturdy herb sprigs (If you're going to eat the confit vegetables on their own, we would argue that the lemons are essential.)

Heat the oven to 300 degrees.

While the oven heats, trim your vegetables to remove any inedible bits (woody asparagus ends for your Kitchen Scrap Stock Bag, broccoli stalk peels for the compost) and cut into bite-size chunks if desired. If we're shooting for a presentation-worthy dish, we leave the vegetables whole or in large pieces (full asparagus spears, carrots halved lengthwise, long celery stalks). But if we're just cooking for family, we cut everything into bite-size pieces so everything is easier to eat and reheat.

Season generously with salt and pepper and place in a small baking dish. Pick a dish that fits your vegetables well, so there isn't a lot of extra space to fill with olive oil. One layer is ideal, with a little overlap, but just wedge in extra bits as best as you can; the parts that don't get submerged will still cook through.

Pour in enough olive oil so your vegetables are roughly three-quarters submerged. Add any lemons, garlic, anchovies, or herbs and spices, cover with a lid or aluminum foil, and place in the oven. Bake until tender, 60 to 90 minutes, or more if you've added any sturdier vegetables. Taste and season with more salt and pepper before serving.

MAKE IT A MEAL

Confit vegetables are so handy to have in the fridge for almost immediate eating. Pull the vegetables out of the cold olive oil to put on tacos, stir into pasta sauce, or fold into an omelet. Put them on top of leftover rice or grains and microwave for an instant meal.

Mix-and-Match Slaw Party

Serves 4 to 6 as a side

Got a bunch of fresh vegetables to use up? Toss them all together in a bright and colorful slaw with hearty greens like cabbage or collards and something crunchy like carrots or fennel. The addition of a sweet-tart apple helps temper any bitter or earthy flavors from the other veggies. The other unusual aspect of this slaw is the nutty tahini dressing, which manages to straddle the line between creamy mayo-based slaws and super tart vinegary slaws—either of which you could choose instead if you prefer. We also like this with raw beets, thinly sliced celery, chopped toasted nuts or sesame seeds, any soft fresh herbs such as parsley or cilantro, and of course we'll never say no to a lavish sprinkling of feta cheese.

4 cups shredded or thinly sliced hearty greens, such as collards or cabbage (reserve any stems for another use)

1 cup grated or thinly sliced crunchy vegetables, such as 2 medium carrots or 1 fennel bulb

1 large apple, such as Honeycrisp, Pink Lady, or Fuji, cored and grated or thinly sliced

2 scallions, thinly sliced on the diagonal (optional)

LEMONY TAHINI DRESSING

¼ cup tahini

3 tablespoons lemon juice or apple cider vinegar (or a combination of the two, or another relatively neutral acid of your choice)

3 tablespoons water

1 tablespoon extra-virgin olive oil

Squirt of honey or maple syrup

Pinch kosher salt

Toss the greens, vegetables, apple, and scallions (if using) together in a large bowl. To make the dressing, put all the ingredients in a medium bowl and whisk until smooth. Taste and adjust as needed, as tahini brands can vary widely in thickness and taste. Pour about half the dressing over the slaw and toss to combine, then add more dressing as necessary—each bite of the slaw should be nicely coated in sauce without being gloppy or wet. With sturdier greens and crunchy vegetables, the slaw can keep in a sealed container in the fridge for a day or two. If the vegetables start to soften too much for the slaw to be good on its own, tuck it into a burger or stuff it into a taco.

Freestyle Vegetable Summer Rolls

Makes about 12 rolls

These light, crunchy, Vietnamese-style rolls are ideal for using up an assortment of vegetables. (Irene likes to put meat in them too; you can freestyle in any direction you like.) Our only must-have is leafy greens and herbs like mint and cilantro, both for brightness and to fill out the rolls so they aren't lumpy, deflated pillows. If you've never rolled with rice paper before, your first attempts may turn out extremely un-cylindrical, but as Mei tells her six-year-old, they will still taste excellent, especially dipped in Nut Butter Sauce (page 318).

NOTE: *This recipe usually makes about a dozen rolls, but we never count—just keep rolling until you're out of filling.*

12 (10-inch) rice paper wrappers, or more as needed

2 cups thinly sliced or shredded crunchy vegetables, such as carrots, bell peppers, or cucumbers (this is a great time to use a mandoline, spiralizer, or box grater)

2 cups leafy greens or herbs, such as lettuce, kale, spinach, cilantro, mint, or basil, torn into palm-size pieces if large

1 cup sliced tofu, scrambled egg, shrimp, or cooked chicken (optional)

3 ounces rice vermicelli, cooked and drained, or another leftover noodle of your choice (optional)

Nut Butter Sauce (page 318) or other dipping sauce, for serving

---

Set up all your ingredients on a flat surface with some room to work, like a clean cutting board. Fill a wide bowl that fits your wrappers (we like to use a pie tin) with an inch or two of very warm water (not too hot, as you'll be sticking your fingers in often).

To make each roll, place a rice paper wrapper in the bowl and let sit for 5 to 10 seconds, until the wrapper softens and begins to crumple in on itself like a piece of fabric. Lift it out carefully, letting any excess water drip back into the bowl. Place the wrapper on your work surface, trying to keep it flat, and unfold any spots that may have stuck together.

The next part is basically a free-form exercise—gather about ⅓ cup of fillings of your choice and place them in a little horizontal rectangle on the bottom third of the rice paper. Fold up the bottom edge of the rice paper and tuck the vegetables in tightly, then fold over both sides, and continue to roll up toward the top edge, like a mini burrito. Repeat until you've used up all your ingredients.

Serve right away with your dipping sauce of choice, or refrigerate in a covered container with a damp towel to keep the rolls from drying out.

Crisp and Crunchy Noodle Salad

Serves 3 to 4 as a side or 2 as a hearty lunch

This flexible noodle salad is ideal for using up odds and ends of raw vegetables (as long as they're not too limp or wilted). Cut everything into thin strips or shreds to make it easy to swirl everything together on a fork so you'll get some cool crisp vegetables as well as chewy noodles in every bite. You could toss in cooked vegetables too—don't let us stop you—but we find the textures of the raw summer veggies are what makes this dish so satisfying. As for the soy-miso dressing, go wild with what you have in your pantry. Add grated ginger or minced shallot or onion. Add some funk and depth with a splash of fish sauce, or spice it up with sriracha, hot sauce, or Scrap Chili Oil (page 86). You'll always want to adjust a dressing like this to taste, given that everyone has their preference on the sweet-savory-tangy scale. Or, if you like, you can swap it out for Whatever-You've-Got Nut Sauce (page 322).

NOTE: *If you're taking the salad to a picnic or not eating it right away, dress it right before eating so your greens don't get too soggy.*

Kosher salt

8 ounces noodles of your choice, such as soba or wheat noodles (or more, if you love noodles)

Neutral or toasted sesame oil, for tossing

1 cup shredded or thinly sliced root vegetables, such as carrots or radishes

1 cup sliced summer vegetables, such as cherry tomatoes, cucumber, fennel, or zucchini

1½ cups roughly chopped hearty greens, such as cabbage or spinach, and/or light leafy greens, such as red leaf lettuce or arugula

2 scallions, thinly sliced

SOY-MISO DRESSING

1 garlic clove, minced or grated

2 tablespoons soy sauce

2 tablespoons rice vinegar or other vinegar of your choice

1 tablespoon toasted sesame oil

1 tablespoon miso

1½ teaspoons sugar, honey, or maple syrup

Bring a pot of salted water to a boil over high heat and cook the noodles according to the package directions. Drain, toss with a splash of oil to prevent sticking, and spread out on a plate or sheet pan to cool.

In a small bowl, whisk together the dressing ingredients and taste. Adjust as needed with more soy, vinegar, or sugar, or a small splash of water if the flavors are too intense. Put your vegetables and any hearty greens in a large serving bowl and toss with a tablespoon or two of the dressing so they have some time to soften. Once the noodles are cool, add them to the serving bowl, drizzle with some more dressing, and toss to coat. Add any light leafy greens and the scallions and toss again. Top with your choice of garnishes and serve.

TOP IT OFF

We like to finish this salad with garnishes such as Quick Pickles (page 37); chopped peanuts or another nut of your choice; sesame seeds; and chopped fresh herbs, such as basil, cilantro, or mint. And if you keep a stash of fried onions or shallots in the pantry (highly recommended—they're good on practically everything!), you might as well sprinkle some on top.

Cream-of-Anything Soup

Serves 2 to 4

A basic creamy soup is one of the most useful recipes to have up your sleeve, allowing you to use up any surplus vegetable with just a few pantry items. Creamy doesn't have to mean dairy. This template recipe is equally good with coconut milk or without any creaminess at all, simply pureed veggies with stock or water (but Anything Soup just doesn't have the same ring). We love it as carrot soup or broccoli soup, and it's absolutely superlative as mushroom soup. Enjoy with crusty garlic bread and a glass of the same dry white wine that you liberally splashed into the soup.

3 tablespoons butter or extra-virgin olive oil
1 medium onion, diced
2 garlic cloves, sliced
3 cups chopped vegetables of your choice, one kind or a mix
Kosher salt and freshly ground black pepper
¼ cup dry white wine, or more to taste (optional)
1 tablespoon soy sauce
2 cups stock of your choice or water, plus more as needed
½ cup cream, coconut milk, or whole milk, whisked with a pinch of flour if you like a thicker soup (optional)

Melt the butter in a soup pot and add the onion, garlic, and vegetables with a good pinch of salt and a few grinds of pepper. Sauté over medium heat, stirring occasionally, until the onion is soft, translucent, and browned on the edges, about 10 minutes. Add the wine (if using) and soy sauce and use a wooden spoon to scrape the bottom of the pan of any flavorful bits.

Add the stock and bring to a boil, then lower the heat and simmer for 10 to 15 minutes, until the toughest veggies are tender. Puree with a blender or immersion blender (if you're using a regular blender, make sure to let some steam escape when pureeing, then return the soup to the pot). You can skip the pureeing step altogether if you're happy with a chunky texture, or add a bit more stock if you'd like a thinner soup.

Bring the soup back to a simmer, then turn off the heat and stir in the cream, if using. Taste and season with salt and pepper as needed, and top with your favorite embellishments.

TOP IT OFF

Smooth pureed soups call for a lavish assortment of garnishes. We like something crunchy (Toasted Breadcrumbs, page 80; Croutons, page 81; or roasted nuts), something green (chopped fresh herbs or a swirl of Green Sauce, page 138) and something a bit luxurious, like bacon bits or a dollop of sour cream.

Noodle Soup How You Want It

Serves 4

In our family, noodle soup is the answer to cold weather, to bruised hearts, to sick days, to questions both existential and mundane. It can be overflowing with silky wilted greens or jumbled up with cubes of potato, chopped tomato, and frozen corn. We know it looks like a lot of ingredients, but many are optional. And if you have a flavorful stock, such as a rich meaty stock or Mushroom Broth (page 216), you can skip making the Quick Broth and just heat and add noodles and vegetables. For more protein, toss in leftover cooked chicken or tofu cubes or top with a cooked egg. We particularly like this with pork meatballs (page 302) cooked directly in the broth.

NOTE: *We've included a wide range of noodle amounts because noodles come in all sorts of package sizes and because you can really eat this with any amount of noodles. If you love noodles like we do, add more!*

QUICK BROTH

2 tablespoons toasted sesame oil, neutral oil, or another fat of your choice

1 medium onion or another allium of your choice, thinly sliced

4 garlic cloves, thinly sliced

1-inch piece fresh ginger, minced

1 pound ground meat or torn mushrooms or 1 (14- to 16-ounce) block tofu, crumbled (optional)

6 cups water

2 tablespoons soy sauce, or more to taste

2 tablespoons Shaoxing wine (dry sherry works as a substitute, in a pinch; optional)

1 tablespoon black or rice vinegar, or another acid of your choice

1 tablespoon fish sauce, or more to taste (optional)

Kosher salt (optional)

6 to 10 ounces dried noodles, such as soba or ramen
Toasted sesame oil or neutral oil, for tossing
1 cup thinly sliced or cubed vegetables of your choice
2 cups thinly sliced hearty and/or light leafy greens

To make the Quick Broth, heat the oil in a soup pot over medium heat. Add the onion, garlic, and ginger and sauté until softened, 3 to 5 minutes. Add the meat, mushrooms, or tofu (if using) and cook, stirring frequently, until lightly browned, 5 to 10 minutes. Add the water, soy sauce, wine (if using), vinegar, and fish sauce (if using) and bring to a simmer. Taste and season with salt and/or more of any other condiments. Keep them close by as you may want to adjust the balance once you've added the rest of the ingredients.

Meanwhile, bring a pot of salted water to a boil over high heat and cook the noodles according to the package directions. Ideally, you want them slightly al dente so they don't overcook in the soup. Drain, toss with a splash of oil, and spread out on a plate or sheet pan to cool.

Add your vegetables to the broth, starting with any firmer vegetables like roots to give them time to cook, while thinly sliced stems and greens need only a few minutes to simmer. Lighter leaves like baby spinach or romaine simply need to be stirred in until they wilt. Simmer until all the vegetables are tender.

Using tongs, portion the noodles into bowls—if you have the space on a counter or table, we like to set out the sheet pan of noodles and let everyone help themselves. Ladle broth and vegetables into each bowl and top with the garnishes of your choice.

TOP IT OFF

We never eat noodle soup without an assortment of toppings, including chopped fresh herbs, sliced scallions, Ginger-Scallion Lettuce Sauce (page 92), and an overflowing spoonful of Scrap Chili Oil (page 86).

Make-It-Your-Own Stir-Fry

Serves 4 as a side dish

When you haven't thought about dinner until it's time for dinner, stir-fries come to a swift rescue. The super fast, high-heat Chinese technique welcomes any quick-cooking vegetable and can be customized with the sauces you have at hand. A stir-fry can be just leafy greens like mild lettuce or hearty kale; it's a great way to use up lots of wilted leaves, as a daunting pile of fresh greens will rapidly shrink to a manageable size in the pan. Or you can go for vegetables with a bit more bite—thin pieces of broccolini, asparagus, or carrots all do nicely tossed in a hot pan for a few minutes.

When making the sauce, your flavor options are nearly endless. Other ingredients that would make good additions include oyster sauce, hoisin sauce, black bean sauce, teriyaki sauce, and a multitude of other items. You just want a balance of saltiness, sweetness, and acidity, so taste your sauce and adjust as needed, keeping in mind that a tablespoon or two of water can help smooth things out. When stir-frying something extremely light like lettuce leaves, you can omit the sauce in favor of just garlic, ginger, and a light drizzle of toasted sesame oil.

SAUCE
1 tablespoon soy sauce
1 tablespoon water
1 teaspoon sugar
1 teaspoon black vinegar, rice vinegar, lime juice, or other acid

1 tablespoon neutral oil, or enough to lightly coat the bottom of your wok or skillet
1 garlic clove, thinly sliced or minced, or more as desired
½-inch piece fresh ginger, minced or grated (optional)
Pinch chili flakes or 1 small chile pepper, diced (optional)

(continues)

MAKE-IT-YOUR-OWN STIR FRY

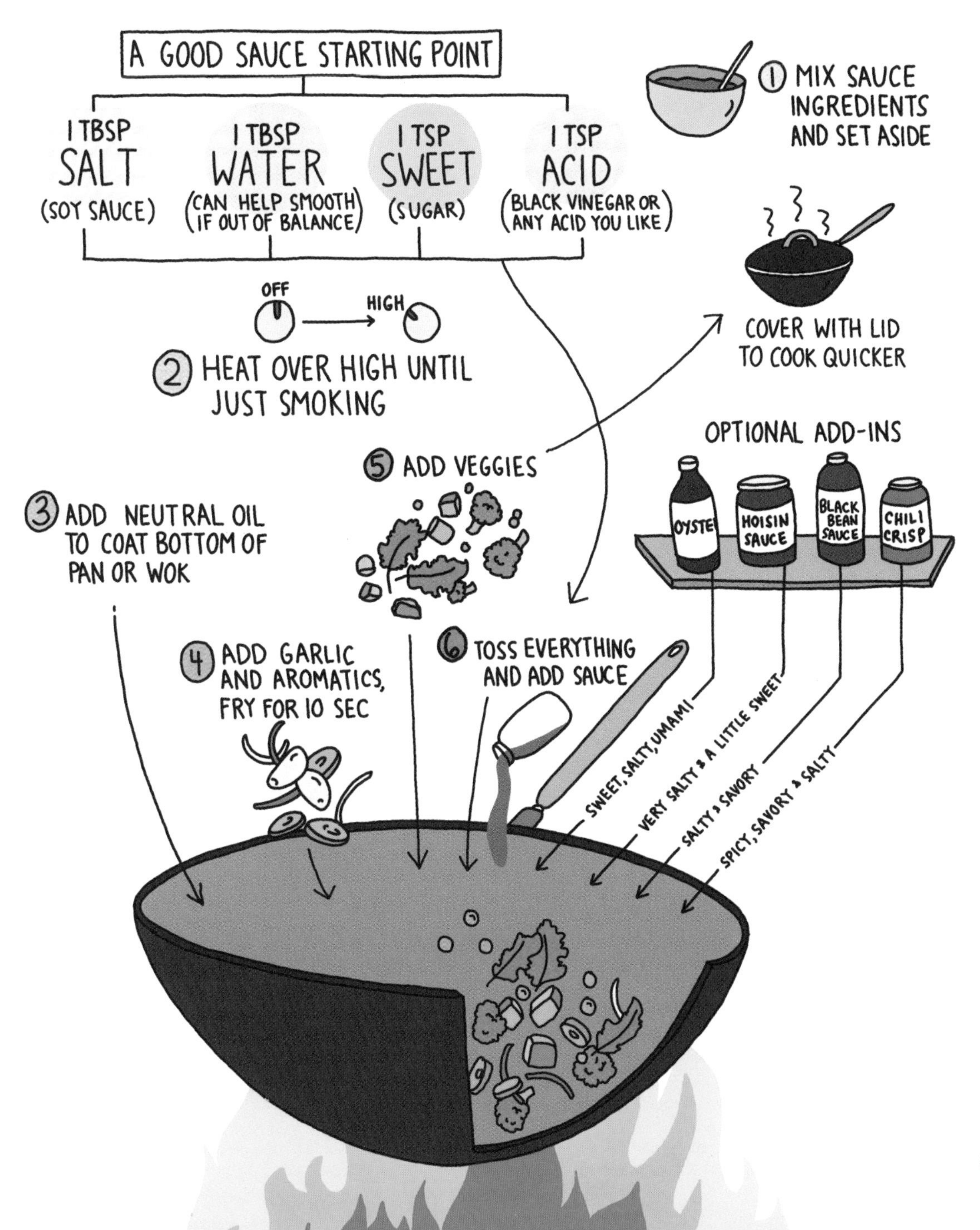

4 cups leafy greens, torn into bite-size pieces, or 1 pound crisp-crunchy vegetables, cut into chunks (for very hard vegetables, slice them thin or blanch first according to the directions on page 23)
Kosher salt

Stir the sauce ingredients together in a small bowl and set by the stove.

Heat a wok or large skillet over high heat until just smoking, then add the neutral oil and tilt to coat the bottom of the pan. Add the garlic, ginger (if using), and chili flakes (if using) and stir-fry for 10 seconds. Add the greens and/or vegetables, in stages as necessary, and toss in the garlicky oil, then add the sauce and cook to your liking, stirring frequently. Vegetable chunks may need 4 to 7 minutes—if you want to speed up the process, cover the pot so the vegetables steam for a minute or two, then uncover and toss again. Sturdy greens may need 3 to 5 minutes to get tender (we like to let them sit for a bit and char for extra texture). Lighter leaves will need less than a minute to wilt down. Stir in a spoonful of any additional sauce you like, season with salt to taste, then sprinkle with your favorite garnishes and a generous drizzle of sesame oil.

TOP IT OFF

A sprinkle of crunch is a great way to finish a stir-fry. Our favorites include crushed cashews or peanuts, toasted sesame seeds, thinly sliced scallions, and fried onions or shallots.

MAKE IT A MEAL

Double the sauce amount and cook 8 ounces chopped boneless chicken thighs, ground pork, or tofu cubes in the garlicky oil, lowering the heat if needed. Sprinkle with salt, then transfer to a plate and let sit while you cook the vegetables in a bit more oil and half the sauce. Once those are cooked, return the protein to the pan, add more sauce to taste, and stir-fry until everything is coated and warmed through. Season and serve over rice or noodles.

Toss-in-Any-Vegetable Stew

Serves 4

Got a lot of different vegetables taking up space in your refrigerator and pantry with no plan in mind? No matter what they are, you can put them in a stew. Thank goodness such a thing exists. As long as you have alliums or aromatics to build flavor, you can get by with the barest minimum of ingredients. Or you can raid the pantry and the spice drawer and toss in all the cans and flavor boosters you can find. This stew is vegan as written, but the notes below offer many ways to add meaty or creamy things as desired. Just keep cook times in mind—roots, tubers, and winter squash need the most time to cook and should go in at the beginning; broccoli and other crucifers get added in the middle so they don't completely overcook (unless you like them that way); and hearty greens get tossed in right at the end for wilting. Look at this super adaptable recipe as an opportunity for cooking creativity and kitchen skill-building. Adding a flexible stew to your repertoire means you can make a spectacular fridge-cleanout meal anytime you like. Plus, it freezes well for those days when a bowl of homemade stew is just the dose of comfort you need.

2 tablespoons extra-virgin olive oil or butter, or more as needed

1 to 2 cups chopped alliums and/or aromatics of your choice (like an onion and a carrot and some garlic, or a shallot and a fennel bulb and an inch of ginger, or 2 leeks and a few stalks of celery)

Kosher salt and freshly ground black pepper

1 to 2 teaspoons curry powder, ground turmeric, garam masala, paprika, harissa, or another favorite spice (optional)

4 cups stock, wine, water, coconut milk, diced tomatoes with their juices, or bean cooking liquid, plus more as needed

4 cups cubed or chopped vegetables of your choice and/or canned beans, roughly divided by cook time

(continues)

2 cups cooked rice or other whole grains (optional)—more is fine; just decrease the amount of vegetables or increase the amount of liquid to achieve the consistency you like

Heat the oil in a Dutch oven over medium heat, adding more if necessary to cover the bottom of the pot. Add your alliums and/or aromatics and sauté for a few minutes until they start to soften and lightly brown on the edges, 3 to 7 minutes depending on your ingredients. It's OK if they start to stick to the bottom of the pot—those browned bits help build flavor; just turn the heat down if it threatens to burn.

Season with a good pinch of salt and a few grinds of black pepper. Add any spices you like and let them bloom in the oil for a minute or two. Add your liquid of choice and use a wooden spoon to scrape up any browned bits from the bottom of the pan.

Now is the time to start layering in your vegetables. Sturdy roots, winter squash, cabbage, and the like should go in first as they need 20 to 30 minutes to soften. Medium-weight vegetables and canned beans take about half that time, and leafy greens go in at the end. Let simmer until all the vegetables are tender, then stir in the cooked grains or beans, if using. Season to taste before topping with your choice of garnishes.

TOP IT OFF

Finishing with fun garnishes takes stew from a basic bowl to a dreamy dish: We love to add a splash of good vinegar, chopped fresh tender herbs, a dollop of sour cream, or a swirl of Green Sauce (page 138).

TOSS-IN-ANY-VEGETABLE STEW

(READ BOTTOM TO TOP!)

A Very Flexible Curried Lentil Stew

Serves 4

Dal is one of Mei's husband's favorite dishes, so she often makes a version with whatever she can find in the fridge. Magic can happen with just a bag of lentils and a cupboard of spices, but stirring in leafy greens, grating in root vegetables, or cooking down some fresh tomatoes adds bulk, texture, and all kinds of fun flavors. If you have harder vegetables like sweet potato or squash, pop them in with the lentils. If you like your vegetables firm and only lightly cooked, add them with the greens.

Red lentils cook up the fastest, but you should absolutely try other lentils or another kind of pulse, adjusting your cook times according to the package directions. Maybe you scored a coveted Rancho Gordo bean club subscription—Can you tell Irene your secret?—in which case most of those beans would be perfect in this dish. You can use water, stock, or coconut milk and adjust the amount of liquid depending on whether you want more of a thick stew or a thin soup.

3 tablespoons extra-virgin olive oil, ghee, or another fat of your choice
1 medium onion or 2 shallots, chopped
4 garlic cloves, minced
1-inch piece fresh ginger, minced or grated, plus more if desired
1 teaspoon ground turmeric
1 teaspoon ground cumin
½ teaspoon ground coriander
Kosher salt
1 cup dried lentils or another pulse or bean of your choice
1 cup diced or grated vegetables of your choice or another ½ cup lentils
4 cups greens, stems and leaves separated and cut into bite-size pieces
3 cups stock of your choice or water, or more as needed
1 (14-ounce) can unsweetened coconut milk, ideally full-fat
Steamed rice or grains, flatbread, or roti, for serving

Heat the oil in a Dutch oven over medium heat. Add the onion, garlic, and ginger and cook until the onion is translucent and starting to brown, about 5 minutes. Add the spices and a good pinch of salt and stir, letting the spices bloom and fry a bit in the oil for another minute or so.

Add the lentils, diced vegetables, and hearty greens stems, then the stock and coconut milk. Season to taste with more salt, then bring the mixture to a simmer. Cook, stirring every so often, until the lentils are soft and the stew has thickened to your liking, about 30 minutes for red lentils. If the stew looks too dry, add a splash of water.

Once the lentils have softened to your liking, stir in the chopped leafy greens and any grated or otherwise quick-cooking vegetable. Make sure they get fully covered with stew so they wilt down and cook until soft, which should take just a minute or two for lighter greens like spinach, 3 to 5 minutes for thicker leaves like collards.

Taste again and season if needed, then serve with your choice of garnishes and a starch.

TOP IT OFF

Stews of all kinds benefit from a swirl of something creamy, like a scoop of plain yogurt or sour cream. Plus, we'll never say no to a handful of chopped fresh cilantro or mint, a squeeze of lime, and a dash of fish sauce to punch up the flavor.

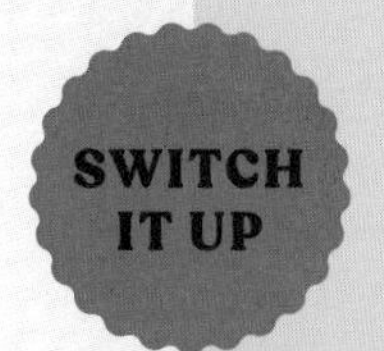

To make a **Thai Curried Stew**, swap the turmeric, cumin, and coriander for 2 to 4 tablespoons curry paste, found in cans and packets at Asian grocery stores and many mainstream supermarkets.

Looking for a rapid-fire dinner? Make a **Quick Bean Stew**: swap the lentils for cooked or canned chickpeas or other beans, which need only 10 to 15 minutes to thicken.

How-You-Like-It Savory Pancakes

Makes 4 pancakes

One of Mei's first dates with her husband was at an okonomiyaki restaurant in London, a choose-your-own-adventure meal where you picked all the ingredients in each savory, eggy, cabbage-stuffed pancake. Options included traditional pork belly, squid, bacon and cheese, and even a Christmas special with turkey and Stilton cheese and cranberry sauce on the side, demonstrating that you can put just about anything into these miraculous creations. It's an ideal vehicle to illustrate the Japanese concept of mottainai, an expression of regret that something has been wasted or not used to its full potential, loosely translated to "What a waste!" In fact, the name *okonomiyaki* proves it is an ultimate Hero Recipe, with *okonomi* meaning "as you like" or "how you like it" and *yaki* meaning cooked or grilled in Japanese, so you might as well take it at face value and make it exactly how you want it.

3 eggs
½ cup water or stock
¾ cup all-purpose flour or a gluten-free substitute
1 teaspoon kosher salt
½ teaspoon baking powder
3 cups shredded cabbage
¼ cup thinly sliced Quick Pickles (page 37) or anything pickled or fermented in your fridge, like sauerkraut or kimchi (not essential, but really delicious)
1 cup diced or shredded cooked meat or raw or cooked vegetables
Neutral oil, for frying
Mayonnaise, for garnish (ideally an easily squirtable option like Kewpie)

EASY OKONOMIYAKI SAUCE

2 tablespoons ketchup

1 tablespoon Worcestershire sauce *or* 1½ teaspoons oyster sauce plus 1½ teaspoons rice vinegar

1½ teaspoons soy sauce

1 teaspoon sugar or honey

Lightly beat the eggs and water in a large bowl, then whisk in the flour, salt, and baking powder until smooth. Stir in the cabbage, pickles, and any additional vegetables or meat until everything is coated in the egg mixture.

Heat a large skillet over medium heat and add a good pour of neutral oil to lightly coat the bottom. Once the oil is shimmering, scoop two large spoonfuls into the pan (roughly a quarter of the mixture each—we like to use a 1-cup measure). Press gently into patties about 5 inches across and 1 inch thick, leaving them puffy rather than dense. Fry until the bottom is set and golden brown, about 5 minutes. Carefully flip both pancakes and cook until the other sides are nicely browned, then transfer to a plate. Repeat, adding more oil if needed before adding the remaining batter.

To make the sauce, whisk together all the ingredients and adjust to taste. Add more Worcestershire or vinegar if you want it tangier, more sugar or honey if you want it sweeter, more soy if it needs salt. This is just a rough recipe; it's up to you to adjust it until you love the taste and want to smear it all over your okonomiyaki.

When you're ready to eat, drizzle on the okonomiyaki sauce and mayonnaise (if you only have thick mayo, you can mix a spoonful into the okonomiyaki sauce and use it as more of a dip), then top with your garnishes of choice.

TOP IT OFF

Traditional okonomiyaki garnishes include katsuobushi (dried bonito flakes), nori (roasted seaweed), sesame seeds, thinly sliced scallions, and pickled ginger.

Fridge-Cleanout Fried Rice

Serves 2, but feel free to scale up

Coming from a Chinese American family that always had leftover rice in the fridge, we've been making fried rice ever since we could handle a frying pan and hot oil. It's the absolute perfect use for leftover rice (even straight from the freezer!) and, given that any quick-cooking vegetable can be swapped in, a truly excellent fridge-cleanout dinner. Do you have frozen carrots, peas, and corn? Go the classic route. Do you have parsnips, asparagus, and chard? Go wild! The technique isn't terribly complicated, but it requires a bit of juggling to get all the individual items cooked. Be sure to have all your ingredients chopped and ready at the side of the stove because the process moves fast, especially when it comes to the eggs. You want them just barely cooked so they're soft and puffy and just the right contrast to your crispy bits of rice.

2 cups cold cooked rice
1 tablespoon soy sauce
1½ teaspoons rice vinegar or black vinegar
1½ teaspoons toasted sesame oil
Neutral oil, for frying
½ cup ground meat or diced tofu (optional)
1 cup bite-size vegetables of your choice
2 eggs, lightly beaten
2 garlic cloves, minced
1 tablespoon minced ginger
2 scallions, thinly sliced
½ cup chopped leafy greens of your choice
Kosher salt

Crumble the rice into a medium bowl to break up any clumps and set aside. In a small bowl, stir together the soy sauce, vinegar, and sesame oil and set aside.

In a large skillet or wok, heat a small splash of neutral oil over medium-high heat until shimmering. If using meat or tofu, add to the pan and cook until lightly browned, about 6 minutes, then transfer to a medium bowl. Add the vegetables and cook, stirring every minute or so, until tender and starting to brown, 3 to 5 minutes. Transfer the vegetables to the bowl with the meat.

Add another splash of oil if necessary and add the eggs. Let them spread out across the pan and cook until just set on the bottom, then use a spatula to fold them over until they are no longer liquid but still soft and just cooked. Transfer the eggs to the bowl with the vegetables and get ready for the last round of cooking.

Heat one more splash of oil until shimmering and add the garlic, ginger, and scallions. Stir-fry until they smell amazing, about 30 seconds, then add the greens and stir to mix everything. Add the rice and spread it out to cook for a minute, then stir and repeat a few times so all the rice gets fried and crunchy. Pour in the sauce and stir to combine, then return the meat, cooked vegetables, and eggs to the pan. Use your spatula to break up the eggs and mix and reheat everything, then season to taste and serve immediately with your favorite toppings.

TOP IT OFF

We never eat fried rice without a ton of random embellishments. Favorites include Scrap Chili Oil (page 86), Ginger-Scallion Lettuce Sauce (page 92), furikake, sriracha, chopped fresh herbs of your choice, and chunks of fresh avocado.

GOT EXTRA RICE?

The following storage instructions and use-up ideas work for nearly all whole grains, from rice to bulgur to wheatberries.

STORE IT RIGHT: Cool cooked grains completely, then store in the refrigerator in an airtight container for up to a week. Rice in particular dries out quickly—in the first day or two, reheat it in the microwave with a small splash of water to approximate freshly cooked rice. As it ages toward a week and dries out, make the fried rice above to take advantage of the dry texture.

SAVE FOR LATER: Cooked grains, including rice and oatmeal, can be frozen in airtight containers or resealable bags with the air pressed out—do this in portions that make sense for the size of meals you tend to make. We prefer using freezer bags as they take up less space, can be stored vertically or horizontally, and are easy to defrost. When ready to cook, stick the frozen sealed bag in a bowl of hot water for 10 to 15 minutes, and you can have cooked grains ready to go by the time you assemble the rest of your meal. This works best for sturdier cooked grains like rice, farro, wheatberries, and barley; softer grains like teff or millet may not maintain their structure as well, so they do better in a soup or a stew than a salad. Frozen grains can also go straight into a soup or a skillet for reheating.

USE-IT-UP IDEAS: Rice Fritters are a great way to use up rice and clean some other leftovers out of the fridge. Mix 1 cup cooked rice or other grain, ½ cup chopped cooked vegetables, ¼ cup shredded cheese, 2 eggs, and 2 tablespoons flour. Form patties and fry in a bit of oil until golden-brown on each side. Sprinkle with salt before serving.

To make **Congee**, combine 1 cup leftover rice with 2 cups water or stock of your choice, and bring to a boil over medium-high heat. Lower the heat to keep the rice at a low simmer and cook for 20 to 25 minutes, stirring occasionally and adding more liquid if needed, until the porridge is a uniform soupy consistency. Top with the same toppings as Fridge-Cleanout Fried Rice (page 62).

Choose-Your-Own-Adventure Vegetable Paella

Serves 2 to 4

Paella is a dish of endless combinations, as you can clearly tell by the abundant variations in Alberto Herraiz's cookbook *Paella*. As Herraiz says, there's no such thing as an "authentic" paella, because it's not a recipe, but rather "a method of cooking linked to a particular utensil: the pan." Despite the importance of the pan, you definitely don't need a traditional paella pan, just a wide skillet of some kind. Once you've got the basic ingredients—tomatoes or sofrito, short-grain rice, and some good stock—you can improvise as you see fit, tossing in your goodies from the farmers' market or whatever calls to you from the fridge or pantry. To ensure your chosen vegetables cook in time, cut or shred harder roots or winter squash into smaller pieces; lighter options such as broccoli or asparagus can be left in larger chunks.

2½ cups stock of your choice

¼ cup extra-virgin olive oil or Garlic Oil (page 90)

1 small onion or ½ bunch scallions, chopped, or another allium or aromatic of your choice

4 garlic cloves, minced

1 cup short-grain rice

½ cup Sofrito (page 89) or pureed tomatoes

½ teaspoon smoked paprika (hot or sweet will work in a pinch)

¼ teaspoon saffron, crushed and mixed with a spoonful of stock (optional)

2 cups chopped vegetables of choice, such as asparagus, mushrooms, or snap peas

Kosher salt

(continues)

In a small saucepan, heat the stock to a simmer. (You want the liquid hot when you pour it into the rice so everything doesn't overcook while it comes to a boil.)

Heat the olive oil in a large skillet over medium-low heat. Sauté the onion and garlic until translucent, about 5 minutes. Add the rice and stir to toast in the oil for a few minutes, until it gets glossy and the edges a bit pearlescent, then add the sofrito. Use a wooden spoon to scrape up any bits from the bottom of the pan, then add the paprika and saffron (if using) and stir.

Add your vegetables, then pour the hot stock into the pan. Season to taste with salt, then turn the heat up to medium-high so it comes to a boil rapidly, moving the pan around a bit if it isn't heating evenly. Turn the heat down slightly and cook at a simmer, without touching, until all the liquid has evaporated, about 20 minutes. If you smell any burning, turn down the heat, but you're aiming for a crisp bottom layer known as socarrat, so the bottom should be browning a bit. Taste the rice—if it's still crunchy, add a splash more stock or water. Once the top is dry and the rice is tender, turn off the heat. Let rest for a few minutes before serving with your favorite accompaniments.

TOP IT OFF

Paella is fun to serve with tiny bowls of garnish like lemon wedges, chopped scallions, chopped fresh parsley, sliced olives, and toasted nuts.

If you'd like to add meat, such as chorizo or chicken, brown bite-size pieces in the pan before sautéing the onion and garlic.

CHOOSE-YOUR-OWN-ADVENTURE PAELLA

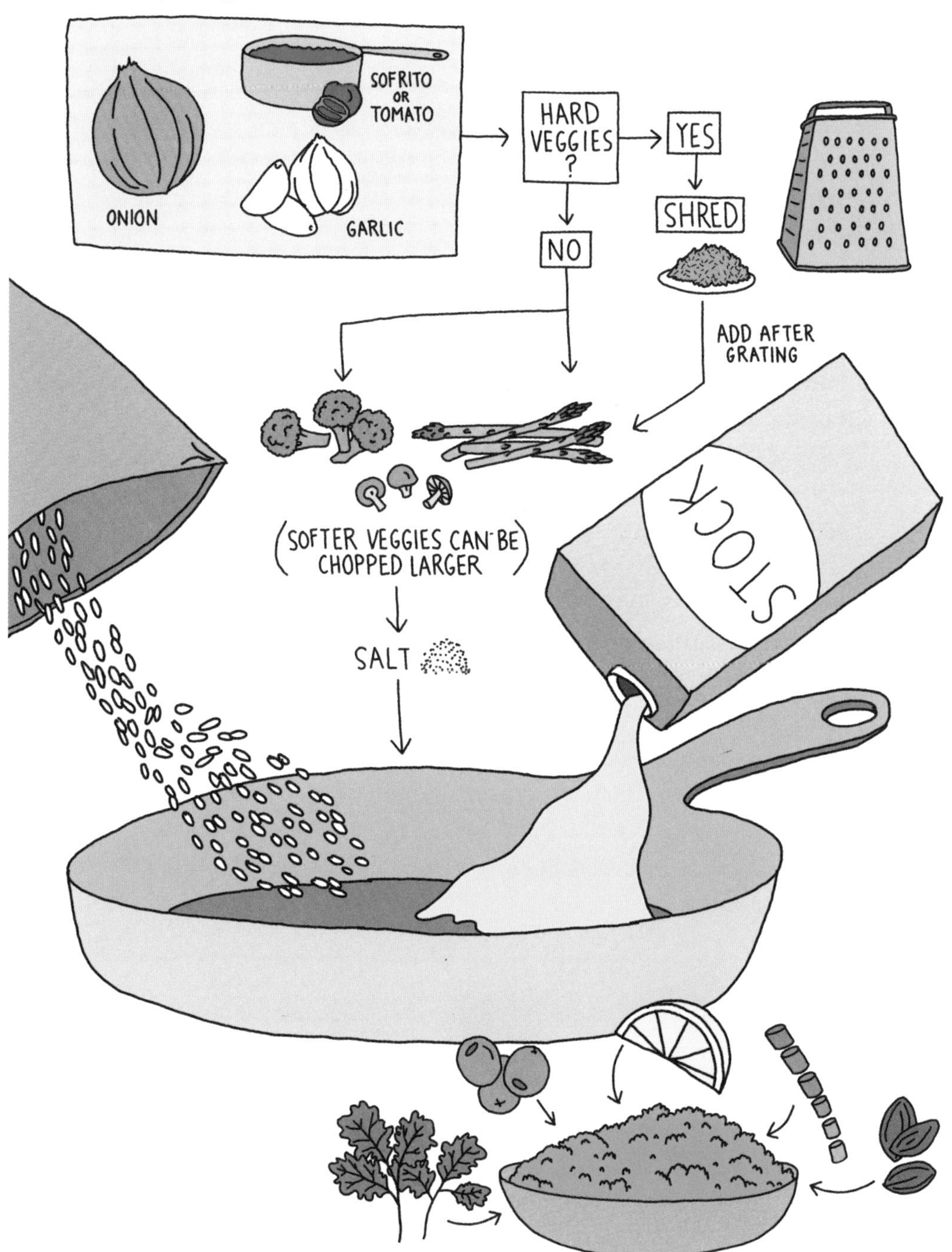

Anything-in-the-Kitchen Pasta

Serves 4

Home late from a party and hungry at midnight? Just back from a long trip with nothing fresh in the fridge? Thank goodness, pasta loves you and will fill your belly and warm your heart with just the barest minimum of ingredients. Break out the leftovers from dinner, the cans in your cupboard, or the bags in the back of the freezer—anchovies, beans, artichoke hearts, frozen peas will all come to your rescue. And if you do happen to have a few fresh items around, even better—toss in some arugula for a peppery bite or stir in a handful of spinach leaves for a hit of greenery. We like to build flavor at the beginning of the pan sauce by adding anchovies, chopped meats like bacon or salami, a spoonful of chili flakes, some capers or olives, or any thinly sliced allium. Sauté some vegetables while your pasta cooks, slice up some deli meat, anything goes.

Kosher salt
12 ounces pasta of any kind
⅓ cup extra-virgin olive oil
4 garlic cloves, thinly sliced
2 cups chopped raw hearty greens and/or tender vegetables, such as asparagus and green beans, frozen corn or peas, or leftover cooked vegetables
¾ cup grated Parmesan cheese or another hard cheese, plus more for sprinkling on top

---

Bring a large pot of well-salted water to a boil, then add the pasta. Cook until just al dente. (We like to set an alarm for 2 minutes before whatever al dente timing they give on the box, since the pasta will finish cooking in the sauce. We also consider the alarm a friendly reminder to dip a large mug into the pot and grab a cup or so of pasta water before draining.)

While the pasta cooks, heat the olive oil in a large skillet over medium-low heat. Add the garlic and maybe some other flavorful things to the pan to start building your pan sauce. If you're cooking meat, let it crisp up a bit and render the fat. If you're using an allium like onion or shallots, let them soften and then just start to crisp up a bit on the edges. If you're using an anchovy or two (or the whole tin with its oil, why not!), let them warm up and dissolve in the oil.

Next, add your raw tender vegetables or cooked leftovers and warm them up for a few minutes; they'll finish cooking once the pasta and pasta water are added.

When the timer goes off, drain the pasta—don't forget to scoop out some pasta water first! Turn the heat up a bit and add the drained pasta and 1 cup of the pasta water. Add the Parmesan and stir until the cheese melts and everything is coated and saucy. If it needs more liquid, pour in a bit more pasta water, and consider stirring in a pat of butter, flavored or regular, or some leaves to lightly wilt. Top with fresh chopped herbs for flavor, breadcrumbs for crunch, or whatever else strikes your fancy.

TOP IT OFF

There are so many ways to finish this dish: We love toppings like a pat of regular butter or Herb Butter (page 142), a sprinkle of grated lemon zest and/or a squeeze of lemon juice, a handful of arugula or radicchio, a few spoonfuls of Toasted Breadcrumbs (page 80), more chili flakes, and lots of freshly ground black pepper. And of course, a free hand with the grated Parmesan.

FAVORITE COMBOS

Spaghetti + salami + spinach + blue cheese

Fettuccine + chorizo (brown, then cook the garlic in the chorizo oil) + lacinato kale + feta

Farfalle + pork sausage (cook same as the chorizo above) + collard greens + sautéed mushrooms

Fridge-Forage Baked Pasta

Serves 4 to 6

If you've got a bunch of veggies to use up and happen to have leftover cooked pasta, why not turn it all into a baked pasta dish? It's super customizable: Swap in any meltable cheeses you've got on hand or use up assorted dairy products in your fridge—use cream if you want a richer version, swap the sour cream for more milk if you don't have any. Crack open a can of crushed or diced tomatoes or some tomato sauce and swirl in a cup with the milk and cheese. Use any cooked meat in place of the sausage; just add some more olive oil to the pan to prevent sticking. Or leave out the meat and just sauté the veggies in a good splash of oil, maybe with some onion and garlic. And if you don't have cooked pasta, boil some up while you brown the sausage and vegetables and give yourself the gift of leftover pasta for tomorrow.

1 tablespoon extra-virgin olive oil or butter

12 to 16 ounces uncooked sausages, removed from their casings, or another ground meat

3 cups quick-cooking vegetables, like chopped asparagus, broccoli, or hearty greens

1 cup shredded mozzarella cheese, plus more for sprinkling on top

1 cup shredded sharp cheddar cheese, plus more for sprinkling on top

½ cup grated Parmesan cheese, or another hard cheese of your choice

½ cup whole milk

¼ cup sour cream

4 cups cooked pasta

Toasted Breadcrumbs (page 80) or chopped fresh herbs, for garnish

Heat the oven to 450 degrees. Heat the oil in a large oven-safe skillet over medium-high heat. Add the sausage meat to the pan and use a spatula to break up the meat a bit and release some fat in the pan. Add the vegetables and stir to combine everything. Sauté, stirring occasionally, until the sausage is browned and the vegetables are reasonably tender (everything will cook further in the oven, so no worries if the sausage is slightly underdone or the greens are still a bit crunchy).

Combine the cheeses, milk, and sour cream in a large bowl and mix thoroughly. Add the pasta and sausage mixture to the bowl and stir to combine (it's easier to mix it well in the bowl than the skillet). Pour everything back into the skillet, top with any extra cheese you want, and bake for 15 to 20 minutes, until the top is bubbling, golden brown, and everything you want it to be. Serve right away, with a scattering of breadcrumbs or herbs.

GOT EXTRA PASTA?

If, like us, you regularly cook too much pasta, don't let it go to waste!

STORE IT RIGHT: Cool leftover pasta completely, then store in the refrigerator in an airtight container. The longer you keep it, the drier it will get, so you'll want to use it up in a baked dish after a day or two.

SAVE FOR LATER: You can freeze cooked pasta into dishes that surround the pasta with moisture, like lasagna, casseroles, or soup. Make sure it's well wrapped (start with a layer of parchment or plastic wrap, then a layer of aluminum foil) and it will keep for a few months. Uncooked fresh pasta can be frozen in its original container or airtight wrapping.

USE-IT-UP IDEAS: Pasta Frittatas with lots of garlic and fresh herbs are a glorious way to reincarnate your leftover pasta. You can also pop it into a **Pasta Salad** (page 162) or **Noodle Soup How You Want It** (page 50).

Anything-You-Like Galette

Makes 1 galette

Once we started keeping store-bought pie crust in the freezer, making rustic galettes for dinner became a surprisingly achievable task. Anything can become a galette filling—sauté some mushrooms or greens, roast up some root vegetables, or just rummage through the fridge for leftovers. As Irene will tell you, baked brie is *technically* a galette! Once you've got your filling, spoon it onto the crust, make a few simple folds (so easy a six-year-old can do it, we promise), bake, and eat. You can also layer a sauce on the bottom of the crust, mix in some herbs or spices, or sprinkle on bits of cheese or meat. Experiment on the outside of the crust too, by dusting on some grated Parmesan, everything bagel spice, or just a few grinds of black pepper and a pinch of flaky salt.

NOTE: *Use the same filling but spread it across store-bought puff pastry to make simple but impressive-looking tarts.*

2 tablespoons extra-virgin olive oil, plus more as needed
1 small onion or large shallot, chopped
4 garlic cloves, chopped
3 cups filling of choice—see "Favorite Combos" on page 75 for some ideas
1 pie crust, thawed if frozen and unrolled
1 egg beaten with a small splash of water, for egg wash (optional; a bit of olive oil or heavy cream works too)

Heat the oven to 400 degrees. Line a rimmed baking sheet with parchment or a silicone baking mat.

Heat the olive oil in a large skillet over medium heat, then add the onion and garlic. Sauté until the onion is tender, about 5 minutes. Stir in any other filling ingredients as directed below, then season to taste with salt and pepper.

Roll out the pie crust and place on the prepared baking sheet. If you're adding a sauce or cheese to the base of the galette, smear it across the center, leaving a roughly 2-inch border around the edges. Scoop your filling on top and spread it around. Fold the edges up over the sides of the filling in all directions (galettes are meant to be rustic, so don't worry too much about the shape), then brush with an egg wash, olive oil, or cream, if using. Bake until the crust is a deep golden brown, 35 to 45 minutes. Let cool slightly before serving.

SWITCH IT UP

It's super easy to add some wow factor to a galette by layering in an ingredient underneath the filling. See what you can find while foraging in the fridge! Our favorite add-ins include a few tablespoons of Green Sauce (page 138); a smear of Dijon mustard or harissa paste; a layer of Caramelized Onions (page 88) or Garlic Confit (page 90); a handful of grated cheese or crumbles of goat cheese; and a handful of chopped nuts or meaty bits like bacon or sliced salami.

(continues)

GALETTE, THREE WAYS

FAVORITE COMBOS

SAUTÉED GREENS GALETTE: Use 1 large bunch hearty greens, or a mix totaling about 8 cups, stems sliced thinly and leaves cut into bite-size pieces. Add the stems and leaves to the pan after the onion and garlic have had a few minutes to soften. Stir until everything wilts down into a manageable pile. Season with salt and pepper until the greens taste good enough to just stand at the stove with a fork and keep eating them. Make sure the greens are relatively dry before transferring to the pie crust; if your greens released a lot of liquid into the pan, transfer to a colander and press with a spoon to squeeze the excess liquid out.

ROASTED SUMMER VEGETABLES: Cut about 3 pounds bell peppers, tomatoes, eggplants, and/or summer squash into small cubes, place on a rimmed baking sheet, and toss with olive oil, salt, and pepper. Roast in the 400-degree oven for about 30 minutes while you prepare the crust and sauté the aromatics. Pull them out of the oven if they start to brown too much—remember that they'll cook a lot longer inside the tart, so this roast is just a push in the right direction. Scatter the sautéed onion and garlic on the crust, then add the roasted veggies. If you feel so inclined, some crumbles of feta or a smear of ricotta would be welcome here.

ROOT VEGETABLES: Cut about 3 pounds root vegetables into ⅛- to ¼-inch slices (this could be just one large butternut or kabocha squash, or a beet, a carrot, and a parsnip for some beautiful color contrasts). Once the onion and garlic are sautéed, scatter them onto the crust—maybe onto a bed of Garlic Confit (page 90) or goat cheese—then layer the root vegetable slices on top. If you're feeling creative, you can arrange your veggies in swirls or other patterns. Brush the tops of the vegetables with a bit of olive oil before baking.

WITH MEI

Eat-Your-Leftovers Pot Pie

Serves 6 to 8, with sides

This is my family's favorite fridge-cleanout meal: My daughter loves flaky pastry, my husband loves meat wrapped in carbs, and I love that I can shove all my leftovers into a single one-pan dish. You could make an entirely vegetarian version or include no vegetables whatsoever, depending which way your pot pie dreams lie. Just keep cook times in mind—start any longer-cooking vegetables in the fat right away or use already-cooked leftovers. Anything you want to keep a bit more bite can be added along with the meat. As long as there is a gloriously rich sauce and a flaky buttery crust on top, the rest is up to you.

1 sheet puff pastry or pie crust, thawed if frozen and unrolled

2 tablespoons butter, extra-virgin olive oil, or your fat of choice, plus more as needed

1 medium onion, chopped

4 cups mixed bite-size vegetables, such as root vegetables, broccoli, or more alliums or aromatics

1 tablespoon minced fresh herbs, such as thyme, oregano, or rosemary

Kosher salt and freshly ground black pepper

¼ to ⅓ cup all-purpose flour, depending on how thick you like your sauce

2½ to 3 cups stock of your choice

4 cups chopped or shredded cooked chicken, turkey, or meat of your choice

1 egg beaten with a small splash of water, for egg wash

Heat the oven to 425 degrees.

Test to see if the pastry fits over your skillet of choice (it should be oven-safe and 9 or 10 inches wide) and if not, roll the pastry out wider with a sprinkle of flour. It's OK if there are square corners hanging off a round skillet; a bit of extra pastry helps keep the entire crust from slowly slipping off the skillet and drowning under the gravy.

Heat your fat of choice in the skillet over medium heat. Add the onion and other vegetables, herbs, and a large pinch of salt and a few grinds of pepper. Cook for 6 to 8 minutes, stirring frequently and adding a bit more fat as needed if the pan seems very dry. Once the vegetables have softened, sprinkle the flour over the pan, stir to mix everything thoroughly, and cook until the flour is completely incorporated and starting to brown a bit on the bottom of the pan, about 3 minutes. Add 2½ cups stock, stir and scrape the bottom of the pan, then let the mixture simmer and thicken for 5 minutes or so. If you want it saucier, add up to another ½ cup stock. Once the sauce has reached the consistency you find appealing, remove the pan from the heat and stir in the meat. Taste for seasoning and add more salt and pepper as needed.

Carefully drape the pastry over the top of the skillet, letting any extra dough hang over the sides. Brush the egg wash over the top of the crust. (If you have leftover egg wash, fry yourself a tiny omelet snack!) Poke a few slits or holes in the top to let steam escape and place in the oven (if the skillet is threatening to overflow, place it on a parchment-lined baking sheet to save yourself an oven cleaning). Bake for 30 to 40 minutes, until the crust is golden brown and the filling is thick and bubbling. If the pastry starts to darken too much, cover it with aluminum foil or lower the oven temperature to 375 degrees.

Let cool slightly, then slice and serve nice and hot. Leftovers will last in the fridge for a few days and can also be frozen once completely cooled and wrapped in airtight packaging.

Savory Bread Pudding

WITH IRENE

Serves 6 to 8, with sides

Bread pudding—sometimes called a strata or bread casserole—is my recipe of choice for when the kitchen starts to overflow with bread products (even slightly stale ones) and assorted vegetables. Sliced supermarket white bread, fancy artisanal ancient grain bread, bagels, waffles, croissants, you name it, I've used it. Toss in whatever you have in the fridge—I'm partial to cheddar and leek tops, thinly sliced—then eat it hot and bubbling, at room temperature, or standing in front of the fridge by the forkful. It's great for a leisurely Sunday brunch with friends: It looks impressive, can be made in advance, and is beloved by all ages. Leftovers reheat well in big squares for breakfast throughout the week. It's the right amount of indulgence while also getting in lots of greens and whatever other veggies you feel like throwing in. Feel free to swap out a cup of the vegetables for chopped meat, ideally something with a lot of fat and flavor, like bacon or sausage.

4 cups whole milk, or 2 cups milk plus 2 cups cream, or a combination of milk and stock—enough to moisten all your bread

2 eggs

8 cups mixed bread chunks, fresh or frozen and thawed

1 cup (or more, don't let me stop you) whatever cheese you have in the fridge, crumbled or shredded, plus more for sprinkling on top if you like

2 tablespoons butter or extra-virgin olive oil

4 cups diced vegetables, ideally an allium such as onion or scallions and a few cloves of garlic, and then any combination of leafy greens, roasted vegetables (keep these separate from the raw veggies), fresh herbs, whatever you like

Kosher salt and freshly ground black pepper

Heat the oven to 350 degrees. Grease a 9 x 13-inch baking dish.

Whisk the milk and eggs together in a large bowl, then add the bread chunks. Mix in the cheese and make sure all the bread is submerged so it can soak up the milk while you prepare the vegetables.

Melt the butter in a large skillet over medium heat. Add your alliums and anything that needs a while to sauté, like kale stems, and cook until softened, 5 to 10 minutes. Once those are tender, add any fresh leaves or already-cooked vegetables and stir to combine.

Remove the skillet from the heat and let cool for a few minutes, then add the vegetables to the bread mixture. Add a generous pinch of salt and a few grinds of black pepper and stir to combine thoroughly.

Pour the bread and vegetable mixture evenly into the prepared baking dish. Bake until the top is puffed and golden brown, 50 to 60 minutes. Serve hot. Cool and refrigerate any leftovers—they'll reheat well in the microwave for snacks all week.

GOT EXTRA BREAD?

Bread pudding is our favorite use-up trick for all bread products, either savory (page 78) or sweet (page 239), along with the bread-crumbs and croutons below. With these techniques and proper storage and freezing, you can save all your bread from a sad death in the trash.

STORE IT RIGHT: Keep bread in paper bags or their original wrapping at room temperature for a few days to a week, after which you risk mold. You can refrigerate bread, but the texture will really only be good for toast, so an easier option is to stick uneaten bread straight into the freezer.

SAVE FOR LATER: Most breads and bread products can be frozen for at least 6 months, if not longer, wrapped tightly to avoid freezer burn. Sliced bread can go into the freezer in its original packaging and then put directly in the toaster to cook.

Whole loaves are easier to deal with when sliced or cubed before freezing; they'll defrost faster and save you the hassle of cutting into an icy loaf. If you did pop a loaf into the freezer whole, let it thaw in the fridge or at room temperature before slicing. If you cut it into cubes or blitzed it into breadcrumbs before freezing, you can put them directly in the oven or pan without thawing (see below for instructions).

USE-IT-UP IDEAS: Toasted Breadcrumbs made from good bread are eat-straight-out-of-the-pan delicious, completely customizable, and best of all, free! (OK, yes, you already paid for the bread, but you didn't have to go out and spend extra money on bland and dusty premade breadcrumbs, and that's what matters.) If you ever have uneaten bread threatening to go stale, cut it into cubes and pop it in the freezer. When you're ready to make breadcrumbs, blitz the bread in the food processor and refreeze any crumbs you don't plan to use.

To toast the breadcrumbs, heat a skillet over medium heat with a splash of extra-virgin olive oil (about 2 tablespoons per cup of bread-crumbs). Add the breadcrumbs and season well with salt and pepper. Stir frequently to toast to a dark golden brown, 3 to 5 minutes. Let cool slightly before sprinkling onto anything and everything. Store in an airtight container in the fridge for a few weeks.

Here are some of our favorite combos to add to ¼ cup oil and 2 cups breadcrumbs:

- 2 minced garlic cloves and 4 minced anchovies
- Grated zest of ½ lemon and a large pinch of chili flakes
- ½ cup finely grated Parmesan or Pecorino cheese
- ¼ cup nori flakes and ½ teaspoon toasted sesame oil

Or you can swap the oil for butter and add 2 tablespoons brown sugar and a sprinkle of ground cinnamon for a crunchy sweet topping for tarts, pancakes, and ice cream.

Croutons are basically giant crunchy breadcrumbs that make artisanal bread worth the extra few bucks because you use up every little piece. Tear or cube any good loaf as it starts to stale and toss lightly with extra-virgin olive oil, salt and pepper, and any flavorings you like from the above list. Spread out on a rimmed baking sheet and bake at 400 degrees for 10 to 15 minutes, until golden brown at the edges.

For both croutons and breadcrumbs:

- Top just about any salad, soup, stew, or pasta dish.
- Make instantly flavorful meatballs (page 302) or use in meat burgers, veggie burgers, or meatloaf.
- Scatter onto roasted vegetables or any baked dish such as Roasted Vegetable Involtini (page 120) or Fridge-Forage Baked Pasta (page 70)

Alliums and Aromatics

IDEAS AND RECIPES

We're kicking off the vegetable categories with the culinary members of the allium family, which includes onions, shallots, leeks, scallions, and garlic, as well as aromatic vegetables such as fennel and celery. We use these ingredients to start off most recipes, so these vegetables tend to be the supporting player rather than the superstar. In particular, onion and garlic are the flavor base for many savory dishes, showing up early and then receding into the background. But we also frequently like to give them a chance to break out into a starring role, perhaps in an unapologetically garlicky stew or an onion tart.

Know What You Got

Onions come in multiple varieties, the most common of which are classified by color (red, white, and yellow). All can be eaten fresh or cooked and can be swapped with each other as well as with shallots. Sweet varieties such as Vidalia and Walla Walla have a higher water content, so they tend to rot faster; eat them quickly or store them in a sealed container in the fridge for a longer shelf life.

Leeks, scallions, ramps, spring onions, chives, and other green-stalked members of the allium family can be eaten from root to tip. They're versatile enough to be cooked into dishes as aromatic bases, but can also be pickled, grilled, lightly steamed, or—especially in the case of scallions and chives—sliced thin and eaten raw as a garnish.

Garlic comes in many variations, including green garlic or baby garlic, which looks like a thick scallion and can be used in the same way. If you get garlic with stems at a farmers' market, the stems can be cooked like leeks. Garlic scapes are the long curling stems that grow from certain varieties of garlic; they can be cooked or eaten raw. You can use them similarly to chives and scallions—they are a particularly good substitute in Green Sauce (page 138) and Ginger-Scallion Oil (page 92).

Fennel and celery fit into many recipes in the Broccoli and Friends chapter (page 180) because of their similar texture and firmness—somewhere between quick-cooking greens and longer-cooking root vegetables. But we've included them here to highlight their aromatic qualities and caramelizing properties with hopes of diversifying your approach to building flavor in savory recipes. They're also especially handy if you're cooking for someone with an allium allergy.

Store It Right

The majority of onions and garlic that you find at the supermarket are "cured," which means they've been dried for storage. These bulbs, with papery skins and no green parts, can last a long time somewhere dry, dark, and cool with a bit of air—don't leave them in plastic bags where moisture can gather, and minimize light, which will cause sprouting. Once an onion or a garlic clove has been peeled or cut, store it in a sealed container in the fridge.

Alliums with green stalks—year-round ones like scallions and leeks, or spring favorites like ramps and green garlic—should be stored in the crisper drawer of the fridge in a breathable produce bag, similarly to fennel and celery. If you don't have breathable bags, store in a sealed container wrapped in a barely damp kitchen cloth or paper towel to provide some humidity.

It's best not to store onions with potatoes, as onions speed up the potato sprouting process (see the illustration on page 195 for more information). Since potatoes are already taking up the dark spot in the pantry, Mei stores onions out in a hanging basket, which helps with ventilation, and they usually last for a few weeks, even in a well-lit area.

Save for Later

- Quick pickling (page 37) is a fantastic way to preserve alliums and aromatics (pickled red onions and fennel in particular add flair to everything from tacos to cheese boards).
- All these vegetables freeze well for use in cooked dishes. Blanch if you like (see page 23), or freeze raw. Chop or dice first, then press the pieces into a flat layer in a freezer bag or pre-portion into small amounts in airtight containers.
    - If you hate dicing onions for dinner every night, cut and freeze a large amount and scoop some out from the freezer every time you cook.

- When it comes to freezing garlic, we prefer to mince and blend with oil rather than freeze the cloves whole. Puree cloves in a food processor with enough oil to get the blades moving, then transfer the paste to a freezer bag and freeze flat or portion into an ice cube tray. When you don't feel like mincing garlic, break off a piece from the freezer bag or unmold a frozen cube and toss it directly into a hot pan.

You Can Still Eat It!

If an allium or aromatic isn't rotten but just doesn't look great—limp celery, dried-out garlic, brown-spotted fennel—pop it into your Kitchen Scrap Stock Bag (page 18) to add oomph to your next soup, stock, or pot of beans. Onions and garlic with green sprouts are fine to eat. If the exterior of an onion or fennel bulb is brown or bruised or has a tiny bit of mold, peel down until you find a pristine layer. The same goes for the slimy outer layer of scallions; strip off the outer pieces and use just the inside. Dried, yellowed, or limp scallions are also fair game—use them up in **Ginger-Scallion Oil** (page 92) or sauté them for **Savory Bread Pudding** (page 78). But once anything is very moldy or rotten, completely collapsed, or seriously slimy, it's time for the compost.

Extra Bits

All parts of the allium are flavorful, so save your onion ends and skins, garlic peels, scallion roots, and leek tops for **Kitchen Scrap Stock** (page 34). If your onions sprout greens, you can treat them like chives. And please—don't waste your scallion greens! In Chinese cooking, scallion greens are an essential ingredient. Ignore recipes where it says to use only the scallion whites—add the greens anyway, or use them thinly sliced as a garnish. Your farmers may even have extra greens, if you ask them nicely like Irene does. Leek tops and fennel stalks can be cooked up in **Sautéed Leek Top Pasta** (page 96) or steamed in a pan with a bit of butter or oil until tender as suggested by the acclaimed Southern chef Edna Lewis.

Scrap Chili Oil

Makes about 1 cup

If you find yourself with lots of allium odds and ends on the side of your cutting board, you've got the perfect opportunity to make our absolute favorite Chinese condiment. We spoon chili oil onto everything we can think of—scrambled eggs, avocado toast, and microwaved pizza. It's fun to customize to your taste—Mei loves fermented black beans and a splash of soy sauce; Irene uses shallots and ham scraps—and play with the amount of chili flakes, depending on whether you want more of a chili oil or chili crisp. And while allium scraps add the most flavor, feel free to toss in other odds and ends, like pepper cores and seeds, herb stems, and ginger peels.

1 cup allium scraps, such as garlic skins, onion peels and ends, and scallion ends

2 star anise pods

2 tablespoons Sichuan peppercorns

1 cup neutral oil, or more if needed

½ to 1 cup chili flakes

Kosher salt

Put the allium scraps, anise pods, and peppercorns in a small pot and cover with the oil, adding more if needed to submerge everything. Heat over medium-high heat until the oil starts to sizzle. Turn the heat down slightly and let it simmer at a lazy bubble for 10 to 15 minutes. Put the chili flakes in a large heatproof bowl, then carefully strain the hot oil over the flakes. Compost the scraps and spices in the strainer and let the oil cool. Season to taste with salt and any other sauces of your choice, then transfer to an airtight container and store in the fridge for a few months.

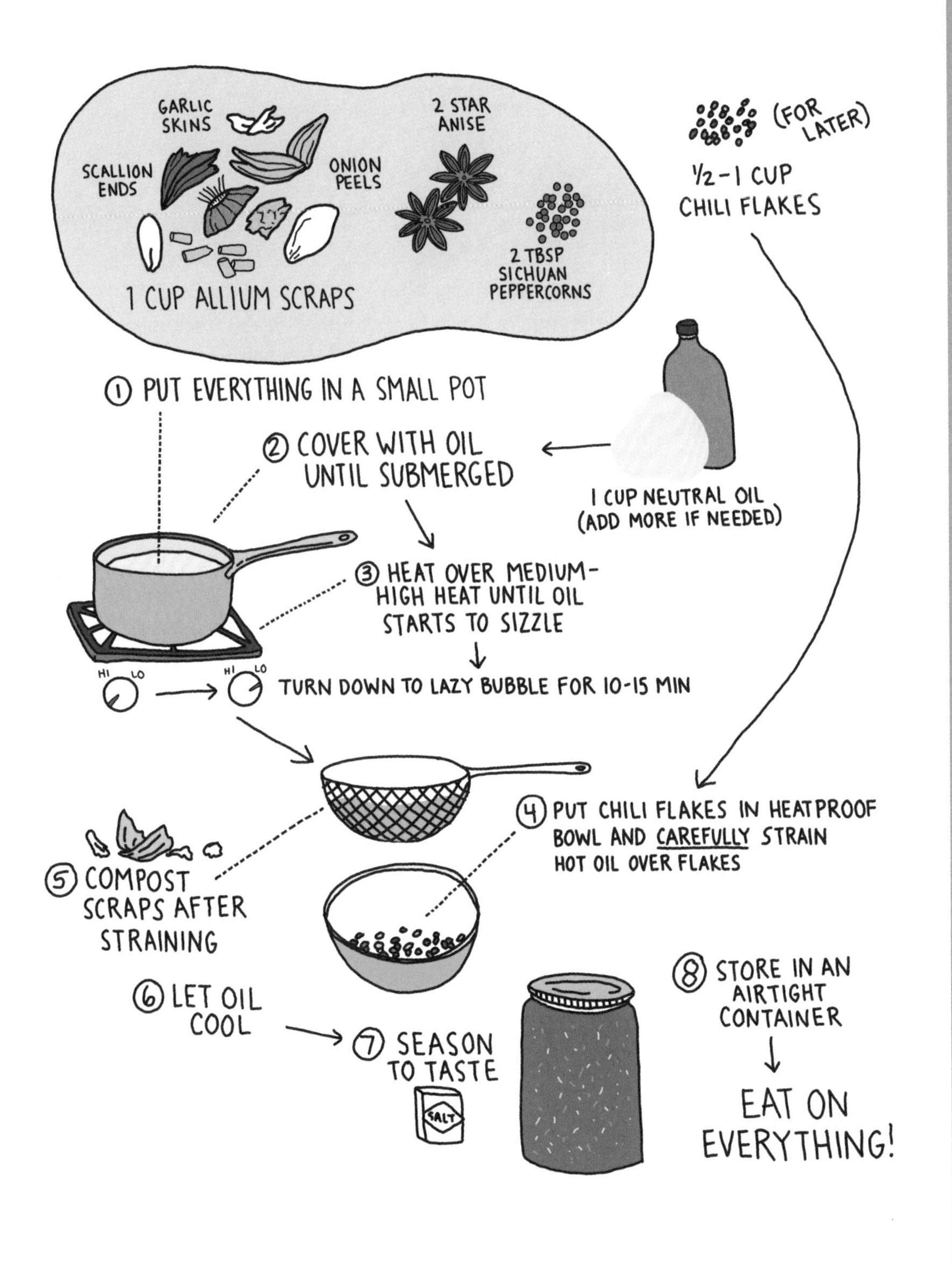

GARLIC SKINS
2 STAR ANISE
(FOR LATER)
SCALLION ENDS
ONION PEELS
½–1 CUP CHILI FLAKES
2 TBSP SICHUAN PEPPERCORNS
1 CUP ALLIUM SCRAPS
① PUT EVERYTHING IN A SMALL POT
② COVER WITH OIL UNTIL SUBMERGED
1 CUP NEUTRAL OIL (ADD MORE IF NEEDED)
③ HEAT OVER MEDIUM-HIGH HEAT UNTIL OIL STARTS TO SIZZLE
HI LO
HI LO
TURN DOWN TO LAZY BUBBLE FOR 10-15 MIN
④ PUT CHILI FLAKES IN HEATPROOF BOWL AND CAREFULLY STRAIN HOT OIL OVER FLAKES
⑤ COMPOST SCRAPS AFTER STRAINING
⑥ LET OIL COOL
⑦ SEASON TO TASTE
SALT
⑧ STORE IN AN AIRTIGHT CONTAINER
EAT ON EVERYTHING!

Use-It-Up Ideas

Onions

- The classic too-many-onions recipe and deservedly so, **Caramelized Onions** are long-lasting, flavor-packed, and usable in practically infinite ways. They punch up all the Hero Recipes and add depth of flavor to quiches, burgers, pizza, and just about anything you're having for dinner. Mix them with sour cream or cream cheese to make caramelized onion dip, stir them into mashed potatoes, or spread them on toast or crackers for a snack.

  Here's how to caramelize: Heat 1 tablespoon butter and 1 tablespoon extra-virgin olive oil over medium heat in a Dutch oven or large skillet for which you have a lid. Add 6 to 8 cups sliced onions with a generous five-finger pinch of salt and cook for a few minutes, stirring frequently, until all the onions have wilted a little. Cover the pan, reduce the heat to medium-low, and let the onions mellow for 30 minutes, stirring and scraping up any flavorsome browned bits on the bottom every 10 minutes or so.

  After this half-hour steam bath, the onions should be a light bronze. Remove the lid, increase the heat to medium, and get ready to stir more frequently, roughly every 5 minutes. Anytime you start developing a browned layer on the bottom of the pan, add 1 or 2 tablespoons water and scrape it up to incorporate that flavor into the onions and let it evaporate off. We usually let this go for about 20 minutes, until the onions reach a rich chestnut brown, but you can go longer and aim for a dark walnut or mahogany—it's up to you. Once cooled, store in an airtight container in the fridge for a week or two, or portion into small containers and freeze for future meals.

- **ANCHOVY-GARLIC CARAMELIZED ONIONS:** Once the onions reach the color you like, push them to the side of the pan and add a tiny splash of extra-virgin olive oil. Plop 4 to 6 minced garlic cloves and 6 chopped anchovies into the pool of oil. Let cook for a few minutes, until the garlic softens and the anchovies dissolve, then add ¼ cup dry white wine. Stir to incorporate everything into the onions. This is excellent for stirring into chicken stews, topping pizza, or just spreading onto puff pastry for a version of the French dish pissaladière.
- **BALSAMIC-BACON CARAMELIZED ONIONS:** Start by cooking 8 slices' worth of chopped bacon in a skillet (easy hack: use scissors to snip bits of bacon straight into the pan). Use the bacon fat in place of the butter and olive oil above, along with 1 tablespoon whole-grain mustard and 2 tablespoons brown sugar. When you remove the lid after the initial 30 minutes, stir in 2 tablespoons balsamic vinegar. This may be the best grilled cheese accompaniment of all time.
- **ONION SOUP:** Once the onions have reached a rich dark brown, add 4 cups broth or stock—beef broth is traditional, but any flavorful broth will work, like Mushroom Broth (page 216) or miso broth—and season to taste with salt and pepper. We like to add a splash of wine, vermouth, or cognac and, of course, French onion–style cheesy toasts are never a bad idea.

Sofrito

Sofrito, the aromatic base for a number of Spanish, Caribbean, and Latin American dishes, also makes quick work of surplus onions and adds instant flavor to stews, braises, or even buttered toast. This long-cooked Catalan-inspired version focuses on the onions, but you can branch out with other alliums or even peppers, carrots, and herbs. It's well suited to the odds and ends of an Eat-Me-First Box (see page 16), welcoming stray garlic cloves, the last sprigs of cilantro, or even the rest of last night's wine.

Heat ½ cup extra-virgin olive oil in a Dutch oven over medium-low heat. Add 6 to 8 cups chopped onions and 1 teaspoon each salt and sugar and cook, stirring occasionally, until the onions are soft and golden, about 35 minutes. Add 2 pounds chopped tomatoes of any kind (fresh, canned, frozen, whatever you have) and any other aromatics you like. Simmer, stirring occasionally, until the sauce is thick and fragrant and the tomatoes have broken down, about 45 minutes. Keep in an airtight container in the fridge for a week or so or in the freezer for many months, either frozen flat in a freezer bag or in an ice cube tray and then transferred to a resealable bag.

MAKE IT A MEAL

Make 15-minute **Shrimp Sofrito Soup** by mixing 1 cup sofrito with 3 cups flavorful stock. Season to taste with savory ingredients like soy and fish sauce, something acidic like lime juice or vinegar, and a pinch of sugar. Bring to a boil, then lower the heat to a simmer and add a pound of peeled and deveined shrimp. Poach lightly until just pink, about 5 minutes.

Other uses for sofrito include adding it to Choose-Your-Own-Adventure Vegetable Paella (page 65), whisking a bit with a little extra-virgin olive oil and vinegar to turn into a salad dressing, or using it as a base for Easygoing Tomato Sauce (page 104).

Garlic

- **Garlic Confit** (with bonus **Garlic Oil**) and **Roasted Garlic** help prep and preserve your surplus garlic. Confit is easiest for peeled cloves, like when we overzealously purchase large bags of peeled garlic and the cloves start to wrinkle, develop spots, or get sticky. Put all your surplus cloves in a small pot and pour in just enough extra-virgin olive oil to cover the cloves. Heat to a gentle simmer—you'll see little bubbles coming up from the garlic—and cook for 30 minutes, or until the cloves are tender and spreadable. Cool completely, then transfer to an airtight container and store in the fridge for up to 2 weeks or in the freezer for a few months. Add the confit to any Hero Recipe or mix it into a creamy dip. Use the garlicky oil to jazz up dressings, soups, and more.

  When you have extra heads of garlic sitting around, it's easier to roast them whole, giving you soft, smushable, easily usable cloves. Slice off the very top of the garlic head, just enough to expose the cloves and make it easier to get them out after roasting. Place one or more heads in a small baking dish and generously drizzle extra-virgin olive oil on top until the heads are well lubricated. Sprinkle with a bit of salt, then cover with aluminum foil or a lid and roast at 400 degrees until the skins are browned and the cloves are completely tender, about 45 minutes. Let cool, then squish the cloves out when you're ready to use them. The garlic heads can be stored in the fridge for up to 2 weeks, tightly enclosed in beeswax or plastic wrap.

SWITCH IT UP

- **STRAIGHT-UP GARLIC SAUCE:** Mash roasted or confit cloves into a paste and stir in some extra-virgin olive oil, lemon juice, salt, and pepper to taste. If you like, add some spices like sumac or cayenne, or some chopped fresh parsley or thyme. Spread on bread, stir into hot cooked pasta, or use it to baste your steak. It's fantastic mixed into Any-Bean Dip (page 306) as well.

(continues)

- **GARLIC BUTTER:** Mix 1 stick softened butter with 8 to 12 mashed roasted or confit garlic cloves and a pinch of salt. Feel free to add more flavorings like chopped fresh herbs, a teaspoon of soy sauce, chili flakes, grated lemon zest, or whatever strikes your fancy. We like this best smeared lavishly on good bread.

Scallions

- Ever tried **Ginger-Scallion Oil** at a Chinese restaurant? It's flavorful, it's punchy, and it is our firm belief in life that GSO makes everything taste better. Heat ½ cup neutral oil in a small pot. Mince a 2- or 3-inch knob of ginger and a bunch of scallions (limp and wrinkled bits unearthed from the fridge work well here!) and put them in a large heatproof bowl with some extra space. Once the oil just starts to smoke, carefully pour it over the ginger and scallions and stand back while it all bubbles up. Let cool, then stir in salt to taste—it should be strongly salty and flavorful.

MAKE IT A MEAL

If you have GSO, you have an instant meal. It totally counts as a vegetable (or so we will continue to tell ourselves). Eat it on everything from breakfast eggs to lunchtime quesadillas to dinnertime meat to late-night pizza. Use it as a dip for fresh veggies, a sauce for grilled meat, or a smear on your sandwich. Mix it into something creamy and make an instant dip. Or go classic Chinese and eat it with poached chicken or on top of fresh steamed white rice or any Asian noodle.

- It's a bold claim, but we think it's possible that we may have improved GSO by adding lettuce, of all things! This turns it into more of a sauce than an oil. The lettuce both adds a pleasantly silken texture and bulks up the sauce so you get greens in every bite. Plus, it's an excellent home for wilted, bruised, older, or generally not-so-pristine lettuce leaves. To make **Ginger-Scallion Lettuce Sauce**, shred 4 cups lightly packed lettuce leaves (we use a food processor), then stir it into the bowl right after the oil stops bubbling.

- We're in love with the **Scallion Oil** from Betty Liu's gorgeous cookbook *My Shanghai*, a sweeter, mellower version of the fast-and-furious GSO above and a great way to use up wilted scallions. Our slightly streamlined version has you chop a bunch of scallions into 1-inch pieces and cook them over medium-low heat in ½ cup neutral oil for about 30 minutes, then stir in ⅓ cup soy sauce, 2 tablespoons sugar, and 1 teaspoon black or rice vinegar. The scallions are so rich and sweet you'll want to fish them out of the sauce and eat them straight, and the oil is good on everything, just like GSO.

Fennel

- We love fennel when crisp and fresh in a **Crisp and Crunchy Noodle Salad** (page 46) or **Mix-and-Match Slaw Party** (page 42), but also cooked in **Braised Fennel with Lots of Lemon and Garlic**. Heat a splash of extra-virgin olive oil in a Dutch oven and brown a few heads of fennel, sliced into wedges. (If you like, toss in celery and onions too and clear out the crisper drawer!) Add a big handful of halved garlic cloves, the grated zest and juice of 1 lemon, and a big splash of vermouth or dry white wine. Bring to a boil, then add 2 cups flavorful chicken or vegetable stock and a few tablespoons of butter. Salt generously to taste, then bake at 350 degrees for 45 minutes, or until super tender. Serve over rice, with crusty bread, or even blended into soup.

Garlicky Red-Cooked Beef

Serves 4

This dish is a mash-up of the old-school classics Chicken with 40 Cloves of Garlic and Chinese Red-Cooked Beef, because soy sauce and garlic love each other deeply and belong together always. Two heads may seem like a lot, but the garlic mellows and softens and then, with a bit of gentle prodding, simply dissolves into the meaty liquid. Like so many stews, this one is flexible—try it with lamb or short ribs, or add turnips or radishes or butternut squash or potatoes. And surprisingly for a recipe with so much garlic, this is a very kid-friendly dish, so it's a good opportunity to swap in a protein or vegetable that you want them to eat. Mei's six-year-old says that the carrots in this stew are her absolute favorite and she has quite literally elbowed her toddler brother out of the way for access to the bowl. And though we rarely feel the need to dictate side dishes, we'd argue that fluffy white rice is an absolutely essential companion to soak up all the intensely savory broth.

NOTE: *Those unfamiliar with Chinese cooking techniques may be surprised by the first step of boiling the meat rather than browning for flavor. The idea is to remove the impurities from the meat proteins by skimming off any scum from the surface and then adding new liquid to braise the meat. This results in an unusually clear broth for a stew, one that's so rich and meaty that we often just drink it straight. Traditional Chinese chefs discard the boiling liquid, but given our anti-waste tendencies, we just skim the foam off with a fine-mesh strainer and then keep the rest for the braise.*

1 pound stew beef, or another similar cut of your choice, cut into 1-inch chunks
3 cups water, plus more if needed
3 cups stock of your choice or more water
½ cup Shaoxing wine (dry sherry or red wine works as a substitute, in a pinch)
3 tablespoons soy sauce
4 to 6 medium carrots, sliced into thick coins
1 to 2 heads garlic (10 to 25 cloves, according to your desired garlickiness), cloves separated and peeled
1-inch piece fresh ginger, lightly smashed
1 tablespoon sugar
3 star anise pods
Kosher salt and freshly ground black pepper
Steamed white rice, for serving

Put the beef and water in a Dutch oven, adding more water if needed to cover the beef, and bring to a boil over high heat. Boil for 10 minutes, skimming the scum off the surface regularly with a fine-mesh strainer or a large spoon. By the end of the boiling, the remaining liquid should be relatively clear and reduced to about 2 cups (pour it out and measure if you like, or just keep an eye on the liquid level as you go and add more water as necessary).

Add the stock to the pot, along with the wine, soy sauce, carrots, garlic, ginger, sugar, and star anise. Bring to a boil over high heat, then reduce the heat to low, partially cover the pot, and simmer for 2 hours, stirring every so often. Add a bit more water or stock if the liquid starts to get low in the pan. Toward the end of the cooking, use tongs to fish out the star anise and ginger, then poke at the garlic cloves so they fall apart and thicken the broth. Cook until the beef is soft and tender and easily breaks apart when poked with a fork or chopstick. Season to taste with salt and pepper, then ladle over copious amounts of white rice.

Sautéed Leek Top Pasta

Serves 4

Every time we make a dish with leeks, it pains us when the recipe says to discard the dark green leek tops—you're throwing out more than half the vegetable! At the very least, pop them into your Kitchen Scrap Stock Bag (page 18). Even better, make them so soft that you'll scoop them up with the rest of your pasta in this comforting recipe. You can keep it simple, with the magic of Parmesan and pasta water to create a sauce, or splash in heavy cream or crème fraîche, a squeeze of lemon juice, a sprinkle of grated lemon zest, a scatter of fresh herbs, or a glug of really good olive oil.

Kosher salt and freshly ground black pepper
2 tablespoons butter
2 tablespoons extra-virgin olive oil
3 large leeks with tops or 6 dark leek tops (the exact amount doesn't matter too much)
12 ounces pasta of any kind
¾ cup grated Parmesan, plus more for garnish

Bring a large pot of salted water to boil.

Meanwhile, melt the butter and olive oil together in a large skillet over medium-low heat. Separate the leeks into white and light green parts and dark green stalks. Slice the white and light green parts and add to the pan with the butter and olive oil and let caramelize slowly for about 10 minutes, stirring occasionally.

Add the dark green leek stalks to the boiling water, saving any extremely tough bits for the Kitchen Scrap Stock Bag in your freezer. Boil for 5 minutes, then use tongs or a slotted spoon or spider to carefully remove from the boiling water and place on a cutting board. Roughly chop, then add to the skillet with the rest of the leeks.

Add the pasta to the still-boiling water and cook until al dente, 1 to 2 minutes before the suggested cook time on the package. Drain, reserving about ½ cup pasta water (we like to scoop up the water with a large coffee mug right before draining). Transfer the cooked pasta to the skillet with the sautéed leeks, then add the Parmesan and ¼ cup of the pasta water. Stir to combine, scraping any browned bits off the bottom. If you feel like the pasta needs more sauce, add more pasta water or a splash of cream. Salt and pepper to taste and eat right away, although reheated leftovers are still pretty spectacular.

SWITCH IT UP

Follow Irene's lead and make this same recipe with fennel, treating the bulb like the white parts of the leek and the stalks like the dark green leek tops.

Summer Vegetables

IDEAS AND RECIPES

Let's chat about all that beautiful produce that spills from gardens and farmstands in warm weather: tomatoes, peppers, summer squash, cucumbers, corn, and eggplant. Whether you've pulled an armful of zucchini from the dirt or just bought too many supermarket tomatoes, people often find themselves with an overabundance of these vegetables. Or, to be precise, these vegetables *and* fruits. All the above except corn have seeds, which makes them fruits, botanically speaking. Is this important to your life? Unlikely, except possibly as bar trivia or to explain why they might be stored or cooked in certain ways, so we'll refer to them as vegetables from now on to avoid confusion.

These vegetables taste best when eaten during their optimal growing season. Try buying from farmers near you whenever possible. Not only will the vegetables be fresher, but your dollars will go to support the local food system and you can avoid lots of unnecessary plastic packaging. If you've got a surplus of straight-from-the-field vegetables, try the raw vegetable recipes to showcase their heightened summer flavors. If you end up with less-than-optimal ingredients out of season, try cooking methods that amplify their flavor, like roasting or slow-cooking.

Know What You Got

TOMATOES: They come in all colors, shapes, and sizes, from adorable round cherry Sungolds to ovoid Romas to gargantuan beefsteaks. Try to eat flavorful, expensive, in-season heirloom tomatoes—the unusually shaped, distinctively colored ones—in a raw preparation, while out-of-season tomatoes do best when slow-roasted or cooked down into sauce.

CUCUMBERS: The most common cucumbers in supermarkets are the classic thicker-skinned American version and the longer, skinnier English kind, which, unfortunately, generally comes wrapped in plastic to protect its thin skin. Both can be eaten raw, pickled, or even cooked (!), with any tough skin on an American cucumber peeled off fully or in stripes. We don't bother peeling English cucumbers or small, firm varieties such as Kirby and Persian cucumbers.

EGGPLANTS: While most of us are familiar with the classic globe eggplant—large, bulbous, thick at the bottom—eggplants come in all sorts of other shapes, sizes, and colors. Asian varieties tend to be long and thin, while Italian varieties range from spherical to pear-shaped. They all cook up similarly; just keep in mind that larger eggplants typically mean tougher skin and more seeds. They're the only vegetable in this chapter we always recommend cooking—raw eggplant isn't unsafe, it just tastes better cooked.

SUMMER SQUASH: Green zucchini are the most famous of the summer squash, but squash comes in all shapes and sizes. Did you know zucchini comes in yellow, round, and striped varieties? You'll find bulbous shapes with straight or crooked necks, as well as the pattypan, which looks like a flying saucer. No matter the variety or color, all these squashes can be cooked or eaten raw—best when super fresh and sliced very thin.

CORN: If you've gotten fresh or heirloom corn from a farmstand, it's usually best to eat it as soon as possible so the sugars don't convert into starches. Cook them any way you like, or just eat the juicy, sweet kernels raw. Supermarket varieties, husked or not, are more likely to be chosen for high sugar content already, so there's not as much pressure to consume right away. Frozen corn is also a great option; the kernels are usually frozen at the peak of freshness so you get that summertime flavor with a minimum of fuss.

PEPPERS: Did you know that all bell peppers start out green? They turn different colors as they ripen, which is why green peppers aren't as sweet as yellow or orange. Red bell peppers have ripened the longest and are the sweetest of the bunch—useful info if you're planning to eat them raw. If you find yourself with spicier chile peppers, such as shishitos, jalapeños, or serranos, they can be stuffed, grilled, sautéed, or used to punch up a pickle or sauce. You might want to wear disposable gloves when handling hot peppers as the oils can irritate your skin—especially your eyes if you touch your face!

Store It Right

Cucumbers, peppers, and all the summer squashes will last the longest unwashed and stashed in breathable produce bags in the crisper drawer of the fridge. Eggplants and tomatoes maintain the best texture and flavor when stored out of the fridge. Put the eggplants somewhere cool and dark and keep tomatoes on the counter but out of the sun. Both can be moved to the refrigerator in a pinch if getting old or overripe. Store corn in the fridge; corn on the cob comes handily swathed in its own protective carrying case, so keep the husks on until you're ready to cook. Husked corn can be wrapped in a damp cloth and then a plastic bag or airtight container to extend their life. Once any of these vegetables are cut, store them in an airtight container in the fridge.

Save for Later

If you have an abundance of fresh tomatoes, place them whole on a sheet pan in the freezer so they maintain their shape. Once frozen, transfer to a resealable bag and use in a cooked dish within a few months, as all the air between them will eventually lead to freezer burn. Chopped tomatoes and leftover canned tomatoes can also be frozen in an airtight container. However, tomato pastes and cooked dishes like tomato sauces and soups maintain texture and flavor best, so if you have time, cook your tomatoes before freezing.* Diced peppers can be frozen raw but should be cooked afterward for the best texture. You can also blanch, sauté, or make Peperonata (page 130) before freezing. Summer squash and corn kernels should be blanched (see page 23) or sautéed before freezing. Eggplant freezes best when already in a mush, so make a dip or puree (pages 117–19) before freezing. Cucumbers don't freeze well; they get mushy and floppy once thawed, so plan to pickle them (page 37) if you need a longer-term storage option.

You Can Still Eat It!

Summer vegetables may rot more quickly than other produce, especially when stored out of the fridge. A spot of mold on your expensive heirloom tomato is unlikely to be extremely toxic; if you want to eat around it, just

*If you want to know more about the cellular mechanics of freezing, there's a great essay by science writer Lina Tran in *Cooking at Home* by David Chang and Priya Krishna. Basically, ice crystals grow within the cells of food as its freezes, and these crystals can break down the cell walls that cause food to have a certain texture. But the cells of cooked tomatoes have already gone through structural changes, so the freezing won't affect them as much as with raw tomatoes. Thus, it generally helps to cook ingredients before freezing, which is why we recommend blanching (see page 23) or making soup or sauce.

remove the mold itself and an inch or so beyond it. Use your common sense though; don't eat anything too overgrown with mold and don't serve to anyone other than a healthy adult. And if you do take a bite of something blemished and it tastes terrible, spit it out immediately and discard. Wrinkled peppers, limp zucchini, and shriveled corn kernels are fine to eat but will do better cooked into a dish. Even soft cucumber can still be eaten—try the Stir-Fried Pork with Cucumber and Zucchini (page 114) for a new way of looking at this vegetable.

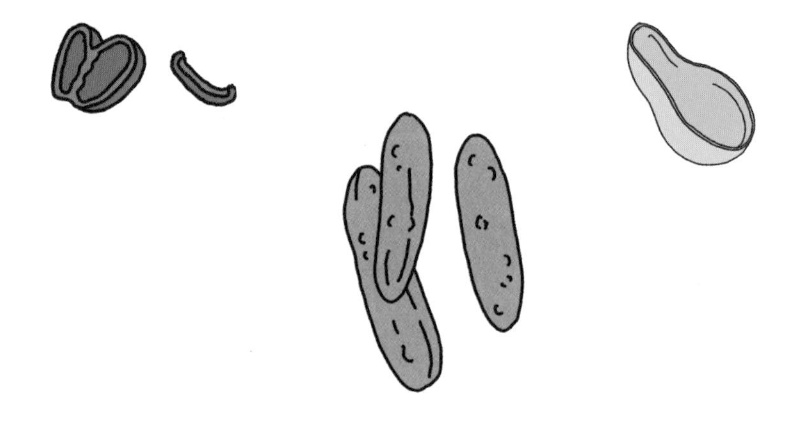

Tomatoes

Use-It-Up Ideas

- Got a bunch of lightly wrinkled tomatoes? Make **Slow-Roasted Tomatoes** by halving or quartering your tomatoes depending on size, tossing them in extra-virgin olive oil and a sprinkle of salt and sugar, then popping them in the oven at 300 degrees. Let them slow-roast for an hour or two for a concentrated jammy flavor that works in nearly every Hero Recipe. Let cool, then store in an airtight container and keep in the refrigerator for about a week or in the freezer, well wrapped, just about indefinitely.
- If you've got big ripe tomatoes around, make **Tomato Butter** to smear on steaks and crusty bread. Core and chop the tomato and squeeze the juices out. (A perfect opportunity to make the **Tomato Water Martini** on page 104!) Blend the tomato flesh with a stick of softened butter and season with salt, garlic, fresh herbs, or the spices of your choice. Store in an airtight container in the fridge for a week or two or form into individual portions and freeze.
- Deal with multiple pounds of tomatoes at once by combining them in an oven-safe pot with a quartered onion, a few garlic cloves, and a small splash of extra-virgin olive oil to make **Roasted Tomato Soup**. Cover and roast at 425 degrees for about 25 minutes. Let cool slightly, then transfer to a blender and add stock, coconut milk, or water until you reach your desired soup consistency.
- Blitz a pound of tomatoes, half an onion, a chile pepper, and a handful of fresh cilantro leaves in a food processor and you've got an easy **Salsa Fresca**—make it as chunky or smooth as you like. Season with salt and maybe a splash of lime juice, and consider

adding bell peppers, corn kernels, mango, pineapple, or whatever else looks good in your fridge. Switch things up and roast all the vegetables first for a smoky version rather than a fresh salsa.

- When we're faced with an abundance of tomatoes, an **Easygoing Tomato Sauce** always comes to mind. We like to riff on the various versions of tomato sauce from renowned Italian chef Marcella Hazan (roughly 2 pounds tomatoes, ½ cup extra-virgin olive oil or 5 tablespoons butter, a chopped onion, a teaspoon or two of salt, sometimes a diced carrot or celery stick, simmered for 45 minutes) by adding vegetables to our puree, like steamed squash or roasted peppers. Despite Marcella's well-known preference for good ingredients, we find this tomato sauce a particularly useful landing place for surplus ingredients like limp celery, wrinkled tomatoes, or wilted herbs. And once you've got sauce, it's easy to make **Baked Eggs** by slipping in some eggs to simmer on the stovetop or bake in the oven until the whites are just done and the yolks are still runny. Spice it up with paprika or harissa, bulk it up with beans or greens, and dinner's on the table in moments.

Summer Vegetable Gazpacho

Serves 8 to 10

If you're turned off by the idea of cold soup, it's time to rethink what you know of gazpacho. After much research and several large bottles of olive oil, we have learned that an ample quantity of good extra-virgin olive oil magically takes you from just sipping on pureed vegetables to a rich, full-bodied, extremely drinkable tomato experience. Once you've gotten used to the idea, feel free to start experimenting. We follow the lead of the celebrated Spanish chef José Andrés, who merely asks: *Will it gazpacho?* And if it's fruit or vegetable, if it's juicy and soft, his answer is *Probably yes.*

2 to 3 pounds tomatoes of any kind, roughly chopped
1 large cucumber, peeled and roughly chopped
1 bell pepper (any color), seeded and roughly chopped
1 small onion or shallot, roughly chopped
1 to 3 garlic cloves, roughly chopped
1 tablespoon vinegar of your choice (sherry vinegar would be traditional)
½ to ¾ cup extra-virgin olive oil
Kosher salt and freshly ground pepper

Put all the vegetables in a blender with the vinegar and ½ cup olive oil and blend until smooth. Taste, and consider adding up to ¼ cup more olive oil if you used a lot of tomatoes. Refrigerate until chilled, then season to taste, drizzling in a bit more oil or brightening with a bit more vinegar if you like. Drink straight from cups or serve as a soup with fun garnishes.

TOP IT OFF

We love the contrast of smooth gazpacho with Toasted Breadcrumbs (page 80) or Croutons (page 81). To plate it chef-style, top with chopped fresh herbs and some tiny diced bits of the vegetables.

Fresh Tomato Bloody Mary

Serves 4 to 6

After copious testing of this recipe and drinking Bloody Marys at all hours of the day, we learned several important things. Firstly and unsurprisingly, it is difficult to continue recipe testing after dedicating yourself to ensuring no Bloody Mary goes to waste. Secondly, the real secret weapon in this recipe is the pickle juice, which takes the drink from just boozy, spicy tomato juice to a bright, tangy, and seriously quaffable beverage. If you don't have any to hand, try kimchi or sauerkraut juice. Worst case, add a splash of vinegar and adjust your salt and sugar levels, and consider how you can survive without a ready stash of pickles in your fridge.

4 large tomatoes (about 5 cups chopped)
Juice of 1 lemon
Grated zest and juice of 1 lime
1 tablespoon horseradish
5 dashes hot sauce, or more to taste
¼ cup pickle juice
1 tablespoon Worcestershire sauce or soy sauce
1 or 2 pinches sugar, if your tomatoes aren't super flavorful
1 teaspoon kosher salt
A few grinds of fresh pepper, or more to taste
Optional spices for the mix or for the rim: celery salt, garlic powder, paprika, chili powder, etc.
1 ounce vodka per glass

Combine all the ingredients, except for the vodka, in a blender and puree. Taste and adjust as needed. Pour an ounce of vodka over ice in each glass, then add ⅔ to ¾ cup of the tomato mixture. Stir and garnish with anything you like.

TOP IT OFF

There's no end of fun ways to finish off a Bloody Mary. To rim your glass with spices such as celery salt, garlic powder, paprika, or chili powder, rub your spent lemon or lime wedge all around the edge of the glass to coat the rim. Place the spices on a plate, flip the glass upside down, and press into the spices. Go wild with fun garnishes like pickles, olives, cucumbers, slices of bacon, you name it.

SWITCH IT UP

Yes, you should absolutely customize your fresh Bloody Mary to your taste, your preferences, or what alcohol you currently have on hand. Leave out the vodka if you'd prefer not to drink alcohol. Swap the vodka for tequila in a version known as a Bloody Maria, maybe garnished with a pickled jalapeño. Spice it up further with sriracha or gochujang. You could even slip in a spoonful of clam juice for a version of Canada's favorite brunch cocktail, the Bloody Caesar, also affectionately known as just a Caesar. Make it your own and have fun with it. Cheers!

Chinese Scrambled Eggs with Tomatoes

Serves 4, ideally with some rice on the side

This classic Chinese stir-fry reminds us of childhood, when we found this dish immensely comforting but were also slightly weirded out by eating stir-fried tomatoes with sugar. (And in Irene's opinion, for a classic version, you'll need a lot more sugar than you think.) As adults, we find this to be an incredibly useful dish to have in your toolbox of quick-cooking vegetable + protein dinners, especially if you have cooked rice or noodles at hand. Like most Chinese-style stir-fries, this dish demands that you have all your ingredients ready to go once you turn on the heat. The eggs cook in seconds, as do the aromatics, and the tomatoes only take a few minutes more. The whole thing requires a bit of focus and possibly a little juggling, but it also means that dinner can be on the table in mere moments—and that's worth all the scrambling (ha!).

6 eggs
1 teaspoon toasted sesame oil
Kosher salt
2 tablespoons neutral oil, plus more if needed
1 garlic clove, minced
½-inch piece fresh ginger, minced
2 large tomatoes, cut into chunks, or 1 (14-ounce) can tomatoes, crushed if whole
1 teaspoon rice vinegar or white vinegar
Big pinch sugar
Small pinch ground white pepper, if you have it, or black pepper (optional)
2 scallions, thinly sliced

Lightly beat the eggs in a mixing bowl with the sesame oil and a pinch of salt. Heat the neutral oil in a large skillet or wok, ideally nonstick, over high heat. Once the oil starts to shimmer, add the eggs and cook, stirring constantly with a spatula, until just barely set, 30 seconds to 1 minute. Return the cooked eggs to the mixing bowl.

Add another small splash of oil to the pan if it looks dry, then add the garlic and ginger. Sauté until fragrant—this will also just take seconds—then add the tomatoes and any juices. Stir in the vinegar and sprinkle with a big pinch of sugar and another pinch of salt, plus white pepper (or black pepper, if you like). Cook until the tomatoes are soft and there's a little bit of a sauce, 2 to 4 minutes. If there's not enough sauce, loosen it with a teaspoon of water or two. Return the eggs to the pan and toss to coat, then stir in the scallions. Season to taste before serving.

Tomato and Crispy Tofu Salad

Serves 4 as a side

This take on the Italian bread salad known as panzanella swaps out the traditional stale bread for Crispy Baked Tofu Bites (page 303), a satisfying way to get some extra crunch and protein while also being vegan and gluten-free. It's a great dish for using up overripe summer tomatoes—the abundant juice adds tomatoey oomph to the dressing—but it works all year round, especially with a mix of tomato colors and sizes. Add any other summer vegetable, like roasted peppers or grilled eggplant or raw corn kernels, or mix in pops of salt with capers, anchovies, or olives. And if you don't have any dietary restrictions, some creamy cheese like mozzarella or feta or a few slices of salami or prosciutto wouldn't go amiss. Raid your pantry and fridge and see what needs to be used up.

3 or 4 large ripe tomatoes or about 1 pound mixed tomatoes, cut into chunks

Kosher salt

½ cup thinly sliced cucumber (cut any larger slices into half-moons)

½ cup thinly sliced onion, red if you have it

½ cup chopped fresh herbs, such as basil, mint, or parsley, including any tender stems

1 recipe Crispy Baked Tofu Bites (page 303)

VINAIGRETTE

2 tablespoons extra-virgin olive oil

1 tablespoon rice vinegar or another vinegar of choice

1 teaspoon Dijon mustard

1 garlic clove, minced

Kosher salt and freshly ground black pepper

In a large bowl, toss the tomatoes with a generous amount of salt and let sit so the juices ooze out while you prepare the rest of the ingredients. Add the cucumber, onion, herbs, and tofu and toss to combine.

Whisk together all the vinaigrette ingredients and season with salt and pepper to taste. Pour over the salad and toss to coat everything before serving.

If you have stale bread to use up, swap the tofu bites with roughly 3 cups Croutons (page 81).

Cucumbers

Use-It-Up Ideas

- Of course, cucumbers are the prime ingredient for **Quick Pickles** (page 37). Experiment with spices and flavorings; we like lots of garlic, chile peppers, fresh dill, and ground turmeric.
- Crisp and crunchy cucumbers make a delicious addition to the **Tabbouleh-ish Herb Salad** (page 149) and the **Tomato and Crispy Tofu Salad** (page 110), or riff on your own using the **Leafy Greens Salad Builder** on page 160.
- The Chinese dish **Smashed Cucumbers** uses a technique that releases liquid and seeds and creates lots of jagged edges, so the pieces have more textural interest and absorb more flavor. (It was the thrill of a lifetime for Irene to do this on camera for the Food Network—if only all our cooking techniques were so culinarily useful and gleefully satisfying!) Thin-skinned cucumbers work best for smashing, such as a large English cucumber or smaller Persian or Kirby cucumbers; if you have only thick-skinned cucumbers, peel fully or in stripes. Cut about a pound of cucumbers crosswise into thick rounds, roughly 1 inch wide. Place in a resealable bag, press most of the air out, and close, then use a skillet or rolling pin to smash the cucumbers so they release their juices. (Alternatively, place the cucumbers in a mortar and use the pestle to do the smashing.) Transfer the cucumber pieces to a sieve or colander, sprinkle with a pinch each of salt and sugar, and let sit for 15 minutes before tossing with **Fridge-Door Dressing** (page 165) or one of the following options:

- For a more traditional Chinese dressing, whisk together 2 teaspoons soy sauce, 1 teaspoon rice or black vinegar, 1 teaspoon toasted sesame oil, and 1 minced garlic clove, plus a pinch of chili flakes if you like.
- The famed French chef Jacques Pépin suggests tossing the cucumbers with 1 cup chopped white onion, ½ cup sour cream, and a few dashes of hot sauce.

- **Cucumber Yogurt Dip** is an excellent use-up for slightly older cucumbers that may not be fresh and firm enough for a salad but are still worth rescuing from the compost. If you have thick Greek yogurt, this recipe works well as a dip; thinner regular yogurt works best as a sauce for drizzling onto roasted vegetables or spiced meat. Grate or dice a cucumber, salt generously, and leave to drain in a colander for 10 minutes before mixing with 1 cup plain yogurt. Here are two fun variations:

- To make **Irene's Favorite Indian-Inspired Raita**, add 2 pinches cayenne pepper, 2 tablespoons chopped fresh cilantro, ½ teaspoon garam masala, and ½ chopped serrano pepper.
- For a **Greek-Style Tzatziki**, add 2 tablespoons finely chopped fresh mint or dill, 1 minced garlic clove, a good squeeze of lemon juice, and a few grinds of black pepper.

- If your cucumbers end up quite soft (but still aren't moldy or off-smelling), blend them up into **Summer Vegetable Gazpacho** (page 105) or even an **All-the-Fruit Smoothie** (page 228).

Stir-Fried Pork with Cucumber and Zucchini

Serves 3 to 4, with rice or noodles

Irene once heard a Chinese chef ask, "Why do Westerners only eat their cucumber raw?" Once hit with a blast of heat, a cucumber's texture is virtually indistinguishable from a zucchini. Feel free to make the dish with all cucumber or all summer squash of any kind if you don't have both.

1 tablespoon water
1 tablespoon soy sauce
1 tablespoon Shaoxing wine (dry sherry works as a substitute, in a pinch)
1½ teaspoons toasted sesame oil
1½ teaspoons rice vinegar
½ teaspoon cornstarch
8 ounces ground pork
Neutral oil, for stir-frying
1 garlic clove, minced
½-inch piece fresh ginger, minced
1 small cucumber, peeled, seeded, and sliced into half-moons
1 zucchini or yellow squash, sliced into half-moons
Steamed white rice, cooked noodles, or lettuce cups, for serving

---

Whisk together the water, soy sauce, Shaoxing wine, sesame oil, rice vinegar, and cornstarch in a small bowl. Transfer 2 tablespoons of the sauce to a medium bowl and mix it into the ground pork.

Heat a splash of oil over high heat in a wok or large skillet. Once the oil starts to shimmer, add the pork and stir-fry until lightly browned, then push it to the side and add the garlic and ginger to the center. Stir-fry the garlic and ginger for 30 seconds, then add the cucumber and zucchini and fry for 2 minutes. Pour the remaining sauce over everything and stir-fry until the vegetables are tender but still a bit firm, about 3 minutes. Add kosher salt to taste and serve immediately with rice, noodles, or lettuce cups.

Sautéed Shrimp and Cucumber with Fermented Black Beans

Serves 2 to 3

Quick-cooking protein + intense umami + juicy, crunchy fresh vegetable = a dinner win in our books. This dish marries the magical garlic and shrimp pairing of Italian scampi with Julia Child's French cooked cucumbers with butter, then nods to our Chinese heritage with the addition of fermented black beans. If you haven't tried fermented black beans, we highly recommend picking up a stash from your local Asian grocery store or ordering them online—they keep forever in the fridge and add a uniquely funky-salty punch to stir-fries, stews, and so much more.

NOTE: *Fermented black beans are quite salty, so you probably won't need additional seasoning. If you prefer your food less salty, give them a quick rinse before adding.*

2 tablespoons butter

1 bunch scallions, thinly sliced (set aside some of the sliced green ends for garnish)

2 garlic cloves, minced

3 tablespoons fermented black beans, roughly chopped

12 ounces shrimp, peeled and deveined

1 cup diced cucumber (peeled, if the skin is very thick)

Kosher salt (optional)

Steamed white rice or cooked noodles, for serving

(continues)

Melt the butter in a large skillet or wok over medium-high heat. Add the scallions, garlic, and black beans and cook for about a minute, until softening and fragrant.

Add the shrimp and cook, stirring occasionally, until they're pink around the edges but still a bit translucent, about 2 minutes. Add the cucumber and toss to combine with the shrimp, then cook until the shrimp are fully pink and opaque, about a minute per side.

Taste and season with salt if needed (the black beans are pretty salty, so you probably won't need any). Garnish with the reserved scallion greens and your choice of toppings and serve with rice or noodles.

TOP IT OFF

Add some crunchy texture with a scattering of sesame seeds or crushed peanuts, plus a generous spoonful of Scrap Chili Oil (page 86).

NO-WASTE TIPS

Do you have a package of fermented black beans still sitting in your fridge from making this recipe last month . . . or even last year? No judgement—good on you for trying out a new ingredient! Let's help you use them up. Their intense umami flavor adds savory depth to Scrap Chili Oil (page 86) and punches up the Braised Tofu on page 311. And of course, you can always add chopped beans to a Make-It-Your-Own Stir Fry (page 52) using just about any vegetable; they go especially well with strongly flavored aromatics like garlic and ginger.

Eggplant

Use-It-Up Ideas

- If we're ever at a loss for what to do with an on-the-verge-of-going bad eggplant, we roast it and store it in the fridge in an airtight container, giving us a few more days to eat it straight or incorporate it into another recipe. Cut it into slices or chunks, lightly oil, salt, and roast at 425 degrees for 25 to 35 minutes, until golden brown, tossing halfway through. Use the chunks in **Anything-in-the-Kitchen Pasta** (page 68) or **Grain Salad** (page 162) or simply toss in **Fridge-Door Dressing** (page 165) with lots of fresh herbs and a hit of honey or maple syrup.
- When looking to use up a bunch of eggplants, the least fussy preparation is roasting them whole in a very hot oven. Once the eggplant is cooked and collapsed, it's easy to remove the skin and use the softened flesh in any number of dips/spreads/side dishes, like the versions of **Baba Ghanoush** and **Baingan Bharta** that follow. Eat them on their own, smeared onto crusty bread, dolloped onto rice, or scooped with naan or pita.

  To start either dish, heat the oven to 500 degrees (or as close as your oven comes) and line a rimmed baking sheet or baking dish with aluminum foil. Stab one or more whole eggplants a few times with a sharp knife. Place the eggplants on the sheet and roast until the skin gets blackened and crackly and the flesh is completely soft and starting to collapse, 40 to 60 minutes. Let cool for at least 15 minutes—slicing open the eggplant will help steam escape faster—before removing the skin. If the eggplant flesh is very juicy, drain it in a colander for a few minutes. Roughly mash the flesh with a fork and proceed with the recipe. You can do this in advance and keep the cooked eggplant for a few days in a sealed container in the fridge.

Make-It-Your-Way Baba Ghanoush

Makes about 2 cups

There are endless versions of baba ghanoush out there, so adjust the ingredients based on your preferences or how much eggplant you have (feel free to halve the recipe if you only have one eggplant). Stir in some yogurt for creaminess, add lots more fresh herbs or pomegranate seeds, and store in the fridge in an airtight container for a few days.

2 medium globe eggplants, cooked, peeled, and mashed as instructed on page 117
2 tablespoons lemon juice
2 tablespoons tahini
1 to 2 tablespoons extra-virgin olive oil, plus more to taste or for drizzling
1 garlic clove, minced
Handful chopped fresh parsley or mint, for garnish (optional)
Kosher salt and freshly ground black pepper

Stir all the ingredients together in a bowl and season to taste.

NO-WASTE TIPS

In a delightfully unexpected use-it-up trick, Eden Grinshpan suggests using burnt eggplant skins to make a charred tahini sauce in her vibrant cookbook *Eating Out Loud*. Our scalable version blends roughly equal amounts of blackened eggplant skins and tahini, plus half as much ice water (say, ½ cup skins, ½ cup tahini, and ¼ cup water). Add minced garlic, fresh lemon juice, and salt and pepper to taste, then blend in more ice water as needed to achieve a saucy consistency you like.

Spiced-How-You-Like-It Baingan Bharta

Makes about 2½ cups

This smoky, Punjabi-inspired eggplant dish has many variations, but the main idea is the sautéed tomato-onion mixture. Otherwise, riff as you like with more or less garlic or tomatoes and the spices of your choice. We like coriander and garam masala, but feel free to add or substitute turmeric, cumin, or chili powder.

2 tablespoons neutral oil
1 medium onion, chopped
1 jalapeño or serrano pepper, seeded if desired and finely chopped
4 to 6 garlic cloves, minced
1-inch piece fresh ginger, minced
2 or 3 medium tomatoes, chopped
2 medium globe eggplants, cooked, peeled, and mashed as instructed on page 117
1 teaspoon ground coriander
1 teaspoon garam masala
Handful chopped fresh cilantro leaves and stems, for garnish
Kosher salt

Heat the oil in a large skillet over medium-high heat. Add the onion and cook until golden brown, about 10 minutes, then add the chile pepper, garlic, and ginger and fry for another minute. Add the tomatoes and cook, stirring frequently, until soft, then add the mashed eggplant and spices and cook for a few more minutes to let all the flavors meld. Stir in the cilantro and season with salt to taste.

Roasted Vegetable Involtini

Serves 4, with sides

This rolled vegetable dish looks impressive but is surprisingly easy and open to improvisation with an assortment of summer vegetables. Use any cheese in a pinch here, but the fluffiness of ricotta, feta, and mozzarella roll up nicely in the vegetables. Go fridge foraging too—add salty things like capers, anchovies, or chopped olives; green things like sautéed spinach or steamed broccoli, chopped into tiny pieces; and meaty bits like salami or bacon or the hot dog you stole off your kid's dinner plate.

1 large globe eggplant or 2 Asian eggplants

1 large summer squash or zucchini

Extra-virgin olive oil, for drizzling

Kosher salt

8 ounces fresh mozzarella or ricotta, plus more for sprinkling if desired

Heaping ¼ cup Toasted Breadcrumbs (page 80), plus more for sprinkling if desired

Grated zest of 1 lemon

¼ cup mix-ins, chopped into small pieces (optional; see headnote)

1 cup Easygoing Tomato Sauce (page 104) or tomato sauce of your choice

---

Heat the oven to 450 degrees.

Slice the eggplant and squash lengthwise into roughly ¼-inch-thick slabs. Lay in a single layer on a rimmed baking sheet and lightly coat with olive oil and a sprinkling of salt. Roast until the vegetables are tender and can easily be rolled, 10 to 20 minutes depending on the thickness of your slices. Set aside to cool while you make the filling.

Tear or chop the mozzarella into small pieces and mix in a medium bowl with the breadcrumbs, lemon zest, and any other ingredients you like. Taste and season with salt as needed. Put a large spoonful onto the end of an eggplant or squash strip and roll the strip up until the cheese mixture is tucked inside like a little swaddled baby. Continue with the remaining strips until all the mixture is gone or all the veggie strips have been used (eat whatever is left over—chef's snack!). Spread a thin layer of tomato sauce in a 9 x 13-inch baking dish, then place the rolls of filled vegetables inside, seams down. Spoon on the rest of the tomato sauce and top with any extra cheese and breadcrumbs. Bake until the cheese has melted and the rolls have collapsed slightly, about 20 minutes. Serve right away.

Zucchini and Summer Squash

Use-It-Up Ideas

In an odd bit of vegetable syllogism, eggplant and cucumber are almost never eaten in the same way, but zucchini and summer squash can be eaten like either one. And also in **cake** (page 123)! **Stir-fry squash with cucumbers and pork** (page 114) or layer with eggplants and melty cheese in lasagna or **Roasted Vegetable Involtini** (page 120). Shred, squeeze the liquid out, and add to **How-You-Like-It Savory Pancakes** (page 60) or **Rice Fritters** (page 64). Pan-sear or roast in chunks or slices and use to top salads, stuff sandwiches, add to pasta, and so much more. We like to let freshly cooked chunks of summer squash sit in a garlicky marinade made from equal parts extra-virgin olive oil and vinegar, a minced garlic clove or two, a pinch of salt, and any tender fresh herb we have on hand. Eat a few straight while still warm and save the rest in the fridge in an airtight container and use the same way you'd use the plain roasted versions.

Also, when zucchini and cucumber are so similar, why do we tend to only cook one and only eat the other raw? Try it the other way around and see what you think. Make **Raw Summer Squash, Two Ways** by slicing a zucchini or summer squash crosswise into thin rounds, or lengthwise into thin ribbons and tossing with:

- crumbled feta, a drizzle of extra-virgin olive oil, a good squeeze of lemon juice and a pinch of the grated zest, a handful of chopped fresh mint, parsley, or basil, and salt and pepper to taste; *or*
- 1 tablespoon soy sauce, 2 teaspoons toasted sesame oil, and 2 teaspoons fresh lime juice, or more to taste. Finish with a pinch of chili flakes, a sprinkling of chopped peanuts or cashews, and a scattering of chopped scallions or fresh cilantro.

Summer Squash Cake (aka Zucchini Bread)

Makes 1 loaf or 12 muffins

Why limit yourself to zucchini when you can make a summer squash cake? It's a very flexible recipe depending on what you have in the pantry and how you like your cake. We generally prefer a lightly sweetened loaf, but sometimes add more sugar and some cocoa powder if we're more in the mood for chocolate cake. And psst: We don't bother squeezing the liquid out of the squash. This recipe doubles easily to make two loaves, or one loaf and 12 muffins. The muffins are prime kid food (a cupcake, but with vegetables), and extra loaves make excellent gifts for endearing yourself to others. Should you want to save the extra loaf for future you, this cake-bread freezes very well, sealed tightly in a layer of plastic wrap, and then in aluminum foil or a resealable bag with the air pressed out.

2 cups grated summer squash

¾ cup extra-virgin olive oil or neutral oil

⅔ to 1 cup sugar, depending on how sweet you want your cake (either brown or white works)

2 eggs

1½ teaspoons vanilla extract

1½ cups all-purpose flour *or* 1 cup all-purpose flour plus ½ cup whole wheat flour

½ cup cocoa powder (optional)

1½ teaspoons ground cinnamon

1 teaspoon baking powder

1 teaspoon baking soda

1 teaspoon kosher salt

(continues)

Heat the oven to 350 degrees. Grease either an 8-inch loaf pan or a 12-cup muffin tin.

Mix the squash, oil, sugar, eggs, and vanilla in a large bowl until well combined. In a separate bowl, whisk together the flour, cocoa powder (if using), cinnamon, baking powder, baking soda, and salt. Mix the dry ingredients into the wet ingredients and stir with a spatula until the mixtures are thoroughly combined.

Pour the batter into the prepared pan. Bake until a sharp knife or fork tines poked into the middle come out clean, 40 to 50 minutes for the cake-bread or 18 to 22 minutes for cupcake-muffins.

Corn

Use-It-Up Ideas

- Cooked or fresh raw corn kernels are fantastic in any salad, whether it's built around **leafy greens** (page 186), **noodles** (page 46), or a **protein** like chicken or fish (page 297).
- Put a handful of kernels into just about any Hero Recipe, from soup to stew to **Savory Pancakes** (page 60).
- Corn pairs well with all its summer vegetable besties—go ahead and add corn to **Roasted Vegetable Involtini** (page 120), **Salsa Fresca** (page 103), or **Peperonata** (page 130).
- Corn is one of the few vegetables that translates well to sweet dishes—add corn to **Use-It-Up Pancakes** (page 232) or **Any-Fruit Snack Cake** (page 236) or even a **Smoothie** (page 228).
- Don't let all the flavor in your corncobs go to waste! Make **Corn Stock** by putting any corncobs you have in a soup pot and covering with a few inches of water. Hunt around the kitchen and toss in some aromatics like a quartered onion, some celery stalks, and a few fresh herb sprigs. Bring to a boil, then reduce the heat and simmer for at least an hour, two if you have the time. Strain, compost the solids, and let cool completely before storing in the fridge or freezing for use in chicken stew, **Cream-of-Anything Soup** (page 48), or, of course, the **chowder** on the next page.

Corn Chowder

Serves 4 to 6

Although we grew up in New England with a very specific idea of chowder (white, thick, creamy, potatoes, clams, maaaaaybe corn, and THAT'S IT), this soup leans more toward the brothy side of the spectrum. And we're willing to let go of rigid conceptions of chowder in favor of this very flexible, very achievable recipe that's hearty and warming without being overly rich. You should absolutely tailor the chowder to the contents of your fridge. Leave out the hearty greens. Add bell peppers, fennel, or mushrooms with the other aromatics. Add cubed potatoes or carrots or squash once the soup comes to a boil and simmer until tender before adding the corn. Slip in some cod or salmon to lightly poach at the end and then break into flakes. You could even, if you must, leave out the bacon or the wine.

8 ounces bacon, chopped (optional; if not using, start the pan with a splash of oil or butter)

1 medium onion, diced

2 celery stalks, diced

2 garlic cloves, minced

1 or 2 cups chopped hearty greens, such as collards, cabbage, or spinach, with any thicker stems chopped and reserved separately

1 tablespoon all-purpose flour

½ cup dry white wine

6 cups Corn Stock (page 125) or another stock of your choice

Kernels from 6 corncobs or about 3 cups frozen corn

Kosher salt and freshly ground black pepper

Thinly sliced scallions or chopped fresh herbs, for garnish (optional)

Heat a soup pot over medium-high heat and add the bacon (we like to cut bits of bacon straight into the pan with scissors to avoid greasing up a knife and cutting board with bacon fat). Fry the bacon until just crisp, then use a slotted spoon to transfer the bacon bits to a paper towel–lined plate. Pour out most of the fat, aiming for a thin layer in the bottom of the pot to sauté the vegetables. (If you pour the fat over a paper coffee filter into a heat-safe jar, it will become beautifully pure bacon grease that you can refrigerate and use for cooking eggs or pancakes or potatoes or whatever you like.)

Reduce the heat to medium and add the onion, celery, garlic, and green stems. Cook until soft, about 8 minutes, then sprinkle the flour over the vegetables and stir to coat them. Cook for a minute or two, then add the wine and scrape up any browned bits from the bottom of the pot. Add the stock and bring to a boil, then add the corn and simmer for 5 minutes. Add the greens and simmer for another 5 minutes to let all the flavors meld. Season to taste, then stir in half the bacon, leaving the remaining half to sprinkle on top right before serving, maybe with a scattering of scallions or herbs.

Odds and Ends Maque Choux

Serves 4, as a side

This Cajun dish, based on a version in Toni Tipton-Martin's wonderful cookbook *Jubilee,* is an easily adaptable, low-key way to use a few extra ears of good summer corn. While it's typically made with fresh corn and bell peppers, you can always use frozen corn, leftover cooked corn, and any other odds and ends waiting to be plucked from your Eat-Me-First Box (see page 16). If you've got some stray tomatoes or summer squash or chile peppers sitting around, chop them up and toss them in too. And while it makes an ideal vegetarian side dish, there's no reason you can't toss in some leftover grilled shrimp or chunks of grilled chicken you might have in the fridge.

3 or 4 ears of corn, shucked
4 tablespoons butter or another fat of your choice, plus more as needed
½ medium onion, diced
1 bell pepper (any color), seeded and diced
2 celery stalks, diced (optional)
2 garlic cloves, minced
Kosher salt and freshly ground black pepper
3 scallions, thinly sliced
½ cup cream or water or a mix
Hot sauce or chili flakes, for garnish (optional)

Stand a corncob upright in the base of a large bowl and use a sharp knife to cut off the kernels and let them fall into the bowl. Use the back of the knife to scrape the cob on all sides and release any remaining corn bits and the "corn milk" into the bowl, then repeat with the remaining ears. Set the cobs aside for Corn Stock (page 125) or freeze in your Kitchen Scrap Stock Bag (page 18).

Melt the butter in a large skillet over medium heat until it sizzles and foams. Add the onion, bell pepper, celery (if using), garlic, and a pinch of salt and cook until softened, about 5 minutes. Add the corn, half the scallions, and another small pinch of salt and stir to mix everything thoroughly. If you have a lot of vegetables, you may want to add another pat of butter.

Cook for about 5 minutes, until the corn is tender but not browning, then add the cream or water. Let the mixture simmer and thicken for another 5 minutes, then taste and adjust as needed. Serve with the remaining scallions sprinkled on top and possibly a dash of hot sauce or a sprinkle of chili flakes.

MAKE IT A MEAL

If you find yourself with leftover maque choux, consider yourself lucky. You're already on your way to making a version of Jerrelle Guy's fabulous **Maque Choux Strata**, a richly spiced bread casserole from her cookbook *Black Girl Baking*. Flip over to the Savory Bread Pudding recipe on page 78 and use the maque choux in place of the other vegetables. We also highly recommend her addition of chili flakes to the sautéed onions and hot sauce to the egg and milk. You could also mix leftover maque choux into How-You-Like-It Savory Pancakes (page 60) or Rice Fritters (page 64) or use it as a condiment, like a corn relish, for spooning onto burgers or sausages or tacos. Or make it a main taco ingredient, topped with sour cream and a few spoonfuls of Salsa Fresca (page 103).

Bell Peppers

Use-It-Up Ideas

- If we've got bell peppers hanging around, we usually toss them into a **Stir-Fry** (page 52) or roast them with extra-virgin olive oil and salt. You can also char them on the grill or gas stovetop burner or put them whole under the broiler until the peppers blacken and collapse, then let cool until you can safely scrape away the seeds and remove the charred skin. Toss the cooked peppers in an omelet, on a salad, or into a stew, or freeze in an airtight container for several months.
- The tangy Italian condiment/side dish **Peperonata** is useful for quickly dealing with any peppers you have sitting around, whether smooth and pristine or wrinkled and drooping. Heat a splash of extra-virgin olive oil in a skillet, then add 2 bell peppers (any color), seeded and cut into strips, along with ½ onion, sliced. Fry, stirring occasionally, until the peppers have softened and their brightness has gone, about 5 minutes. Pop in a tablespoon of chopped olives or capers, if you like, then add 2 tablespoons vinegar. Turn the heat down to low and let the peppers stew for a few minutes in the vinegar. Let cool and store in the fridge in an airtight container for a week or two or in the freezer for a few months. Pile the peperonata on top of sausages or burgers, tuck some into omelets, stir into pasta or rice, or just shovel onto a piece of crusty bread smeared with ricotta or goat cheese. Peperonata also makes a great addition to **Easygoing Tomato Sauce** (page 104) or **Baked Eggs** (page 104).

Snacky Stuffed Peppers

Serves 4 as a side

We love stuffed pepper wedges for small bites that pack a wallop of flavor and texture, more umami-rich and crispy than their larger main course siblings. Put in all the salty tidbits in the pantry like anchovies and olives; swap in capers if you want to keep it fish-free. And if you want these crispy mouthfuls to be dinner—maybe with something green on the side—that's cool too.

3 bell peppers (any color), seeded and cut lengthwise into quarters or halves depending on the size
1 cup roughly chopped tomato
1 cup Toasted Breadcrumbs (page 80) or crushed Croutons (page 81)
¼ cup chopped olives of your choice
3 anchovies, minced
2 garlic cloves, minced
2 tablespoons vinegar of your choice
3 tablespoons extra-virgin olive oil

Heat the oven to 400 degrees.

Place the peppers in a 9 x 13-inch baking dish, cut sides up. Mix all the other ingredients in a bowl and place a few spoonfuls in each pepper slice.

Cover with aluminum foil and bake for 20 minutes, then remove the foil and bake for an additional 10 to 15 minutes, until the tops get all browned and crispy.

(continues)

MAKE IT A MEAL

For main-course **Stuffed Peppers**, slice off the very tops of 6 large bell peppers, then scoop out the ribs and seeds. Stuff the peppers with a mixture of 2 cups cooked rice or whole grains, 1 cup or so chopped vegetables, and 1 cup shredded or crumbled cheese. Amp up the filling with sautéed or Caramelized Onions (page 88), cooked sausage or bacon crumbles, chopped fresh herbs or Green Sauce (page 138), or other flavor boosters. Stand them upright in an oven-safe pot, splash with a bit of water or stock to keep things moist, and cover the pot. Bake at 350 degrees for 1 hour.

Dim Sum–Style Stuffed Peppers

Serves 2

This take on smaller stuffed peppers has all our favorite Chinese flavors. We see variations on these every so often on carts zooming around dim sum restaurants—another version has the meat sandwiched between two slabs of eggplant. With all the rich umami meatiness from the mushrooms and soy sauce, the peppers recede into the background as just a handheld meatball delivery structure, which makes this dish a nice way to use up peppers for people who don't really like peppers (aka both of us).

2 bell peppers (any color), seeded and cut lengthwise into quarters or halves depending on the size
Neutral oil, for brushing
Kosher salt
8 ounces ground pork
2 cups chopped mushrooms
3 garlic cloves, chopped
2 scallions, thinly sliced
½-inch piece fresh ginger, minced
1 tablespoon chopped fresh cilantro
1½ tablespoons soy sauce
1 tablespoon Shaoxing cooking wine (or dry sherry, in a pinch)
1 teaspoon cornstarch or all-purpose flour
¼ teaspoon sugar
Pinch ground white pepper

(continues)

Heat the oven to 450 degrees.

Place the peppers in a 9 x 13-inch baking dish, cut sides up. Brush with neutral oil and give them a light sprinkling of salt. Bake for 10 minutes while you mix up the filling.

Combine all the other ingredients in a large mixing bowl and test by heating a tiny spoonful in a skillet. Taste and season as desired. Once you're happy with the taste, scoop it into the pepper quarters and bake for an additional 10 to 15 minutes, or until the pork is fully cooked.

Fresh Herbs

IDEAS AND RECIPES

Fresh herbs are one of the best tricks out there for adding flavor, texture, brightness, and depth to a meal. Fresh herbs are also expensive; 3 bucks for a small plastic box of fresh thyme seems reasonable, but that's a staggering $96 per pound! And the thin, fragile leaves of many fresh herbs tend to turn brown or slimy quickly. Most written recipes don't help matters—a typical cookbook recipe might call for a tablespoon of chopped parsley—now what do you do with the bunch-minus-a-tablespoon? All this combines to create a costly level of herb waste in many home kitchens.

When you've got an abundance of herbs, try a recipe piled high with leaves, like the Tabbouleh-ish Herb Salad (page 149) or our Thai-Style Tofu with Lots of Herbs (page 151). For smaller amounts, or to prep for future meals, take a look at the Use-It-Up Ideas, packed with lots of flexible sauces and condiments to save your herbs and spark up your meals. Serve them as dips or spreads, or mix them into other dishes, especially all the Hero Recipes, for a quick and easy flavor boost.

Know What You Got

The most common cooking herbs can be divided into two groups:

TENDER HERBS: The leafier, lighter herbs include mint, parsley, cilantro, basil, tarragon, dill, fennel fronds, chervil, and chives. They can be cooked into dishes but are especially delicious raw.

HARDY HERBS: The woodier, tougher herbs, such as sage, rosemary, thyme, oregano, and lemongrass are more likely to be cooked into dishes than eaten in salads or as a garnish. Remove the leaves from the stems and chop finely or leave in whole sprigs for easier removal.

Store It Right

Herbs need a bit of extra protection but also some access to air. Two good ways to achieve this: (1) loosely wrap in cloth, then place in a breathable bag or (2) fold into a reusable beeswax wrap. Store herbs in the crisper drawer of the refrigerator, with the exception of basil, which browns quickly in the cold. Keep basil with trimmed stems in a glass of water, like cut flowers, on the counter away from the sun. A plastic bag loosely covering the leaves will help keep them from drooping too much.

Save for Later

- Got any empty ice cube trays or muffin tins? Put a spoonful of chopped herbs into each cube, cover with extra-virgin olive oil or melted butter, and freeze. Once the cubes are frozen solid, transfer them to an airtight bag and use in soups, stews, and other cooked dishes.
- Freeze whole sprigs of sturdier herbs like rosemary or lemongrass wrapped in plastic in a sealed container—their flavor will keep even as the herbs brown and dry out.
- Tie up your extra herb sprigs with twine or rubber bands and let them air-dry upside down like dried flowers. Ideally, place them in a cool room with a reasonable amount of air circulation. After a few days, once fully dry, crumble and store in airtight containers at room temperature.
- Dana Gunders's *Waste-Free Kitchen Handbook* suggests drying herbs in the microwave to retain flavor better than an oven or dehydrator. Remove the stems, place the leaves on a plate between two paper towels, and microwave for 1 minute, then in 20-second intervals until completely dried.
- Dried herbs and spices will last indefinitely in your pantry as long as there's no moisture. Keep in mind that they will lose potency over time, though, so try to use them up within a few months to a year.

You Can Still Eat It!

Even if herbs don't look vibrant and pristine enough to garnish a salad, they're still usable in cooked dishes or sauces, condiments like herb oil or dipping sauce or herb butter, or dishes like bread pudding and frittata. A bit of wilting or yellowing is totally fine, and if a few unsalvageable sprigs need to be picked out, you can still rinse and use the rest. But once the majority of the bunch is slimy, browned, or rotting, it's time for the compost.

Extra Bits

We tend to focus only on the leaves of most herbs, but there's so much more that can be eaten. You paid for the whole pricey bunch, so get the most out of it! We use the soft stems of cilantro in the same way that we use the leaves. If you're lucky enough to have cilantro roots, they can be used in curry pastes. The lighter stems of basil, parsley, mint, and dill can sometimes be eaten raw like the leaves, if chopped finely. They can get bitter, though, so if you're not inclined to eat them straight, toss them into any of the pureed sauces or condiments below or add them to your Kitchen Scrap Stock Bag (page 18).

Woodier stems like rosemary and oregano can be saved for use as flavor boosters, similar to the ends and roots of other vegetables. Pop them into your Kitchen Scrap Stock Bag to help flavor soups and broths or include them in an herb sachet while making a stew. They can be stuffed inside a roast chicken along with lemon rinds, then composted before eating.

Chive and basil flowers are among the herb flowers that are absolutely edible, although they range in tenderness. Chive blossoms are the most versatile and can be eaten raw or cooked, just like the rest of the chive.

Use-It-Up Ideas

Our favorite way to deal with herbs, whether it's just a few sprigs or an entire bunch, is making condiments of all kinds. Depending on the ingredients in your kitchen and the time on your hands, you can create a zippy sauce, a creamy dressing, a fragrant butter, a refined oil, and more.

- When you've got herbs and no plan, **Green Sauce** comes to the rescue. Use any combination of tender herbs—take it easy on the strong, woody herbs like rosemary or sage—and tilt toward the flavor profile of your choice. Go for an Italian salsa verde or an Argentinian chimichurri or an Italian pesto, depending on what condiments and seasonings you have in your kitchen. And it's a great landing spot for tender stems of cilantro and parsley, as well as greens like arugula, spinach, or even kale.

(continues)

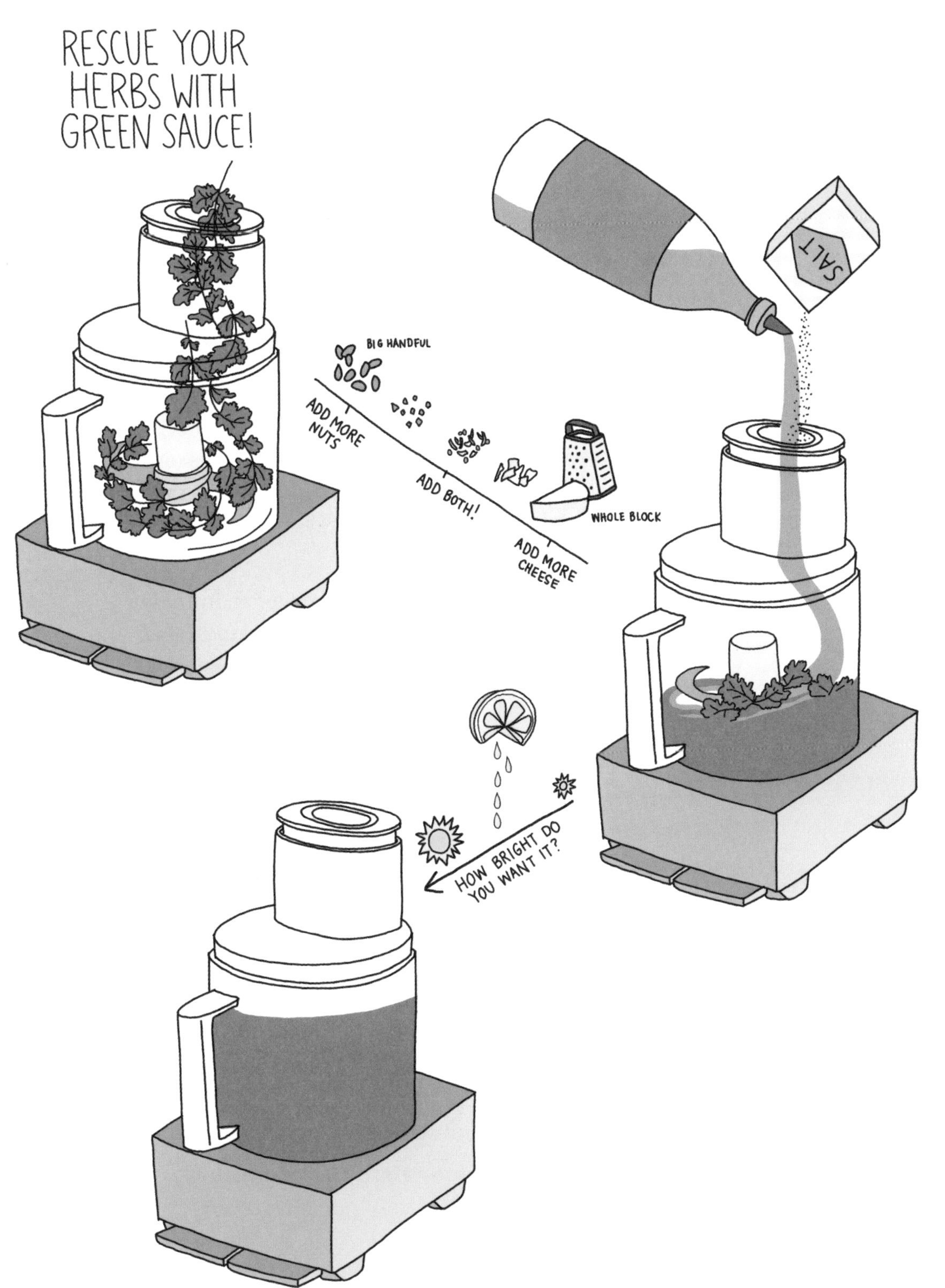
RESCUE YOUR HERBS WITH GREEN SAUCE!
BIG HANDFUL
ADD MORE NUTS
ADD BOTH!
ADD MORE CHEESE
WHOLE BLOCK
SALT
HOW BRIGHT DO YOU WANT IT?

Here's our method: Put your herbs and greens in a food processor or blender—this could be anywhere from 1 to 4 cups or more. Add a clove or two of garlic (maybe more if you have tons of herbs) and drizzle extra-virgin olive oil on top until it's wet enough to puree easily. Pulse until it's roughly chopped—we like a chunkier salsa verde style, but if you're going for more of a pesto, you can process until smooth. Keep adding olive oil slowly until it gets to a good consistency—you want enough oil to make a cohesive sauce, but not so much that you have pools of oil. Finally, splash in a teaspoon of lemon juice or vinegar and adjust to taste. And make sure to season with salt—proper seasoning is what makes this sauce addictively, spoon-it-on-everything level delicious. Keep it in the fridge for mixing into dishes for a few weeks. If you don't think you'll eat it all within a week or two, portion the remaining sauce into ice cube trays or small containers and freeze.

- Blend Green Sauce into something creamy for an infinitely customizable **Creamy Green Dip**. We like cream cheese, but you can use anything thick and creamy like feta, ricotta, yogurt, or sour cream. You can even swirl it into **Whatever-You've-Got Nut Sauce** (page 322) and avoid dairy altogether. Start with the creamy item and blend in the herb sauce, then taste and adjust for acidity and saltiness. A splash of extra-virgin olive oil can help loosen up a very thick spread; more cream cheese or crème fraîche can help thicken or rebalance if you accidentally oversalt. Up the ante by adding spices like curry powder or onion powder or any of the Switch It Up ingredients on the next page. Whatever ingredients you choose, it's an ideal opportunity to practice your tasting instincts to achieve a texture and flavor balance you like. You may need many potato chips for this process, which is unquestionably the right of the chef and should be doubted by no one.
- Turn your Green Sauce into an **Herby Vinaigrette** by mixing with equal amounts extra-virgin olive oil and

vinegar of your choice. Taste, then add more vinegar if you want it zingier, or more oil if it's too tart. As much as we'd like to tell you exactly what to do, it's going to depend on how your herb sauce turned out. It's a fun exercise in developing your own vinaigrette palate—just make sure to season well with salt to finish.

Green Sauce is incredibly flexible. Great add-ins include capers, grated citrus zest, anchovies, alliums like scallions or shallot, chili flakes or fresh chiles, a handful of nuts of any kind, or pitted olives of any variety.

Green Sauce stands on its own but is also a magical starter ingredient for so many other sauces and full dishes. Swirl into a frittata, quiche, or bread pudding, stir into any soup or stew, or mix into Four-Ingredient-Meatballs (page 302). Use to top Anything-in-the-Kitchen Pasta (page 68) or stir into rice, polenta, mashed potatoes, or your favorite starch.

- The absolute favorite sauce in Mei's household is **Herby Ranch**. Everyone loves ranch, and it's a delicious way to use up various herbs and random dairy products. It's good on everything from pizza crust to a simple bowl of lettuce. Whizz ½ cup mayonnaise, ½ cup sour cream, ½ cup packed fresh herbs and/or chopped alliums, and 1 tablespoon lemon juice in a food processor or blender. Thin with buttermilk, milk, or half-and-half, season with salt and pepper, and basically tinker with it until it's so good you kind of want to drink it. You can store it in the fridge for at least a week or two, but ours never lasts that long.

- Need to use up extra sprigs of herbs that are wilted and sad? Thankfully, texture doesn't matter when the herbs are smashed to smithereens in a savory **Herb Butter**. Mix a softened stick of butter into ½ to 1 cup finely chopped herbs and add salt or any of the Switch It Up additions suggested for **Green Sauce** (page 138). We like to roll the butter into a log on top of plastic wrap or parchment and then wrap it up and twist the ends like an enormous Tootsie Roll. Store in the fridge for a few weeks and cut a slice off the end whenever you want some, or pop it into the freezer for a few months. Let it come to room temperature and slather it on good bread and top with sliced radishes. Melt onto hot pasta, sautéed vegetables, corn on the cob, fried eggs, or omelets. Stir into rice or mashed potatoes or soup or grits. Stick cold slices under the skin of a chicken before roasting. Drop a cold slice on top of a just-cooked steak or pretty much any seafood, whether lobster rolls or grilled fish.
- **Herb-Infused Simple Syrup** is an unexpected but excellent way to get the most out of older herbs, especially the woodsier ones like thyme and rosemary. Make a basic **Simple Syrup** by heating a small pot with 1 cup water and 1 cup sugar (it's equal parts sugar and water, so scale up or down as needed). Add 3 to 10 herb sprigs and bring to a boil, then turn the heat down and let simmer for 5 to 10 minutes. Turn off the heat and let cool with the herbs still in the pan. Once the syrup is completely cool, strain out the herbs and discard, then store the syrup in an airtight container in the fridge for ages. Here are some of our favorite uses:
    - **Boozy drinks:** Substitute your herb infusion for a plain simple syrup in any number of cocktails, including our favorites on page 143.
    - **Nonalcoholic options:** Try flavoring iced tea or coffee with mint simple syrup, adding any syrup to whipped cream, drizzling over cake, or spooning a bit onto sliced fruit for dessert.

HERB-INFUSED COCKTAILS

- Make deliciously fragrant **Herb Oil**, which can be a choose-your-own adventure activity depending on the time and tools at your disposal:
    - **2 minutes:** Pop sprigs of any fresh herbs into a jar or bottle of extra-virgin olive oil. It'll keep in the fridge for a few days; just take it out a few minutes before you use it to let the oil warm up a bit. Try it anywhere you regularly use olive oil, like whisking into salad dressings or drizzling onto avocado toast.
    - **10 minutes:** Put ½ cup tender herb leaves and stems into a blender or food processor with 1 cup extra-virgin olive oil (scale up if you have more herbs to use) and blitz until as smooth as possible. Strain out the solids and compost (or leave them in), then store in the fridge for about a week. Use for making salad dressings, dipping good bread, or drizzling onto soup or stew.
    - **20 minutes:** For sturdier herbs like thyme and rosemary, heating the oil will help release more flavor. After pureeing the herbs with the oil as above, gently heat the mixture in a pot on the stove until it just starts to sizzle. Let cool, then strain through a fine-mesh strainer and keep in the fridge for a week or so. Spoon onto cooked eggs, fish, chicken, or another protein, or toss onto roasted vegetables.

A Simple (Yet Infinitely Adaptable) Herb Salad

WITH IRENE

Serves 2 to 4

Opening a restaurant and working with experienced chefs taught me a lot about the versatility of herbs. Lots of home recipes ask for a tablespoon or two of herbs, but restaurant chefs will go ahead and throw an entire fistful atop a dish. They'll liberally use herbs in addition to or in place of lettuces in salads, creating dishes that absolutely sing with flavor. To make this vibrant salad, you can use just about any tender herbs—my ultimate combo is cilantro + basil + mint—and any kind of lettuce. I love the sharp bite of spicy mizuna or arugula, while butter lettuce or a spring green mix provides a gentle balance. And although it calls for equal parts lettuce and herbs, you should adjust as you like depending on your palate or the contents of your fridge, and scale up or down depending on how many people you're feeding. You can stick with just herbs and leaves (a nice accompaniment to a luxuriously rich main dish) or add thinly sliced cucumber or very ripe summer cherry tomatoes. You could mix it up with a light yogurt dressing and even plop a huge ball of burrata on top and let the cream ooze out and mix with the dressing. You could add toasted pine nuts or sesame seeds or Croutons (page 81) or Toasted Breadcrumbs (page 80). It's a salad worthy of any restaurant, but you didn't even have to leave the house.

3 cups salad greens of any kind

3 cups mixed fresh tender herbs, such as parsley, cilantro, tarragon, mint, basil, chives, or shiso

Extra-virgin olive oil (this is a good time to break out that special olive oil you've been saving)

Grated zest and juice of ½ lemon or about 1 tablespoon flavorful vinegar

Kosher salt (or another fancy salt of your choice) and freshly ground black pepper

(continues)

Tear any larger salad leaves into bite-size pieces and run a knife through the herbs to chop up any tender stems, but try to leave the leaves whole. Toss everything together in a large salad bowl to mix the herbs and leaves together thoroughly.

Drizzle the greens lightly with olive oil and toss to coat (we like to do this with our hands to avoid bruising any tender leaves) so every leaf is a bit glossy but not heavy with oil. Sprinkle on the lemon zest and squeeze the juice over or drizzle your nice vinegar on top, then toss on your salt and some grinds of black pepper. Taste and adjust as needed until you find the right balance of salt and acidity that makes it so you can't stop eating, then serve immediately.

Eat-the-Whole-Herb Tempura

Serves 2 to 4 as a snack

While we waited for our food truck to be built back in 2012, Irene worked at an Italian restaurant called La Morra famous for its cicchetti, or little snacks or appetizers. One of their specialties was salvia fritta con acciughe, a large anchovy sandwiched between two whole sage leaves, battered and deep-fried, and Mei loved drinking at the bar and yelling at Irene through the pass while eating dozens of them at a time. Fried herbs are salty and crispy, complex and crunchy, and the perfect accompaniment for an amaro cocktail or a citrusy IPA. We were reminded of those days when paging through Yotam Ottolenghi's *Flavor* and finding his recipe for Tempura Stems, Leaves, and Herbs, an inventive idea for using up anything from beet stems to dill fronds, as well as most quick-cooking vegetables like beans or asparagus. It's fun to experiment with spices and garnishes; Ottolenghi suggests mixing sesame seeds into the batter and sprinkling with Sichuan peppercorns after frying. Feel free to double or triple the recipe to feed more people or provide yourself with more snacks.

Neutral oil, for frying
½ cup all-purpose flour
½ cup cornstarch
1 teaspoon kosher salt, plus more for sprinkling
¾ cup cold beer (nothing too dark or heavy) or sparkling water
1 bunch mixed herb leaves and tender stems cut into 2-inch pieces
Herby Ranch (page 141) or another creamy sauce, for dipping

Pour 2 to 3 inches oil into a Dutch oven, aiming to fill it no more than one-third of the way. Heat the oil to 350 degrees, or until a drop of batter sizzles and floats but doesn't immediately darken.

(continues)

Meanwhile, make the batter by whisking together the flour, cornstarch, and salt in a large bowl, then pouring in the beer or sparkling water. Stir so that it just comes together; lumps are fine. Line a plate or wire rack with paper towels to get ready for frying.

Make sure your herb stems and leaves are dry. Place a few pieces at a time into the batter and use your hands to coat each piece. Lift the herbs out of the batter, letting any excess drip back into the bowl, then slip the pieces into the hot oil, holding your fingers close to the surface to reduce splashing. Using a slotted spoon or spider, separate any stuck pieces and add herbs until the pot can't comfortably fit any more. Cook for about 1 minute, until the batter turns a pale golden blond and the pieces are crisp and don't wilt when lifted out. Lift the tempura, transfer to the paper towels, and sprinkle with salt right away. Repeat until everything has been fried and eat immediately with the ranch.

Tabbouleh-ish Herb Salad

Serves 4

This salad starts with our interpretation of the intensely herby Middle Eastern dish tabbouleh and offers lots of options from there. Tabbouleh traditionally includes a lot of parsley—enough that it's arguably a parsley salad—and a very small amount, comparatively, of bulgur wheat. Ratios vary from cook to cook, though, so balance the herbs and grains to your taste. We like to switch it up with different grains as we're more likely to have quinoa or couscous in the pantry already. And beyond the classic mint and parsley, we toss in whatever other tender herbs are in the kitchen, from basil to fennel fronds, and possibly a few extras like tiny cubes of cucumber or just-barely-cooked kernels of corn, crumbles of feta or fresh goat cheese, bacon bits, or leftover shredded chicken. And while we like the simple dressing of olive oil, lemon, and a spiky hit of flavor from your allium of choice, many versions of tabbouleh call for spices, such as cinnamon or allspice, so feel free to season to your taste.

1 pound tomatoes, chopped, or 1 pint cherry tomatoes, halved
Kosher salt and freshly ground black pepper
¼ small onion or 1 small shallot, minced
⅓ cup extra-virgin olive oil
3 tablespoons lemon juice, plus a pinch or two of grated lemon zest
1 to 2 cups cooked whole grains of your choice, such as bulgur wheat, couscous, or farro
2 cups finely chopped fresh flat-leaf parsley (about 1 large bunch)
1 cup finely chopped fresh mint (about 1 small bunch)
½ cup finely chopped other soft fresh herbs of choice, if desired
4 scallions, thinly sliced

(continues)

Put the cut tomatoes and any juices in a bowl and sprinkle with salt. Let some more juices run out, then stir in the onion, olive oil, and lemon juice and zest and season to taste with salt and pepper.

Combine the grains, herbs, and scallions in a large bowl and pour the tomatoey-onion dressing on top. Toss to combine and season to taste with salt and pepper, with maybe an additional squeeze of lemon.

Thai-Style Tofu with Lots of Herbs

Serves 4

This dish is loosely inspired by laab or larb, a Laotian and Thai dish made of minced or ground meat with lots of spicy, sweet, sour, and savory flavors. As with so many well-known dishes around the world, every cook makes larb with their own customizations and opinions. We find larb incredibly valuable as a loose concept—chopped protein with lots of aromatics and herbs—that we can easily adapt to what's in the kitchen and who's eating dinner. Do you have spice-fearful children who frantically chug milk if anything mildly hot creeps onto their plate? Mei does, so she leaves out the dried chiles that others might consider an essential characteristic of the dish. She likes to add chopped lettuce, hearty greens, or leftover vegetables like sautéed mushrooms, steamed broccoli, or boiled edamame. Do you frequently impulse-buy 5-pound bags of Meyer lemons and always keep a gallon of maple syrup on hand? Irene does, so she's always ready to substitute different ingredients for the acidity and the sweetness. And we love this as a vegetarian meal with tofu, but feel free to swap in the ground meat of your choice.

NOTE: *If you have ½ cup uncooked sticky rice and some extra time, toast the rice in a skillet until golden brown, then grind it into a powder and stir it into the larb. Mei's Thai friend Jibbie considers its nutty flavor a must for larb and also includes spices like lemongrass and galangal. But if you don't have any (or a friend like Jibbie who you can steal it from), you'll still have a fantastic dinner.*

SWEET-SPICY-SOUR SAUCE

1½ tablespoons fish sauce

1½ tablespoons soy sauce

2 teaspoons lime juice or a neutral vinegar

1 teaspoon sugar or honey

Pinch chili flakes

(continues)

1 tablespoon neutral oil

½ cup diced shallots or another allium of your choice

2 garlic cloves, minced

1 (14- to 16-ounce) package firm tofu, wrapped in a kitchen towel and pressed with a heavy skillet for 10 minutes, then crumbled into bite-size pieces

1½ cups chopped hearty greens of your choice, such as kale or spinach

2 cups roughly chopped or torn fresh herbs, such as a mix of basil, cilantro, and mint (make sure to include any soft stems!)

Kosher salt

Steamed rice, cooked noodles, or lettuce leaves, for serving

Mix the sauce ingredients in a small bowl and taste. Consider our measurements a starting point from which you can adjust if you want the dish more sour or spicy or savory.

Heat the oil in a large skillet over medium-high heat. Add the shallots and cook until softened, about 4 minutes, then add the garlic and stir-fry for 1 minute. Stir in the tofu and cook, pressing it into the hot pan to help it brown a bit. Once the tofu is cooked, 6 to 8 minutes, mix in the hearty greens and sauce. Cook until the leaves wilt, then turn off the heat and stir in the herbs. Taste and adjust with salt or other sauce ingredients as needed. Garnish however you like and serve with steamed rice, cooked noodles, or lettuce for wrapping.

TOP IT OFF

Larb is so much fun to customize: our preferred accompaniments include crushed peanuts or cashews, shredded carrots, more herbs or greens, lime wedges, sliced shallots or scallions or chiles, and Quick Pickles (page 37).

Herby Green Rice with Meat or Tofu

Serves 4

If you've got Green Sauce (page 138) and cooked rice, you can simply stir them together to make a last-minute side dish that feels way more special than just plain rice. If you don't have either, cook them both along with a protein in this one-pot meal inspired by Mark Bittman's Best Green Rice. This dish is great for all eaters as it works with any kind of ground meat, from plain beef to spiced pork sausage, as well as tofu or other plant-based meat alternatives. Well, except for the avowed cilantro haters; for them, try swapping the cilantro for a mix of parsley and basil.

4 tablespoons neutral oil, divided
1 pound ground meat or crumbled firm tofu or other meat alternative
Kosher salt
1 cup fresh cilantro stems and leaves, or another tender herb or mix of your choice
½-inch piece fresh ginger
2 scallions, roots trimmed
4 garlic cloves, peeled
2 tablespoons toasted sesame oil
1 cup white rice
2 cups water

Heat 2 tablespoons of the oil over medium heat in a large skillet for which you have a lid. Add the meat or tofu with a pinch of salt and cook, stirring frequently, until lightly browned, 5 to 7 minutes depending on what you're using. Don't worry about it being fully cooked, it'll have time to cook with the rice.

(continues)

Meanwhile, combine the cilantro, ginger, scallions, garlic, sesame oil, and remaining 2 tablespoons neutral oil in a blender or food processor. Puree, then season to taste with salt.

Add the rice to the skillet and stir it with the meat or tofu to lightly toast for a few minutes. Stir in the herby mixture until all the rice and meat is fully coated, then add the water. Stir, scraping the bottom of the pan, and raise the heat to high to bring the mixture to a boil, then stir again and cover. Turn the heat down to low and cook for 15 minutes. Taste a grain of rice—if it's not tender, cover and cook for another minute or two. Once the rice is done, turn off the heat, fluff the rice with a fork, cover again, and let sit for 5 to 10 minutes before serving.

Light Leafy Greens

IDEAS AND RECIPES

If there's anyone out there who has never had to throw out wilted lettuce, good for you. For the rest of us, here are our favorite tips and recipes to save your light leafy greens from the trash. We're talking about tender leafy greens in this section, which range from mild and watery to pungent and peppery. If you'd like to switch up your salad game and find new ways to combine these greens, take a look at the Leafy Greens Salad Builder (page 160). But keep in mind that lettuces can be grilled, stir-fried, or cooked into soup, too, so don't be afraid to try subbing in these leaves for any in the Hearty Greens chapter or Hero Recipes.

Know What You Got

Here are a few of the more common varieties:

- **Mild lettuces**, such as romaine, red leaf, green leaf, Bibb, Boston, Little Gem, iceberg, butter, mesclun, and spring mix, have a high water content and a subtle flavor. These are the ones we tend to reach to for fresh salads. Baby spinach is also on the milder side and good for salads, but has enough heft to stand up in pesto, Green Sauce (page 138), or any Hero Recipe.
- **Bitter or spicy greens**, such as radicchio, endive, escarole, mizuna, dandelion greens, mâche, watercress, and arugula, are versatile and taste great as a bold addition to salad or cooked into a dish.

NO-WASTE TIPS

Reducing wasted lettuce can start even before bringing it home; when grocery shopping, we look at the shelf life of lettuces and start thinking about how they can be eaten before purchasing anything. Adding a leafy green to your shopping cart is often done on autopilot, just to tick the box of including something fresh and healthy in your diet. But purchasing out of habit can lead to waste if you have plans to eat out the next few nights or you have a fridge full of more enticing ingredients. When possible, buy lettuce when you know you'll be eating the next few meals at home. If you're buying to eat later, lettuces with roots still attached, such as Bibb and Boston lettuce, will last longer than individual leaves or heads. Irene's trick for when she wants to eat more healthy greens but also knows that she may not get to them immediately: Buy a lighter leaf that's delicious in salads but can easily be cooked into omelets, pastas, and more, such as arugula or spinach.

Store It Right

Refrigerate leafy greens in an airtight container like a lidded food storage tub, a reusable produce bag, or even your salad spinner. When storing delicate greens, your goal is to maintain a balance of moisture and humidity. Too wet, and your greens get slimy and moldy. Too dry, and the lettuces can go limp and soft instead of staying crunchy and fresh. You can help by wrapping very dry greens in a damp cloth or paper towel or, conversely, stashing a dry cloth in with wet greens to soak up any excess moisture. The high humidity of the crisper drawer can help leafy greens last longer, but we often find it more useful to store greens where they can be seen and therefore eaten, given their short shelf life.

If you have the time and plan to eat them soon, you may want to wash your greens once you get them home from the market. Cleaned greens can be pulled from the fridge and eaten immediately, which makes it less likely they'll go to waste. Submerge cut or torn greens in a large bowl of cold water and swish them around gently with your hands, letting any dirt fall to the bottom. Drain and dry the leaves well as excess moisture will cause wilting; use a salad spinner and/or paper towels or kitchen cloths to blot off extra water. But if you're not sure when you'll get to them, leave greens unwashed to minimize moisture.

NO-WASTE TIPS

Leafy greens are increasingly likely to be sold and stored in clear plastic clamshell boxes. They're certainly handy for popping straight into the fridge, but moisture tends to condense inside, leaving your expensive and delicate salad leaves to collapse in a puddle of green goop. If you notice condensation, stick a cloth or paper towel inside to soak up any excess moisture. If we're eating these leaves raw, we usually give them a quick rinse even if they're labeled "washed." And unfortunately, many of these plastic containers can't be recycled, so we try to repurpose them for food storage or kid art projects whenever possible.

Save for Later

Lighter leafy greens can be frozen, as long as you're not expecting to eat them in raw salads. Thicker leaves hold up better in the freezer, especially the sturdier bitter greens like escarole, which can be blanched according to the directions on page 23. Tender lettuces can be washed and dried, then frozen in a resealable bag with the air pressed out, for use in cooked dishes like soup or stew. We like to pop mild or sweet frozen greens straight into smoothies, especially baby spinach.

You Can Still Eat It!

Did you know you can revive wilted lettuce? Amazingly, you can reverse the droop factor of your salad greens using the process of osmosis, whereby water molecules work their way into the lettuce cells and reinvigorate the leaves. Submerge wilted greens in a cold-water bath with a few ice cubes and let sit for 5 to 10 minutes. As long as they haven't reached total collapse, this should get your greens close to salad worthiness. If you're still not loving the texture, try a cooked dish like a Stir-Fry (page 52) or Ginger-Scallion Lettuce Sauce (page 92), both great uses for lightly wilted leaves. And if a few leaves wilt or go brown or slimy, you can pick them out and save the rest.

Use-It-Up Ideas

Some unexpected uses for leafy lettuces:

- Stir-fry them! Use the **Make-It-Your-Own Stir-Fry** recipe (page 52) to quickly wilt your lettuces in a garlicky sauce.
- Use larger leaves in place of burger buns or tortillas, or as lettuce wraps for **Thai-Style Tofu with Lots of Herbs** (page 151).
- Use any kind of leaf in a **Pasta Salad** (page 162) or **Anything-in-the-Kitchen Pasta** (page 68).

- Char whole heads of romaine or other sturdier heads like **Grilled Greens** (page 174).
- Add sweeter leaves like baby spinach to an **All-the-Fruit Smoothie** (page 228).
- Chop and stir lettuce into a stew or soup right before serving.

Leafy Greens Salad Builder

Lettuces on their own make a wonderful salad, but sometimes they need help from their friends. Putting together new salad combinations is a chance for kitchen creativity *and* an opportunity to clean out the fridge. Do you have cooked grains or roasted vegetables or pickles in there? Would last night's leftovers go well with your greens? Remember that you don't need to pile a dozen different ingredients on every time—simplicity lets your leafy greens shine.

Here's how we think about building a salad:

1. **What kind of greens do you have?** Are they thin and delicate or on the sturdier side? Are they mild and sweet or sharp and pungent? Generally, you'll want to pick lighter accompaniments for more fragile lettuces so they don't get overwhelmed by large chunks of roasted vegetable or heavy cream-based dressings.

2. **Is this a main or a side?** If you're just looking for something fresh and green to accompany your dinner, maybe lettuce plus one other vegetable—like chunks of perfectly ripe avocado or thin slices of sugar snap peas—is enough. If you're looking for lunch in a bowl, you'll probably want at least one additional vegetable that could be raw, roasted, blanched, sautéed, or generally cooked in any fashion. Cooked grains like farro, wheatberries, and quinoa add bulk, texture, and flavor. Cheese adds salt, creaminess, and richness. Then, consider what you can add for protein: eggs of any style, leftover meat or fish, sliced cold cuts, cooked beans, etc.

3. **Sweetness:** We've grown to love fresh or dried fruit in salads as a contrast to robustly flavored leaves. This is a fun time to think outside the typical fruit box. Is there half an apple left over from your kid's lunch? Do you have a random half-opened bag of dried peaches in the pantry? If you have a hard time going too far over the sweet-savory line, you can quick-pickle dried fruit (see page 37) while you make the rest of the salad.

4. **Crunch:** Unless we're focusing just on greens, we ~~usually~~ always want some form of crunch on top of a salad. Croutons (page 81) or Toasted Breadcrumbs (page 80) are classic, as are any kind of nut, whether raw, toasted, or candied. What's hanging around the snack section of your pantry? Consider pumpkin seeds, tortilla strips, roasted corn kernels, the last of the pretzels, whatever you think would taste good. Raw vegetables like carrots and radishes add cool crisp textures too.
5. **Flavor accents:** To finish off your salad and spark up your palate, consider garnishes like fresh herbs, capers, olives, anchovies, sauerkraut, kimchi, or any kind of Quick Pickles (page 37). Pops of salt and acid can give a big personality boost to an otherwise simple salad.
6. **Dressings:** Now look at what you've created and make your dressing. Leafy salads work best with a lighter dressing, like the Fridge-Door Dressing (page 165). Heavier salads with grains, cooked meat, and sturdy greens can handle a thick dressing like Herby Ranch (page 141) or Lemony Tahini Dressing (page 42).

(continues)

FAVORITE COMBOS

FRUIT AND GREENS SALAD: Toss together 6 cups greens + 1 cup sliced strawberries, not-super-ripe peaches, or another somewhat tart fruit of choice + ¼ cup Quick Pickles (page 37) + ½ cup chopped or crushed nuts, such as pecans, walnuts, or almonds. Top with a sprinkle of creamy soft cheese such as feta, goat cheese, or queso fresco and Maple-Dijon Dressing (page 167).

GRAIN SALAD: We love grain salads because they're customizable for picnics or dinner parties, tweakable for seasonality or transportability, and scalable to serve just one or a crowd. Add what brings you joy (or at least, what you have in the fridge). As a starting point, combine 6 cups leafy greens, 3 cups cooked grains, 2 cups raw or cooked vegetables, and 2 cups protein or 4 soft-boiled eggs, everything chopped into bite-size pieces and tossed with the dressing of your choice.

PASTA SALAD: We're deeply into the pasta + salad kind of pasta salad, where the pasta is used like a crouton—sparingly, as a novel textural contrast to the light and leafy crunch of lettuce. (Of course, you should also feel free to include actual croutons—the two are not mutually exclusive by any means.) Our Platonic ideal of this salad consists of 2 to 3 cups cooked pasta, 4 cups chopped mixed leafy greens of your choice, 4 thinly sliced scallions, 1 cup halved small tomatoes, ½ cup Quick Pickles (page 37), ½ cup crumbled feta or ricotta salata, ½ cup chopped fresh tender herbs, and ¼ cup something crunchy—toasted pine nuts are worth splurging on for this salad, but Toasted Breadcrumbs (page 80) and Croutons (page 81) are much cheaper and just as enjoyable alternatives. And perhaps due to unpleasant memories of monotonously gloopy pasta salads, we avoid creamy dressings in favor of zippy vinaigrettes like Preserved Citrus Dressing (page 279) or Fridge-Door Dressing (page 165).

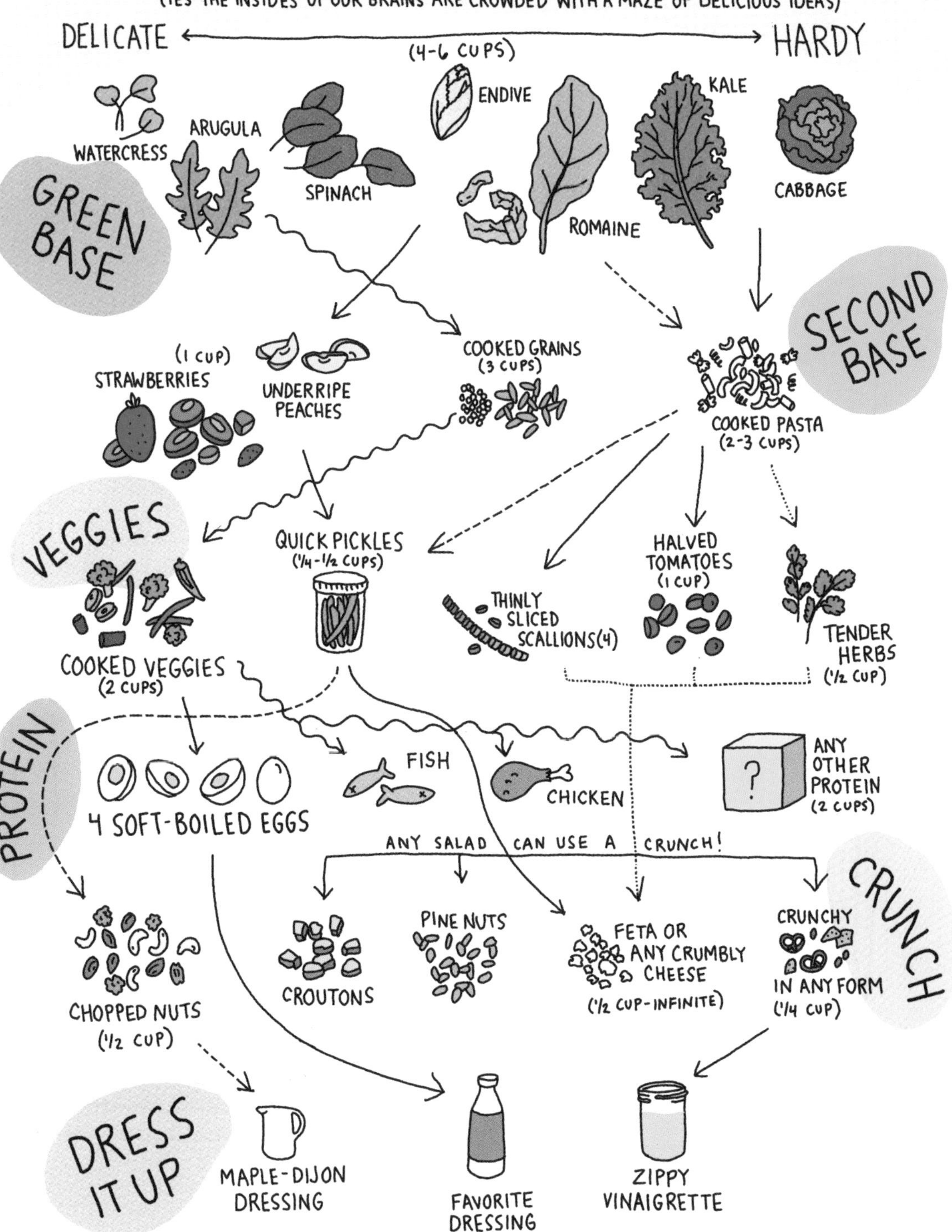
ALL DAY WE DREAM OF SALAD
(YES THE INSIDES OF OUR BRAINS ARE CROWDED WITH A MAZE OF DELICIOUS IDEAS)
DELICATE
HARDY
(4-6 CUPS)
GREEN BASE
WATERCRESS
ARUGULA
SPINACH
ENDIVE
ROMAINE
KALE
CABBAGE
SECOND BASE
(1 CUP)
STRAWBERRIES
UNDERRIPE PEACHES
COOKED GRAINS
(3 CUPS)
COOKED PASTA
(2-3 CUPS)
VEGGIES
COOKED VEGGIES
(2 CUPS)
QUICK PICKLES
(1/4-1/2 CUPS)
THINLY SLICED SCALLIONS (4)
HALVED TOMATOES
(1 CUP)
TENDER HERBS
(1/2 CUP)
PROTEIN
4 SOFT-BOILED EGGS
FISH
CHICKEN
?
ANY OTHER PROTEIN
(2 CUPS)
ANY SALAD CAN USE A CRUNCH!
CRUNCH
CHOPPED NUTS
(1/2 CUP)
CROUTONS
PINE NUTS
FETA OR ANY CRUMBLY CHEESE
(1/2 CUP-INFINITE)
CRUNCHY IN ANY FORM
(1/4 CUP)
DRESS IT UP
MAPLE-DIJON DRESSING
FAVORITE DRESSING
ZIPPY VINAIGRETTE

MAPLE
DIJON
MAYONNAISE
JAM
BUTTER
HONEY
TAHINI
CAPER

Fridge-Door Dressing

When I'm making a salad, I'll often just open up the refrigerator and stare at the array of condiments. If I'm feeling particularly lazy, I'll close the door and just go with the simplest dressing of extra-virgin olive oil plus fresh lemon juice or vinegar. But if I'm in the mood for something more exciting—or if I see a mustard that's almost gone, or a jar of capers on its last legs—then I'll use the oil + acid combination as a base to play around with other fun things in the fridge. Here are a few ingredients you can add or use up in dressings for A Simple (Yet Infinitely Adaptable) Herb Salad (page 145), Grain Salad (page 162), and so much more.

To start, you want to make a vinaigrette base that is roughly 2 parts extra-virgin olive oil and 1 part acid. I like dressings on the acidic side; if you don't, you could go up to 3 parts olive oil, or somewhere in between. For one salad, this might be 2 to 3 tablespoons olive oil to 1 tablespoon lemon juice or vinegar of your choice.

Use a relatively neutral option such as rice, wine, or apple cider vinegar, or something more flavorful like sherry or balsamic vinegar. Plain white vinegar is more aggressive and not ideal for dressings—but if it's all you have, balance it with more sweetness. Measure everything out and whisk together in a bowl, or eyeball using a glass jar, then put on the lid and give it a good shake to combine (this is a great task to outsource to kitchen helpers, like a six-year-old). Add kosher salt to taste, plus freshly ground black pepper if you like, and that's your basic vinaigrette.

From there, there are endless ways to customize using the contents of your fridge doors and shelves. Check out the Switch It Up box on page 167 for lots of ideas.

(continues)

BASE
OLIVE OIL
OLIVE OIL
+
APPLE CIDER VINEGAR
+
SALT
=

A BIT SWEET:
+
DIJON MUSTA
+
MAPLE SYRUP
TANGY & CREAMY:
+
YOGURT
+
NUTTY & CREAMY:
+
TAHINI
+
+
HONEY
SALTY & UMAMI:
+
CAPER
+
+
MAYO
+
DIJON MUSTA

- Add a small spoonful of Dijon, whole-grain, or any other kind of **mustard** to the basic vinaigrette, then balance it out with one of the sweet or creamy items below, if you like. When I'm at the end of a mustard jar, I make vinaigrette straight in the jar to use up the last bits of mustard stubbornly clinging to the inside.
- If you like sweeter dressings, whisk or shake a small spoonful of **honey**, **maple syrup**, or **jam** into your basic vinaigrette.
    - Mei's kids love **Maple-Dijon Dressing**: Whisk together ¼ cup extra-virgin olive oil, 2 tablespoons lemon juice or vinegar, 1 tablespoon maple syrup, 1 teaspoon Dijon, and a pinch of salt.
- **Buttermilk** and **yogurt** are both tangy cultured dairy products, fantastic in dressings. Mix a spoonful into your basic vinaigrette or start with a mix of half yogurt and half buttermilk, then add lemon juice, extra-virgin olive oil, salt, and pepper to taste.
- If you perpetually have a jar of **tahini** in the fridge, make the nutty, almost creamy **Lemony Tahini Dressing** (page 42) or freestyle your own version.
- **Capers**, **pickles**, and **olives** all live in acidic liquids, so why not make use of these concoctions that someone has already prepared for you? Beyond dressings, pickle brine in particular adds oomph to soups, meat marinades, potato salads, dips (pickle brine + mayo = instant makeshift tartar sauce) and makes for an excellent **Bloody Mary** (page 106).
    - When you want an easy take on a Caesar salad, make **Caper-Mayo Dressing**: Whisk together (or use an immersion blender to blend) ¼ cup extra-virgin olive oil, 1 minced garlic clove, 1 tablespoon capers, 2 tablespoons mayonnaise, 2 tablespoons any kind of mustard, and 1½ tablespoons caper, lemon, or pickle juice, plus salt and pepper to taste.

Lettuce Soup

Serves 2 to 4

Sautéed in fat with aromatics and then simmered in a savory broth, lettuce deserves the chance to become soup just like any other vegetable. You can use any kind of lettuce; make a milder version with romaine or Bibb or dial up the flavor with a spicy green like arugula or watercress. We like to thicken it up with a potato and a swirl of heavy cream, but you can make a light vegan version without either one.

2 tablespoons extra-virgin olive oil or butter
1 medium onion, diced
4 garlic cloves, sliced
1 bunch lettuce or a mix of any light leafy greens (about 8 cups), roughly chopped
Kosher salt and freshly ground black pepper
3 cups stock of your choice or water
1 medium potato, such as a russet, peeled or scrubbed and chopped
¼ cup tender fresh herbs such as parsley or chives (optional)
½ cup heavy cream or full-fat coconut milk (optional)
Lemon wedge
Optional garnishes: dollop of sour cream, chopped fresh chives or scallions, Croutons (page 81), Toasted Breadcrumbs (page 80)

Heat the olive oil in a medium pot over medium heat. Add the onion and garlic and cook until softened, about 5 minutes, then add the lettuce with a good pinch of salt. Stir until wilted, then add the stock, potato, and fresh herbs, if using. Bring to a boil, then simmer until the potato is completely cooked, about 20 minutes.

Carefully puree the soup. If you have an immersion blender, you can puree it in the pot; if you have a regular blender, let the steam escape when blending so it doesn't explode on you. Stir in the cream or coconut milk, if using, then season to taste with more salt and pepper and a good squeeze of lemon for brightness. Serve with your choice of fun toppings.

Hearty Greens

IDEAS AND RECIPES

Here we focus on the sturdy greens that typically come in bunches and encompass stems as well as leaves. We're also including the leaves of other vegetables, which often get discarded, such as beet, radish, sweet potato, and turnip greens. While the roots of those vegetables typically get all the attention, why discard their flavorful and nutritious leaves when they're just as good as the ones we spend money on? We'll take two veggies for the price of one anytime.

From side dishes in the Use-It-Up Ideas to main dishes later in the chapter, these recipes are perfect for when you find yourself with a bunch or two of greens. Or if you've got a few different varieties, combine them into one recipe. And don't forget most of these greens can be worked into a Hero Recipe or treated as a Light Leafy Green; the possibilities are endless!

Know What You Got

The flavor of greens can vary considerably according to age and variety, but here we've listed a few of the more common varieties you might encounter. It's by no means an exhaustive list—you may find new and unusual options at farmers' markets and grocery stores—but this starter roundup can help you learn how to use unfamiliar new greens you may encounter, like amaranth or borage. Taste them—are they mild or assertive, bitter or cabbage-like? Once you've tried them, you can swap and substitute in any of the recipes in this chapter with a sense of how the final dish will taste.

More neutral-tasting, sometimes a bit sweet

- **Bok choy:** There are many varieties of Asian cabbage (and many ways of spelling the same vegetable, which adds to the fun), including Shanghai bok choy, with pale green stalks; regular bok choy, with white stalks; and baby or dwarf varieties, which are tiny and adorable. They're members of the Brassica family but have a much milder taste than many other cabbage-y vegetables.
- **Sweet potato greens:** These are popular in many African dishes and a totally underrated green vegetable.
- **Spinach:** We're talking about the mature, full-leaf spinach that you'd buy in a bunch—milder baby spinach that comes in bags is covered in the Light Leafy Greens chapter.
- **Swiss chard:** Chard comes in multiple varieties with different-colored stems and can range from mild to more bitter, but we treat them all the same way.

- **Beet greens:** They're related to chard and can be cooked in exactly the same ways.

Cabbage-like, a bit more bitter

- **Kale:** Whether red Russian, curly, Tuscan (also known as cavolo nero, dinosaur, black, or lacinato)—kale is the new "it" vegetable for raw salads, but it's also good in many cooked dishes.
- **Collard greens:** Collards are popular in the Southern part of the US when cooked until soft, but they're also surprisingly good served raw.
- **Turnip greens:** These are also common in the South and are as versatile as collards.
- **Broccoli leaves:** Those tiny leaves you see on your broccoli stalks also come full-size!
- **Cabbage:** Red, green, savoy, napa—all are delicious raw in salads as well as roasted in the oven or charred on the grill.

Spicier, more pungent

- **Mustard greens:** These can be frilly or leafy, green or purple—tame their bitterness by eating in cooked dishes or add to a salad to spice things up.
- **Radish greens:** Taste and feel them before eating—sometimes the leaves have little prickles that are uncomfortable to eat raw, in which case you can cook them or whizz into Green Sauce (page 138).

Store It Right

For hearty greens in bags or bunches or attached to root vegetables: Remove any rubber bands or twist ties to minimize stem bruising, slice off any attached roots (storage info can be found on page 192), then store the bunch in a resealable bag or airtight container in the crisper drawer of the refrigerator. Wrapping in a damp cloth or paper towel can help dry greens maintain some humidity. When ready to wash, submerge the cut leaves in a large bowl of cold water and swish them around gently with your hands, letting any dirt fall to the bottom. Drain and dry the leaves well to extend their life; use a salad spinner and/or paper towels or kitchen cloths to blot off extra water. Put any greens you're not using back in the container. If they're not completely dry, stash a dry cloth or paper towel in the bag to soak up any moisture.

For hearty greens in a head, like cabbage: You can pop a cabbage straight into the fridge with no wrapping, although we often have trouble getting larger ones to fit in the crisper drawer. If that's the case, either leave it on a higher shelf or cut it into large wedges and store in a resealable bag. If the exposed sides start to discolor, slice off any dark edges before using.

Save for Later

Blanching (see page 23) can help keep your greens a few days longer, and they'll be soft enough to add straight to a Hero Recipe. Keep blanched greens in the fridge in an airtight container or, once they've cooled, freeze them in a sealed bag with the air pressed out. When you're ready to use them, place the bag in the refrigerator or in a bowl of cold water to thaw, or pop the frozen greens directly into a soup or stew.

You Can Still Eat It!

If leaves start to turn yellow or wilt, cook them into a soup, stew, or another Hero Recipe. You can also perk the leaves back up in an ice-water bath (see page 158 for more).

Extra Bits

In all too many greens recipes, the stems get ignored completely. And yes, if you're making a light, refreshing salad, it may not make sense to include a tough kale stem or crunchy cabbage core. But if you're cooking the greens, we encourage you to treat the stems as an integral part of the vegetable. Treat them the same way you're treating the leaves, but with a longer cooking time. Add them to the pot first, let them soften a bit—usually 3 or 4 minutes will do—then add the rest of the greens. Cutting stems into small equal-size pieces or slicing them thinly will shorten cooking times and help them cook more evenly. And if stems don't really fit in your dish, chop and blanch them as on page 23, or keep them raw. Stored in a bag in your fridge or freezer, they'll keep until you figure out which Hero Recipe needs a dose of healthy green stems.

Use-It-Up Ideas

- **Braised Greens** are an easy way to use up any assortment of greens you have hanging around the kitchen. Heat a splash of extra-virgin olive oil and a minced garlic clove in a large skillet. Add 4 to 6 cups chopped greens and stir just until wilted. Add 1 cup stock or water, plus maybe a splash of wine, cover, and let the greens simmer until tender, 3 to 8 minutes depending on the greens. Season well to taste, then pile onto toast, top with a fried egg, or stir into a bowl of rice or pasta.

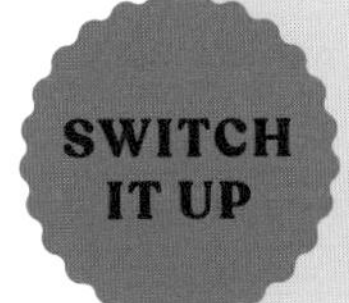

Add minced ginger with the garlic, then stir in a pinch each of ground turmeric, coriander, and cayenne before adding the greens. Finish with a spoonful of yogurt or coconut milk.

- Hearty leaves of any variety—even nontypical salad ingredients like chard, collards, and Brussels sprouts—can soften up to salad or slaw quality with a bit of love. Set aside any thick stems, slice the leaves into thin ribbons for easier eating, and consider mixing in a mild lettuce to temper any bitterness. If the leaves are tough, use your hands to massage in a splash of vinegar or lemon and a pinch of salt until the leaves are thoroughly coated and lightly wilted. Let sit while you put together the rest of the salad with the help of the **Leafy Greens Salad Builder** (page 160), or follow the **Mix-and-Match Slaw Party** instructions (page 42).
- **Grilled Greens** make for an incredibly easy last-minute side dish if you've already got a grill going. Greens that come naturally in a head work well, like bok choy or romaine, as they hold together instead of falling through your grill grates. However, we've laid sturdier, large-stemmed leaves like kale directly on the grate too; they're more likely to stay put if you keep the stem in, then you can eat or compost the stems as desired. Toss lightly with extra-virgin olive oil and sprinkle lightly with salt, then place directly on the grill grates until tender and lightly charred. To soothe the charred bitterness and crunch, whisk together a simple **Yogurt Dressing** with ½ cup plain yogurt, 2 tablespoons extra-virgin olive oil, the grated zest and juice of ½ lemon, 1 minced garlic clove, and a pinch of salt. Other cooling sauce options include the Caesar-ish **Caper-Mayo Dressing** (page 167) or **Herby Ranch** (page 141).
- **Roasted Greens** are another great option if you've already got the oven going for dinner. Lightly drizzle leaves (keep the stems in or discard if they're very tough) with oil and sprinkle with salt, then roast at 400 degrees for 4 to 6 minutes for leaves like kale, 15 to 20 for thin wedges of cabbage. Arrange on a platter and sprinkle with stuff—bacon bits! feta crumbles! **Toasted Breadcrumbs** (page 80)! chopped nuts!—and you've got an impressive vegetable dish for a relatively small amount of work.

Try the never-fail dress-it-up options in the illustration below for braised, grilled, oven-roasted, or otherwise cooked hearty greens.

Steamed Soy-Butter Fish with Greens

Serves 2, but feel free to double if you have room in your steamer setup

This dish is a take on the classic Cantonese whole steamed fish but with butter (yum) and no tiny bones or fish eyes (only yum for some of us). Using fillets and steaming them over greens like kale or chard results in a super healthy meal in one easy setup. And lest you think steaming means no flavor, welcome to the Chinese method of frying aromatics in oil, adding soy sauce, and pouring it over your fish. You may want to start splashing this mixture over everything you eat, and we highly recommend fluffy white rice for soaking up the sauce.

1 bunch hearty greens, leaves roughly chopped (stems saved for another use)
12 ounces white fish fillets, such as cod, sea bass, tilapia, or flounder
3 tablespoons neutral oil
1-inch piece fresh ginger, peeled and sliced into matchsticks
1 tablespoon butter
1 tablespoon minced cilantro stems, or several chopped cilantro sprigs
2 scallions, thinly sliced
1 tablespoon soy sauce
Pinch sugar
Steamed white rice, for serving

Set up a steamer or a heatproof plate and steamer rack over a pot filled with an inch of water. Bring to a boil, then add the chopped greens to the steamer. Cook until the greens wilt, 3 to 5 minutes, then place the fish in a single layer on top of the greens (a bit of overlapping to fit is fine), cover, and steam until the fish is opaque and flakes easily when prodded with a fork, 4 to 6 minutes.

Meanwhile, heat the oil in a small saucepan over medium heat and add the ginger. Fry until starting to brown, about 2 minutes, then add the butter. Stir to combine until the butter melts, then add the cilantro, scallions, soy sauce, and sugar. Stir to combine, then turn off the heat. Taste and adjust as needed—if it's too strong, stir in a small splash of water.

Check your fish—if it's still translucent and sticky, give it another minute or two. When done, use a spatula to transfer the fish and greens to a plate, then pour the soy-butter mix over and serve immediately with freshly cooked rice.

All-the-Greens Saag Paneer

Serves 4, with naan or rice

We've learned many new things about saag paneer, Irene's must-order Indian takeout dish, over the past few years. For years we mistakenly assumed that *saag* meant spinach but learned through many text messages with Mei's friends Rahul and Tara that it in fact refers to leafy green vegetables of any variety. The iconic Indian chef Madhur Jaffrey recommends radish greens (and suggests stirring in a dollop of butter before serving—we like her style). Try broccoli rabe or mustard greens, toss in a few sprigs of carrot tops or extra beet greens—use up any leaves you have, even the wilted ones in the back of your crisper drawer. To change things up further, food writer Priya Krishna suggests substituting feta for paneer in her cookbook *Indian-ish*. It doesn't have the same blocky texture, but it's often in our fridges already (and unlike paneer, is available in every supermarket). Homemade saag paneer, here we come.

NOTE: *We sometimes like to toss the paneer in a bit of ground turmeric, cayenne, and salt (it's not as strongly seasoned as feta) and pan-fry it until crispy on a few sides for a fun textural contrast to the blended greens.*

ANOTHER NOTE: *If you don't have the listed spices in your cupboard, feel free to swap with what you do have—such as mustard seeds, chili flakes, ground cardamom, or fenugreek.*

3 tablespoons ghee or neutral oil
1 teaspoon garam masala, or more to taste
1 teaspoon ground coriander, or more to taste
1 teaspoon ground cumin, or more to taste
1 medium onion, diced
2 garlic cloves, minced

1-inch piece fresh ginger, minced

1 serrano or other chile, chopped (optional)

8 to 10 packed cups hearty greens, roughly chopped, leaves and stems separated

½ lemon or lime

Kosher salt

8 ounces paneer (or whatever your package size, but we firmly believe the more paneer, the better) or feta, cut into bite-size pieces

Steamed white rice or naan, for serving

Chopped fresh cilantro, for garnish

Melt the ghee in a Dutch oven over medium heat. Add the spices and stir-fry for a minute or so, then add the onion. Stir to coat in the spices and cook until translucent and starting to brown, 5 to 7 minutes. Add the garlic, ginger, and chile, if using, and cook for another minute. Add the stems of your greens, if you have any, and cook for 2 or 3 minutes. Then add the leaves and cook until wilted and tender, 5 to 8 minutes (adding a small splash of water to the pan and covering it for a few minutes can help everything wilt faster, especially if your pan is full to the brim).

Remove the pan from the heat and let cool slightly. Transfer the greens to a blender or food processor, squeeze in the lemon or lime juice, and add a generous pinch of salt. Pulse or blend until the mixture reaches the texture you like (we like all the leaves finely chopped but not too smooth). Return the mixture to the pan and heat over medium-low heat. Gently stir in the paneer or feta and season to taste with more salt or the spices of your choice. Once everything is warmed through, serve with rice or naan, and maybe a sprinkle of chopped cilantro and a drizzle of melted butter or ghee. Cooled leftovers will keep for several days in an airtight container in the fridge, or freeze as a thoughtful gift for your future self.

Broccoli and Friends

IDEAS AND RECIPES

Here's where we cover those in-between vegetables, the stalks, pods, and florets that are sturdier than the leafy greens but not quite as weighty as the root vegetables. The most popular of these is broccoli, but we've included a few other brassicas, fresh legumes, and other miscellaneous vegetables as well. Turn here when you're looking to celebrate broccoli and all its friends, whether raw in a salad or cooked into a party dish.

Know What You Got

Here's what we include in this section:

- **Asparagus:** Whether thin- or thick-stalked, purple or green, the flavor of asparagus doesn't change according to shape or color, so it's a matter of preference which ones you bring home.
- **Pods:** This group includes green beans, snow peas, and snap peas. (Dried beans and other longer-storing members of the legume family can be found in the Hero Recipes.)
- **Florets:** Besides regular broccoli, there's Chinese broccoli, Broccolini, and broccoli rabe. We're all familiar with broccoli's thick stems and large head of florets, while Chinese broccoli or gai lan has very thin stems and more leaves. Broccolini is actually a cross between the two, and broccoli rabe (also known

as broccoli raab or rapini) looks like a leafier version but is actually more closely related to the turnip. Broccoli, gai lan, and Broccolini are all on the sweeter side and can be cooked similarly; the more bitter broccoli rabe is often used more like a hearty green similar to mustard greens.

- **Brussels sprouts:** Delicious roasted, fried, sautéed, or raw, Brussels sprouts can also be used in many of the recipes in the Hearty Greens chapter.
- **Cauliflower and romanesco:** Cauliflower comes in a range of colors and sizes, but all can be prepared the same way. Romanesco, a fractal-patterned member of the Brassica family, cooks up similarly to cauliflower.

WITH IRENE

A Botany Nerd Moment

Have you ever noticed that broccoli leaves look like collard greens? Or that those tiny individual broccoli buds are like miniature Brussels sprouts? Why and how? Brussels sprouts, broccoli, cauliflower, and cabbage are all *Brassica oleracea*—they're the same species of vegetable bred for different characteristics. And that's not just a fun fact; it also gives us clues about how to substitute these veggies for one another and cook more creatively. Now you're a botany nerd, just like me.

Store It Right

Asparagus are a bit fussy—to keep them fresh as long as possible, store upright in the fridge with the bottom ends in a cup of water (like how you'd store fresh flowers). If you can't fit an asparagus vase in your fridge, wrap the ends in a wet cloth and store in a breathable bag in the fridge. Store all the pods and florets and Brussels sprouts unwashed in a breathable produce bag in the refrigerator crisper drawer and try to eat any fresh beans sooner rather than later. Cauliflower and romanesco, which usually come wrapped in plastic, can be kept in their original packaging.

If you want to eat any of these vegetables raw, do so in the first few days, when they're at their best. They should still be fresh and firm for at least another few days after that, but will be better cooked into a dish.

Save for Later

All these vegetables freeze well and will keep best when cooked before freezing. Follow the instructions for blanching (page 23) and store in a sealed container with as much air pressed out as possible. Previously frozen asparagus and florets are great for soups, curries, stews, and other softer-textured dishes. Cauliflower and green beans also make great pickles.

You Can Still Eat It!

A number of these vegetables, especially cauliflower, will develop tiny brown spots, a harmless discoloration that can be cut off before cooking. If a few beans out of a bunch look bad, pick them out and discard, then wash the rest well before cooking. After a week or so, any of these vegetables may go soft or limp but will still be fine to eat. Use in a soup or stew or refresh in an ice-water bath to revive the vegetables a little. Roasting is a good way to cook slightly older veggies, as the crispy edges will help add texture that's been lost due to age. Of course, if any of these vegetables are moldy, shriveled, or completely rotten, it's time for the compost bin.

Extra Bits

These vegetables typically require a bit of prep before cooking, from removing the tough asparagus ends to separating the stem and florets of broccoli and cauliflower. However, just because certain parts get broken down differently doesn't mean we shouldn't eat them.

- **Asparagus:** In our opinion, people tend to discard lots of perfectly good asparagus ends by snapping them off where they bend. Give those ends a feel—if they're just a little tougher than the rest of the stalk, slice them crosswise into thin coins and give them a bit of extra cooking time. If the very ends are really dry or woody, toss them into your Kitchen Scrap Stock Bag (page 18) so they don't go to waste.
- **Broccoli:** Cut the stalk right at the base of the florets. Trim a thin slice off the base of the stalk if browned or dry, then use a peeler or sharp knife to remove the tough outer layer down to the lighter core. For quick cooking methods like stir-frying, cut the stem into thin coins; for longer methods like roasting, cut into chunks or planks. Broccoli leaves are not only edible but delicious, if you're lucky enough to find them—treat them like hearty greens. Broccolini and Chinese broccoli stems may or may not need to be peeled; sometimes just slicing the stems crosswise can help break up any tougher stringy fibers. If you're serving either one whole, splitting the stalk in half lengthwise can help ensure the whole stem is evenly cooked.
- **Cauliflower and romanesco:** The leaves and cores are edible and can be treated just like the rest of the cauliflower.
- **Green beans, sugar snap peas, and snow peas:** Many are sold trimmed, but if not, you may want to cut or snap off the ends and pull out the strings. Don't feel you have to trim them, though. We love how the tiny stems get crispy when roasted at high heat. When what could be called laziness is joined with deliciousness, we will always opt for the no-prep route.

WITH MEI

Cheesy Broccoli Stem Soup

When your six-year-old gleefully announces an undying love for broccoli florets and an equally vehement distaste for the stalks, make **Cheesy Broccoli Stem Soup**! Anytime I make broccoli for dinner, I cook the peeled stalk with the rest of the broccoli, then let it cool and pop it into a freezer bag. Once I've got enough stalks, I make **Cream-of-Anything Soup** (page 48) with a bit of extra cream and a cup or two of shredded sharp cheddar. Finally, eaters of all ages can eat stalks with excitement.

Use-It-Up Ideas

- For times when you need to rescue these vegetables before they go bad, cook them any way you like to extend their life a few more days. We like to roast at high heat for caramelized edges, crispy browned bits, and an easy hands-off cooking process. Other options include boiling or steaming, pan-braising with butter and lemon, or sautéing in a simple **Stir-Fry** (page 52). Store cooked vegetables in the fridge for future meals or work the cooked vegetables into any of the Hero Recipes.
- Broccoli and friends have a tender-crisp texture that offers a satisfying level of crunch when served raw. Beyond our **Very Versatile Green Salad** (page 186), try using slender slices of broccoli, asparagus, or cauliflower in **Mix-and-Match Slaw Party** (page 42) or **Freestyle Vegetable Summer Rolls** (page 44)—you can include the stems too if they're shaved thinly with a mandoline or peeler. For more ideas on eating these vegetables raw, see the **Leafy Greens Salad Builder** (page 160).

A Very Versatile Green Salad

Serves 4 as a side

This raw salad is a great way to highlight fresh-from-the-market asparagus, Brussels sprouts, snow peas, or anything else similar. You're looking for very thin slices here, which can be shaved into ribbons with a peeler, mandoline, or careful knife skills. If you're not a fan of raw asparagus, steam or boil it for mere moments before transferring to an ice bath. The rest of this recipe should be taken as a template: Mix a spoonful of yogurt or buttermilk into the dressing to make it creamy; swap the nuts for breadcrumbs or a cooked grain like farro or couscous, toasted a bit in a pan.

1 pound asparagus or Brussels sprouts, very thinly sliced
2 tablespoons fresh lemon juice
Kosher salt and freshly ground pepper
3 tablespoons extra-virgin olive oil, or more to taste
8 ounces arugula or another soft-leaf lettuce
½ to 1 cup good cheese of your choice (about 2 ounces), such as dollops of soft feta or goat cheese, or crumbles of a hard cheese like Manchego or Parmesan
½ cup chopped nuts, such as walnuts, almonds, or pine nuts, toasted or raw

---

If using Brussels sprouts, toss thoroughly with the lemon juice and a generous sprinkle of salt right away and let sit while you get the rest of the ingredients together so they get a bit more tender.

Combine all the ingredients and toss to coat. Try a forkful and see if it needs a bit more of anything—oil, lemon, salt, or pepper—and serve immediately.

Quick Cauliflower and Chicken Curry

Serves 4 to 6

This clever trick for using up an intimidatingly large cauliflower comes from our chief recipe tester and sister-in-law Mel, the curry master of the family. You split the cauliflower into two distinct parts so most of the florets get infused with spicy curry notes while the remaining florets, leaves, and core become cauliflower "rice" in the food processor. It's a great dish to feed anyone avoiding starches, and also a stellar way to use up all the generally discarded parts of cauliflower. The recipe relies on curry paste to do the heavy lifting—perfect for when you don't feel like chopping aromatics—but if you want to punch it up, go ahead and sauté diced onion, ginger, and garlic before adding the paste.

NOTE: *If you want to make this with any of the other vegetables in the chapter, cook them as you do the florets and use actual rice (or another grain) in place of the cauliflower.*

1 large cauliflower
1 tablespoon neutral oil
¼ cup Thai curry paste of your choice
1 pound boneless, skinless chicken thighs, cut into 1-inch pieces
1 (14-ounce) can unsweetened coconut milk, ideally full-fat
1 tablespoon soy sauce
1 tablespoon fish sauce
1 tablespoon lime juice
¼ teaspoon sugar
Kosher salt
Small handful fresh cilantro leaves and stems, plus more for garnish
1 scallion, cut into 2-inch pieces

(continues)

Break down the cauliflower into large chunks, setting aside the stem, core, leaves, and about one-third of the florets. Cut the remaining florets into bite-size pieces.

Heat the oil in a large skillet over medium heat, then add the curry paste and stir-fry for 2 minutes, until toasty and fragrant. Add the chicken, stir to coat in the paste, and cook for 5 minutes, then add the bite-size cauliflower florets. Stir-fry the chicken and cauliflower for 2 minutes, then add the coconut milk. Refill the can halfway with water, swish it around a bit to get all the remaining milk from inside the can, and add the water to the pan. Bring to a boil, then lower the heat to medium and simmer for 8 to 10 minutes, until the chicken is cooked through. Stir in the soy sauce, fish sauce, lime juice, and sugar, then season with salt to taste.

While the chicken is cooking, put the cauliflower stem, core, leaves, and reserved florets in a food processor with the cilantro and scallion and pulse until the cauliflower resembles rice or couscous. Transfer to a microwaveable bowl, cover with a lid or plastic wrap, and microwave on high for 3 to 5 minutes, until it's tender but still has some bite. Stir, season with salt, and serve with the curry. Store leftover curry in a sealed container in the fridge for several days or in the freezer for a few months.

Broccoli and Feta Phyllo Pie

Serves 6 to 8

It's possible that this is our new favorite way to eat broccoli. We're big fans of the Greek pie spanakopita, and the addition of broccoli adds substance and flavor that we're not sure spinach can ever match. And as cute as those little spanakopita triangles are, this version gets you all the flake with none of the meticulous crafting. Yes, the layering of the phyllo sheets into the skillet requires a bit of handiwork, but it's much more forgiving than individual wedges and still presents as an impressive party dish.

6 tablespoons butter, divided

2 tablespoons extra-virgin olive oil

1 medium onion, diced

3 garlic cloves, chopped

2 heads broccoli or 1 head cauliflower (about 1 pound), florets separated and stalks peeled and cut into chunks

½ cup dry white wine

½ cup water

8 to 12 sheets phyllo pastry, thawed

¼ cup chopped fresh herbs of your choice, such as dill and/or parsley

8 ounces crumbled feta (about 1½ cups)

Grated zest of 1 lemon, plus 1 tablespoon lemon juice

Kosher salt and freshly ground black pepper

Melt 1 tablespoon of the butter with the olive oil in a medium skillet over medium-high heat. Add the onion and garlic and sauté for 3 minutes, until slightly softened. Add the broccoli and stir until fully combined, then add the wine and water. Cover and let simmer for 10 minutes, stirring

(continues)

occasionally, until the broccoli is tender. Uncover and cook for a few minutes longer, until the liquid has mostly evaporated.

Meanwhile, heat the oven to 400 degrees.

Melt the remaining 5 tablespoons butter (the microwave is a good place to do this). Use a pastry brush to coat the bottom and sides of a large oven-safe skillet with a thin layer of melted butter, then place a sheet of phyllo so two-thirds of the sheet covers the bottom and sides of the skillet and the last third hangs over the rim. Brush butter onto the part of the phyllo sheet inside the pan, then rotate the skillet slightly, and place another sheet angled to the first one. Continue to add sheets and brush butter all over the sheets inside the pan until the entire base of the skillet is covered and there's phyllo hanging off all sides of the pan.

Once the broccoli mixture is done, add the chopped herbs, feta, and lemon zest and juice, then season with salt and pepper so the mixture is so good you want to eat it straight from the pan. Spoon the filling into the skillet and either fold the overhanging phyllo sheets over the top to make a closed pie or scrunch the sheets around the inside of the skillet to make a crunchy wreath.

Place the skillet on the stovetop and cook over medium heat for 5 to 7 minutes to ensure your pie doesn't end up with a soggy bottom (the horror!). Transfer to the oven and bake for 20 minutes, or until the top is a crisp golden brown. Serve hot or at room temperature. If you end up with any leftovers, we recommend reheating in a skillet on the stovetop with a bit of butter to get the phyllo browned and crunchy again.

Roots, Tubers, and Winter Squash

IDEAS AND RECIPES

Here we cover the sturdiest vegetables—roots, tubers, and winter squash—that abound in the fall and winter and work with nearly every cooking technique out there. We consider these hard vegetables a food waste warrior's best friend: They've got a pretty long shelf life when raw and are also easy to repurpose once cooked. Mashed, pureed, or roasted, these vegetables can easily be transformed into other dishes or used to top a grain bowl or spice up a salad. We've also got lots of ideas for using up the extra bits that come along for the ride, from peels to greens to seeds. And whether a root, a tuber, or a squash, they're all prime ingredients for Hero Recipes, just waiting to be chucked haphazardly into a stew or artfully strewn on a puff pastry tart.

Know What You Got

- **Roots:** With these vegetables, the edible root grows underground, sometimes attached to edible greens. Most can be eaten raw as well as cooked. This category includes but is not limited to beets, carrots, parsnips, turnips, jicama, rutabaga, radishes, kohlrabi, and celeriac/celery root. (Onions and garlic are technically roots, but as they're used quite differently in cooking, you'll find them in the Alliums and Aromatics chapter.)
- **Tubers:** These starchier vegetables also grow underground but typically require cooking to be digestible—think potatoes, sweet potatoes, yams, and sunchokes/Jerusalem artichokes.
- **Winter squash:** Squash are botanically fruits and grow above ground, but their hardness means we tend to treat them like root vegetables. Common varieties include butternut, pumpkin, acorn, delicata, spaghetti squash, kabocha, and Hubbard.

Store It Right

Root vegetables can generally last 1 to 3 weeks, sometimes more, loosely wrapped in a breathable produce bag in the crisper drawer of your fridge. Once cut, store in an airtight container. If you have young root vegetables, such as early summer beets or carrots, they should be eaten sooner, within a few days if you want to consume them raw. Cut off any greens they came with—they pull moisture out of the root—and store the greens as you would any hearty greens.

Potatoes, sweet potatoes, and winter squash should be stored somewhere cool and dark, ideally somewhere well ventilated, but we stash ours in a cupboard, so do your best. If you're using only part of a large squash, store the remaining cut section in an airtight container in the fridge. Storing potatoes near onions speeds the deterioration process, so keep them separate if possible. If your house is very hot, you may want to move squash and new or early-season potatoes to the fridge.

Save for Later

All the roots pickle beautifully (tubers and squash not so much), so extend their life in a Quick Pickle (page 37) whenever the clock starts to run out. Winter squash, sweet potatoes, and most of the roots freeze well when cut into chunks and then blanched or steamed. Once cooled, freeze in an airtight container; when you're ready to eat them, put the frozen chunks straight into soups and stews, or thaw and cook them into an oven dish like Fridge-Forage Baked Pasta (page 70), Savory Bread Pudding (page 78), or a casserole. Purees and soups are a great option for freezing and don't need to be defrosted before heating. Potatoes go mushy when frozen on their own but can be cooked into a dish like a stew or soup and then frozen without too much loss of texture.

You Can Still Eat It!

Slightly wrinkled or shriveled tubers can still be eaten; just remove and compost the dry exterior. If roots start to get a bit limp or floppy, revive them in an ice-water bath or cook them into a mash or puree or any dish where your goal is softness anyway. Browned or bruised areas or even a spot of mold on the outside of these vegetables can often be removed—cut away and discard until you see a good-looking area—leaving the rest of the vegetable fine to eat. But if it's really soft, moldy, or collapsing, it's time for the compost.

NO-WASTE TIPS

If you keep your potatoes near your onions, store them in the sunlight, or forget about their existence for long stretches of time (we have been guilty of all three, particularly the last), you may have found yourself with sprouted or green-tinged potatoes. Although some recommend just discarding a sprouted potato, we remove the sprouts and eyes and cook them anyway. Or pop them into soil and see if you can grow some potatoes! (Look online for tips.) Green skin is more of a warning sign though: These potatoes may contain higher levels of natural toxins, but according to the USDA can still be edible if you remove all the green parts, skin, and sprouts. But don't eat anything you don't feel comfortable eating—if you don't like the look of a potato, if it tastes bitter, or especially if you are immunocompromised, pregnant, elderly, or feeding kids—then toss it in the compost. Use your best judgment, and that includes not judging yourself if you decide to throw something away.

POTATOES & ONIONS: FRENEMIES OF THE KITCHEN

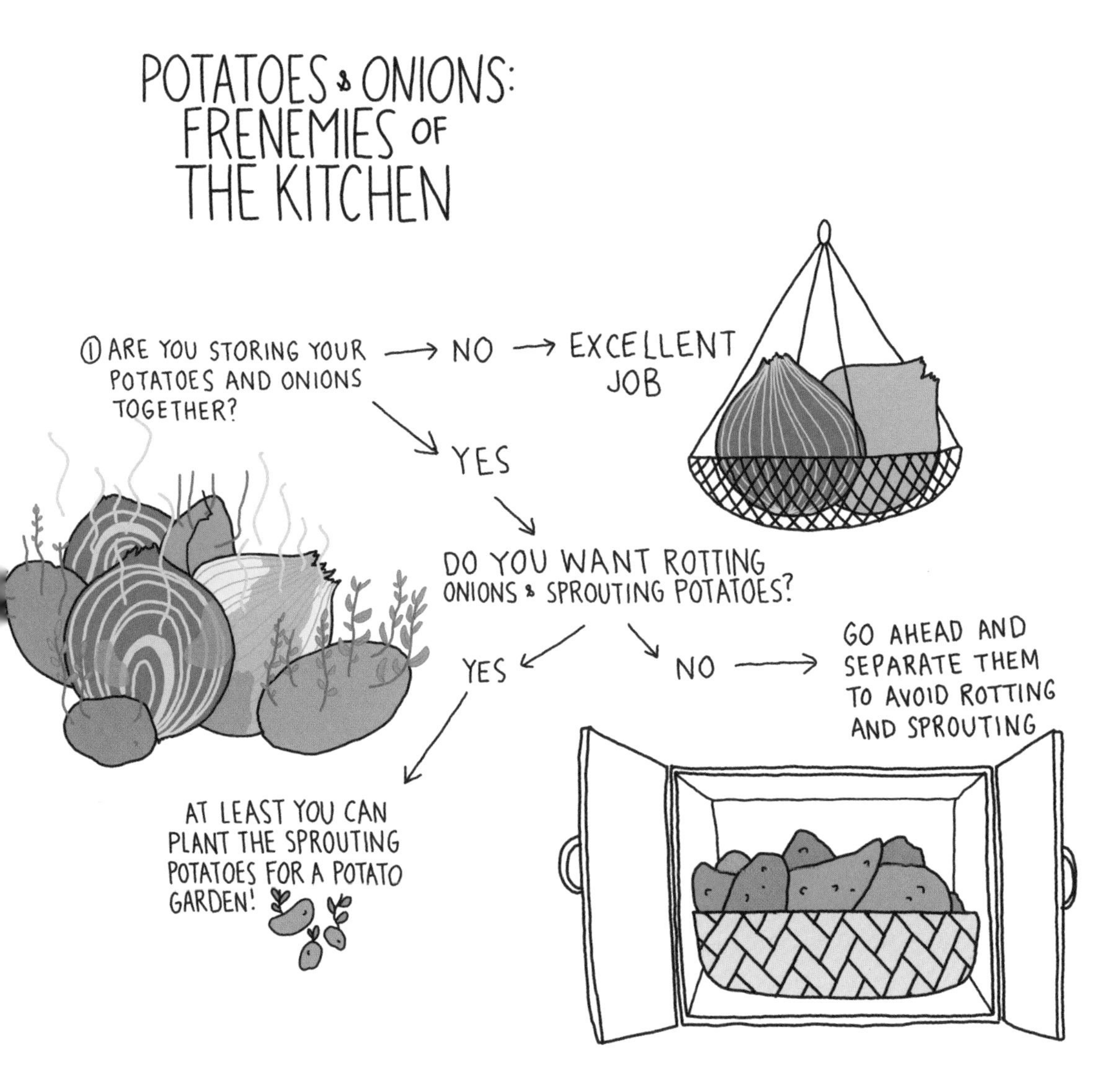

Extra Bits

- **Attached greens:** If you can, buy root vegetables with the greens still attached. First of all, it's a general indicator that the vegetables are fresh and have been harvested recently. Secondly, if the greens are still attached, they're edible (parsnip greens can cause allergic reactions, which is why you don't see them at the store). Beet greens, sweet potato greens, and turnip greens can be eaten like other leaves that you spend money on, like kale, chard, and spinach. If you're not sure what to do with them, it's fun to combine the root and its greens in a single Hero Recipe like **Savory Bread Pudding** (page 78) or **Anything-You-Like Galette** (page 72). Our friend Bryant Terry makes a fantastic soup with roasted turnips and their sautéed greens in his book *Vegetable Kingdom*. Radish greens can be tender enough for salad but sometimes have a bit of a prickly texture, in which case we recommend putting them in cooked dishes. Carrot greens sometimes edge toward tough and bitter, so go for a sauce or pesto or mix a few into **All-the-Greens Saag Paneer** (page 178). Taste the greens and decide—are they fibrous and tough, or tender and sweet? Find tons of ways to use them up over in the Hearty Greens chapter.
- **Seeds:** If you like to eat pumpkin seeds, you know that squash seeds shouldn't be relegated to the trash. And this applies to seeds from all types of winter squash! Toss them in salt and extra-virgin olive oil and roast at 350 degrees for 15 to 25 minutes depending on their size, until golden brown and crispy. Make them even more snackable by sprinkling an array of spices on before you roast, like any combination of ground cumin, coriander, turmeric, cayenne, or garlic powder. Here's what changed the game for us: Don't bother cleaning the seeds of all the squash flesh. Those little strings and thin whispers of squash, wholly at the mercy of the hot roasting pan, get all browned and crispy in a way that thick slices never will. Also, any laziness that makes it more likely you'll actually cook something is a

major power move in our book. Once roasted, you can blitz the seeds into a paste using a blender or food processor. It makes for a rustic, substantial spread, perfect for smearing on toast for breakfast along with a drizzle of good olive oil and a sprinkle of flaky salt.

- **Peels:** One of our no-food-waste mantras: You don't have to peel root vegetables! The outer layers contain fiber, flavor, and additional micronutrients, not to mention crisp or chewy textures. For roots, you'll often find that younger summer vegetables—particularly those with greens—don't need a peel, only a good scrub. If you're planning on eating a carrot or beet raw, try a bite of the skin and see what you think. Fall and winter root vegetables also have peels that can be eaten; we particularly love acorn and delicata squash skin in roast dishes for contrast. Consider also that texture and flavor genius Yotam Ottolenghi does not always peel his butternuts. There are a few roots you'll definitely want to peel: jicama, with its fibrous outer coating, and rutabaga, which is often coated with wax for storage. And don't even bother trying to peel celeriac, aka celery root—just slice off the gnarled and warty outer layer. Peeling is a judgment call and you're in charge. Maybe a beet or butternut squash skin is too tough to eat, or perhaps you're aiming for an elegant and smooth potato puree. In those cases, save your peels! Roast them and make our **Crispy Vegetable Peels** (page 198) to snack on straight, sprinkle onto soup, or dip into a creamy sauce. Other options include adding the peels to pureed soups for extra bulk, stashing them in your **Kitchen Scrap Stock Bag** (page 18), or composting.

Crispy Vegetable Peels

This quick snack and champion use-it-up technique is one of our favorite discoveries to come out of the writing of this book. These cheesy roasted peels combine the crunch of a French fry with the glorious taste sensation that is fried cheese, all combined with the immense satisfaction of using up something that is so often thrown out. They're so good that Mei has actually peeled potatoes just to eat the peels, and then let sad naked potatoes sit in her fridge for two days until she figured out what to do with them (thanks to Irene's suggestion to store them in water, they turned out fine!).

Heat the oven to 400 degrees. Scrub your roots and tubers well, then peel. Scatter the peels on a baking sheet. Drizzle with enough extra-virgin olive oil to lightly cover all the pieces, and sprinkle with salt and pepper. Shower lightly with cheese—Parmesan coats well and crisps up nicely, but any semi-firm melting cheese will work—and toss everything to combine. Roast until the peels shrivel and start crisping up. Most root vegetable peels—beets, turnips, carrots—will take 10 to 15 minutes, depending on their size and thickness, while sturdier potato peels may take 15 to 25 minutes. Snack on them right away—try not to burn your fingers—or use them as a crunchy topping for soups, salads, and more. Store them in the fridge in an airtight container—they might stay crispy for a day or two, and if not they'll still be delicious in a Sheet Pan Frittata (page 308).

①PEEL
②GRATE
③ROAST
④SNACK

Use-It-Up Ideas

- Our go-to cooking method for these sturdy vegetables is a high-heat roast in the oven to achieve tender flesh and toasty caramelized edges. But there's also boiling, steaming, frying, braising, and more, all of which will extend the life of your vegetables for a good amount of time.
- Of course, the fastest way to get any of these hardier veggies ready to eat is not to cook them at all. This works best with the roots—raw potatoes aren't really digestible, although sunchokes are, and some people will make a case for raw winter squash, shaved very thinly. Any roots can be eaten raw—typically carrots, jicama, and radishes, less commonly beets, parsnips, and turnips—but it depends on age and variety. Look for early-season, smaller roots with leaves. A few ideas for eating raw roots:
    - Slice raw roots into batons for a vegetable platter or cheeseboard and dip them into **Any-Bean Dip** (page 306) or **Herby Ranch** (page 141). Or slice thinly and layer them on avocado toast with a drizzle of good oil and a sprinkle of flaky salt, or on a fresh baguette with good butter, a simple but fancy-feeling French snack typically made with radishes.
    - Raw roots can add a delightful crispness to salads and slaws, two semi-interchangeable words for an assembly of mostly raw vegetables and dressing. For slaw, check out the **Mix-and-Match Slaw Party** (page 42); for salad, start with the **Leafy Greens Salad Builder** (page 160).
    - Try mixing raw roots into **Crisp and Crunchy Noodle Salad** (page 46) or **Freestyle Vegetable Summer Rolls** (page 44), or making **Quick Pickles** (page 37).
- Make **A Very General Root Vegetable Soup**, one of Irene's secret-weapon recipes that's simple but impressive, especially with the right garnishes. Start by heating butter or extra-virgin

olive oil in a soup pot and sautéing an onion or other aromatics of your choice with some salt and pepper. Add 4 cups raw or cooked roots, tubers, or squash, cut into chunks, along with 4 cups stock or water. This 1:1 ratio of vegetables to liquid makes for quite a thick soup, which is what we want when it's freezing outside—the soup equivalent of cozy slippers and a super soft hoodie. If you're in a soupier soup mood, just add more liquid until you reach the texture you like. Bring to a boil, then simmer until all the vegetables are tender, typically 15 to 30 minutes depending on your chosen vegetables. (If you're using all cooked vegetables, give it just 10 to 15 minutes to warm the vegetables through. It's OK if you have a mix of cooked and uncooked; the cooked ones won't overcook while you simmer the raw vegetables until tender.) Stir and puree to your desired consistency with an immersion or regular blender (if using a blender, let the hot steam escape while blending to avoid getting pureed carrots on your ceiling). Taste, season with salt and pepper, and garnish with fresh herbs, crunchy things, creamy things, or a swirl of **Green Sauce** (page 138) or **Herb Oil** (page 144). Like most soups, this recipe is very easily doubled, tripled, or otherwise multiplied to feed a crowd or to freeze for future meals. Raid the spice drawer to give the soup a bit more oomph—consider carrots + ground cumin, potatoes + paprika, or celery root + cayenne.

- For infinite variations on **Fancy-Looking Roasted Vegetables**, follow a very simple formula: roasted roots + exciting sauce + something crunchy = magic! Roast your wedges or thick slices of vegetables at 400 degrees until completely tender when speared with a fork, with lots of golden browned bits, typically 20 to 40 minutes (see the box on page 202). Let cool slightly, or store at room temperature for a few hours before you eat—roasted roots taste good hot or at room temperature. Lay the vegetables out on a platter and drizzle a fun sauce on top. Creamy choices like **Herby Ranch** (page 141) or **Garlicky Vegan Mayo** (page 303) will never go wrong, but a straight-up **Green Sauce** (page 138) can stand on its own here too (or you could smear some plain Greek yogurt on the platter underneath the roots for a nice contrast). Scatter something crunchy on top, such as chopped nuts, **Toasted Breadcrumbs** (page 80), savory granola, toasted cooked grains, or sesame seeds.

SWITCH IT UP

Once you start to swap out roots and tubers in various recipes, you'll never run out of ways to use them up. To roast any of the vegetables in this chapter, cut into relatively uniform pieces, peeled if you like. Slices or wedges add visual drama for a more presentation-worthy dish; French fry shapes are good for snacking and selective children. Place on a rimmed baking sheet, drizzle with enough extra-virgin olive oil for a light coating, and sprinkle with salt. Roast at 400 degrees per the times below; start checking at 15 minutes to pull out smaller items like Hakurei turnips or tiny carrots or to flip over sturdier items like squash or sweet potatoes. Although the size of your pieces will affect the cooking time, here's a rough guide:

- Turnips, carrots, radishes, and kohlrabi: 15 to 25 minutes
- Beets: 20 to 40 minutes
- Winter squash and sweet potatoes: 25 to 40 minutes
- Potatoes: 25 to 35 minutes

Any-Root-Vegetable Hash

Serves 4 to 6 as a side

Hash was originally invented to use up leftovers, but now it seems to be found only in diners and inextricably linked with corned beef. Unless you're a person who happens to have corned beef around (Does that person even exist? And are they looking for new friends?), it's time to let go of that association and start making hash at home with anything you happen to have around. The only requirements are some sturdy vegetables—traditionally just potatoes, but let's not limit ourselves—and an allium of some sort. From there, you can add meaty flavor with something breakfast-y like bacon or sausage or leftovers from last night's dinner, or leave the meat out altogether. Toss in any cooked vegetable you can find, chopped into tiny bits. Last, consider adding a good spoonful of ketchup. It's not strictly necessary, but the sugars help caramelize the vegetables for enhanced diner-breakfast-style flavors, and that is always a good thing. And since we're already going for that diner vibe, a sunny-side up egg on top is never a bad idea.

½ to 1 cup chopped cooked meat, or raw bacon or sausage (optional)
Neutral oil, for frying
1 cup diced onion, shallots, or leeks
3 to 4 cups diced root vegetables (aim for ¼-inch cubes)
Kosher salt
1 teaspoon spice(s) of your choice, such as ground cumin, coriander, and/or paprika
1 to 2 cups assorted cooked vegetables and fresh leaves or herbs you might have in the fridge, cut into small pieces
A hefty squirt (roughly 2 tablespoons) ketchup

(continues)

If you're cooking bacon or sausage or something with its own fat, fry it in a large skillet and transfer to a paper towel–lined plate. Otherwise, start by coating a large skillet with neutral oil and heating over medium-high heat. If using leftover meat, fry it until hot and crisp, then transfer to a plate.

Add a splash more oil if needed, then add the onion and cook until softened, about 5 minutes. Add the diced root vegetables and a good pinch of salt, stir to combine, and cook until mostly tender, 10 to 15 minutes depending on the vegetables. Let the vegetables brown a bit on the outside and stir every so often, turning the heat down slightly if needed to prevent burning. Lightly sprinkle with the spices of your choice and add any extra vegetables you want to use up. If they're cooked, you just want to warm them up; if they're raw leaves like chard or kale, cook until they're wilted and tender.

Squirt on a tablespoon or two of ketchup and stir to lightly coat all the hash, adding more if necessary. Using a spatula or spoon, press the hash into the pan and let cook for a few minutes to get a good crust going on the bottom. Stir and repeat for more browning, then taste for seasoning and spice. Continue cooking until all the vegetables are completely tender and satisfyingly browned and crunchy. All you need are some cooked eggs and you get the diner fry cook badge of honor.

A Riff on a Spanish Tortilla

Serves 8 as a side, 4 as a main dish

Spanish tortilla is basically a thick potato pancake, suffused with oniony olive oil, held together with egg, and browned all over. While potatoes are classic, it turns out you can sub in any thin-sliced winter vegetable you want—we love turnip and rutabaga and the pop of pink from a watermelon radish. This recipe makes a very large tortilla that could serve as a side for 8 people or a main for 4, but feel free to size it down depending on what you've got. The basic idea is that you want approximately half as much onion as roots, enough olive oil to cook both, and enough egg to cover everything.

1½ cups extra-virgin olive oil
3 cups diced onion
6 cups thinly sliced root vegetables (about 2 pounds)
Kosher salt and freshly ground black pepper
6 or 7 eggs
Herby Ranch (page 141) or Green Sauce (page 138), for serving (optional)

Heat the oil in a Dutch oven over medium-high heat. Add the onion and root vegetables and cook at a low simmer—you're not trying to deep fry them—until tender, about 15 minutes, stirring occasionally. Scoop the vegetables out with a slotted spoon or carefully strain, reserving the olive oil (you'll use some to fry the tortilla; store the rest in a sealed container for future cooking). Let the vegetables cool slightly, then season well with salt and pepper.

Meanwhile, crack 6 eggs into a large bowl and beat lightly. Gently stir in the cooled vegetables and make sure they are covered by the egg mixture; if not, add another lightly beaten egg.

(continues)

Grab a large skillet—cast iron and nonstick work well—and coat the bottom of the pan with a few spoonfuls of the reserved olive oil. Heat the oil over medium heat, then pour in the egg and vegetable mixture. Cook for 5 to 7 minutes, tilting the pan so the egg continues to flow to the bottom and lifting the edges occasionally with a silicone spatula to check for browning. You're looking for a nice golden brown on the bottom, indicating the eggs are well set and the tortilla will be lightly crisp.

Flip the tortilla by carefully placing a large dinner plate over the skillet and inverting the skillet so the tortilla ends up upside-down on the plate. Add a bit more oil to the skillet and then slide the tortilla back into the pan. Cook until the second side is browned, about 5 minutes. Slice into wedges and eat hot, warm, or at room temperature. Dip it into ranch, drizzle on green sauce, or eat all on its own.

Bubble and Squeak

Serves 4

If you, like my husband and sister-in-law/chief recipe tester, grew up in the United Kingdom, then you're familiar with the concept of mash. If not, think of mashed potatoes, and then replace "potatoes" with any of the vegetables in this section. And if you grew up with mash, you're probably already familiar with the delightfully named Bubble and Squeak. This dish is traditionally made from the remnants of a British roast dinner like potatoes and cabbage, but as a dish invented to use up leftovers, it should be considered infinitely flexible to use up what you have in your fridge. If we got to draft our Bubble and Squeak fantasy team, we'd have leftover Brussels sprouts, sausage, and mashed potatoes in the fridge, but any cooked leftovers and mashable roots or tubers will do just fine.

3 tablespoons butter, extra-virgin olive oil, or bacon fat

1 medium onion, chopped

3 to 5 garlic cloves, minced

1 cup leftover cooked vegetables, such as broccoli or carrots, roughly chopped

2 or 3 cooked sausages, cut into chunks, or another leftover meat (optional)

2 cups leftover mashed potatoes or another mashed vegetable (see box on page 209)

(continues)

Melt the butter in a large skillet over medium heat. Add the onion and cook, stirring occasionally, until softened, about 5 minutes. Add the garlic and cook for 1 minute. Add the leftover cooked vegetables and sausage (if using), stir, and let the vegetables get a little color and the meat crisp up a bit, maybe 5 minutes. Add the mashed potatoes and, using a spatula, mix the potatoes into the rest of the vegetables and meat, then press down so the large mashed-potato pancake you've formed starts browning on the bottom. As the pancake cooks, continue to flip parts of it and mash them back down so all the surfaces get browned and crispy. You're aiming for browned bits throughout the large patty, not just on either side, so just keep turning over bits and incorporating them back in, until everything is nicely browned and warmed through.

Root, Tuber, or Winter Squash Mash

Mashed sweet potatoes, carrots, or butternut squash don't have to be fed to babies or saved for the Thanksgiving table; mash is a simple way to use up any of the vegetables in this chapter without the use of fancy appliances.

Boil, steam, or roast your vegetables, then use a fork, potato masher, or wooden spoon to smash into a chunky paste. It's easiest to do when they're still hot; if using leftovers, a quick reheat in the microwave helps soften things up. Stir in some fat like butter or sour cream, add a splash of liquid like cream, milk, or stock, and adjust for seasoning.

What to do with your mash:

- Bulk up other dishes—layer into a lasagna, stir into pasta, or mix into rice.
- Stir in a bit of flour and an egg to form patties, then pan-fry into cakes or croquettes.
- Sprinkle with crunchy bits and spoon on a sauce, similar to **Fancy-Looking Roasted Vegetables** (page 201), and serve as a side dish for smearing on crusty bread or crackers.
- Mix pureed beet or squash with a bit of pasta water to make a pasta sauce, or mix into **Easygoing Tomato Sauce** (page 104).
- Turn it into a dip, either on its own or by mixing in something creamy like plain yogurt, labneh, sour cream, or **Any-Bean Dip** (page 306).
- Puree until completely smooth and turn into a salad dressing by whisking in an acid and oil in your preferred ratio (2:1 for a punchier dressing, 3:1 for a mellower version).
- Serve as is with cooked meat like seared chicken or meatballs.
- Use in various Hero Recipes, perhaps smeared onto the base of a **Galette** (page 72) or stirred into **Lentil Stew** (page 58) or **Baked Pasta** (page 70).

MASH MORE THAN POTATOES!

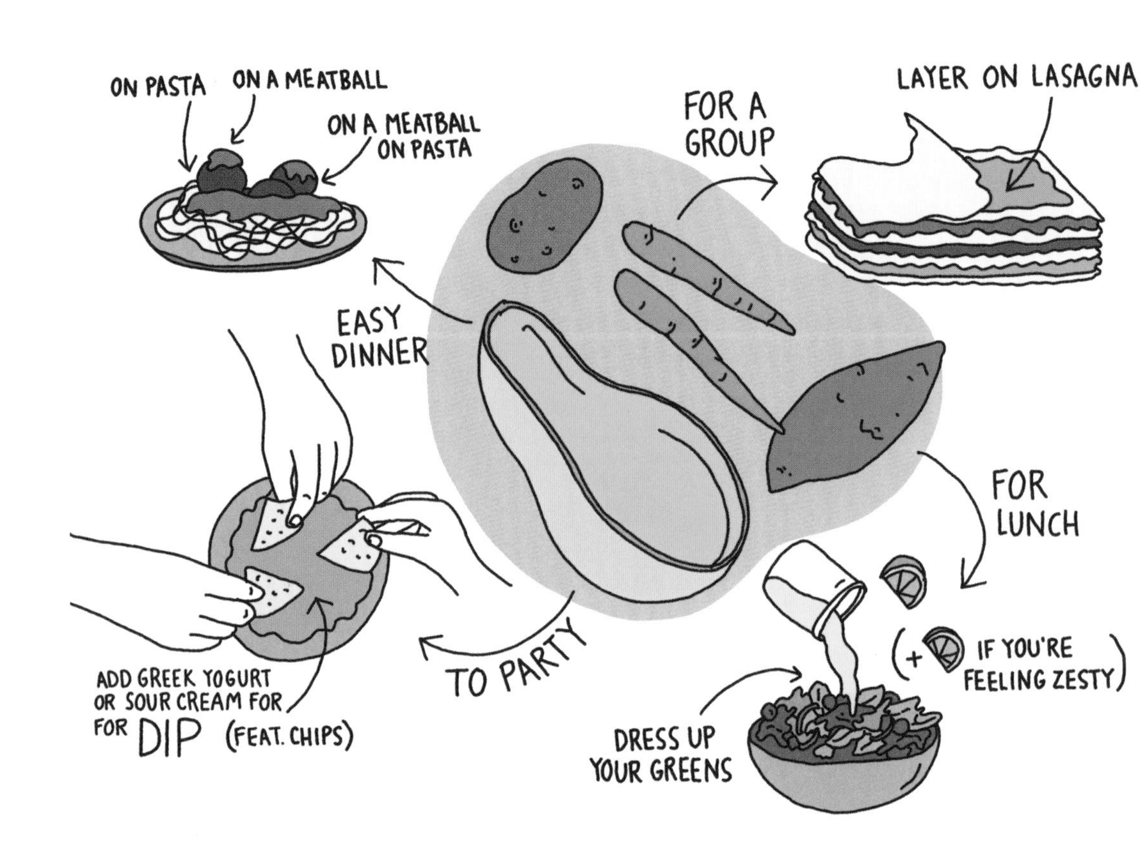

VEGETABLES

Mushrooms

IDEAS AND RECIPES

Mushrooms are in their own special world when it comes to the vegetable kingdom—quite literally, as they aren't vegetables. Fungi don't have leaves, roots, or seeds, and they don't need light to grow. In fact, they aren't even plants! Biological distinctions aside, many mushrooms can be eaten raw, but we tend to cook them alongside many other vegetables, meats, and grains.

Know What You Got

While a nearly endless array of mushrooms grow wild, only some are edible. Here are a few of the most common varieties, some of which can be easily found at supermarkets, others of which are found only during certain seasons or in specific regions:

- **White button, cremini**, and **portobello** are all the same variety of mushroom, harvested at different points in the mushroom's life. The buttons are the mildest; as the mushroom ages it loses more water, which is why the creminis are slightly more flavorful and the portobellos are the meatiest. They're solid, versatile, and, once cooked, can fit into numerous Hero Recipes.
- **Shiitake** and **oysters** can sometimes be found in supermarkets (and you can even grow them yourself!). Shiitakes tend to be thinner, drier, and earthier, while oysters and other larger mushrooms have a higher water content, requiring a bit longer cooking and heavier seasoning.
- The hardest-to-find varieties are generally the most distinctly flavored, from fruity golden **chanterelles** to nutty **morels** to rich **porcinis**. If you can get some from a farmers' market or an experienced foraging friend (make sure to only eat wild mushrooms identified by an expert!), cook them in a simple dish to highlight their unique flavors.

Store It Right

Opinions differ on proper storage of mushrooms, so we simultaneously tested multiple methods. Long story short: Loose mushrooms stored in a paper bag in the fridge kept the longest without getting slimy. Refrigerate prepackaged mushrooms in their original container—it's always nice when the option involving the least amount of work also functions the best, isn't it? Don't wash them before storing, as wet mushrooms go slimy quickly. We typically don't wash mushrooms at all and instead rub away bits of dirt with a kitchen cloth, but you can rinse them if they're really dirty.

Save for Later

Mushrooms can be cooked and frozen as is, but unless you're absolutely desperate to save them quickly, we recommend making them into a dish for improved texture. We'd venture you'll be happier to encounter ready-to-heat Use-It-Up Mushroom Bolognese (page 219) in your freezer over a container of icy mushrooms.

You Can Still Eat It!

If your mushrooms end up sitting around in your fridge for a while, check them for smell and feel. If they smell intense but earthy, like a clod of dirt, they're probably fine to eat. Touch the different parts of the mushroom too—if there's a place that's wet and soft but the rest of the mushroom feels fine, you can discard that part and cook the rest. Save older mushrooms for soups, sautés, or stews—raw or quick-cooking dishes are best with fresh, bouncy mushrooms that you just brought home. Fresh mushrooms that have dried out a bit will plump up as they cook unless they're thoroughly dehydrated, in which case you can toss them into your Kitchen Scrap Stock Bag (page 18). Mushrooms that you've purchased dried will last indefinitely in the pantry; we like to stock up on dried shiitakes at our local Asian grocery store for an amazingly rich and meaty addition to stir-fries and soups. And as a bonus, when you rehydrate dried mushrooms in hot water, you can save the soaking liquid for a major umami boost to add to stocks, stews, and pots of beans. As always, mold and bad smells mean time for the compost.

Extra Bits

Don't throw out your mushroom stems! They are free flavor and should not be dismissed. If the stems feel moist like the rest of the mushroom, tear them into small pieces and cook them alongside everything else. If the base of the stem feels hard, trim a thin slice off. If they're shriveled and/or extremely dry—shiitake stems can be particularly desiccated—pop them into your Kitchen Scrap Stock Bag (page 18).

WITH MEI

A Strong Opinion on Prepping Mushrooms

Once upon a time, I was too lazy to get out a knife and a cutting board (by which I mean almost all the time) and instead just took some mushrooms in my hands and broke them apart with my fingers. What happened next? A revelation! Torn mushrooms are infinitely better for texture and flavor, with all the craggy bits catching more sauce and the uneven ends getting browner and crispier. Torn mushrooms are faster, with tiny button mushrooms and hefty portobello alike breaking up under your fingers within seconds. Torn mushrooms are prime lazy person cooking, leaving you without a knife and a cutting board to wash. I haven't gone back since.

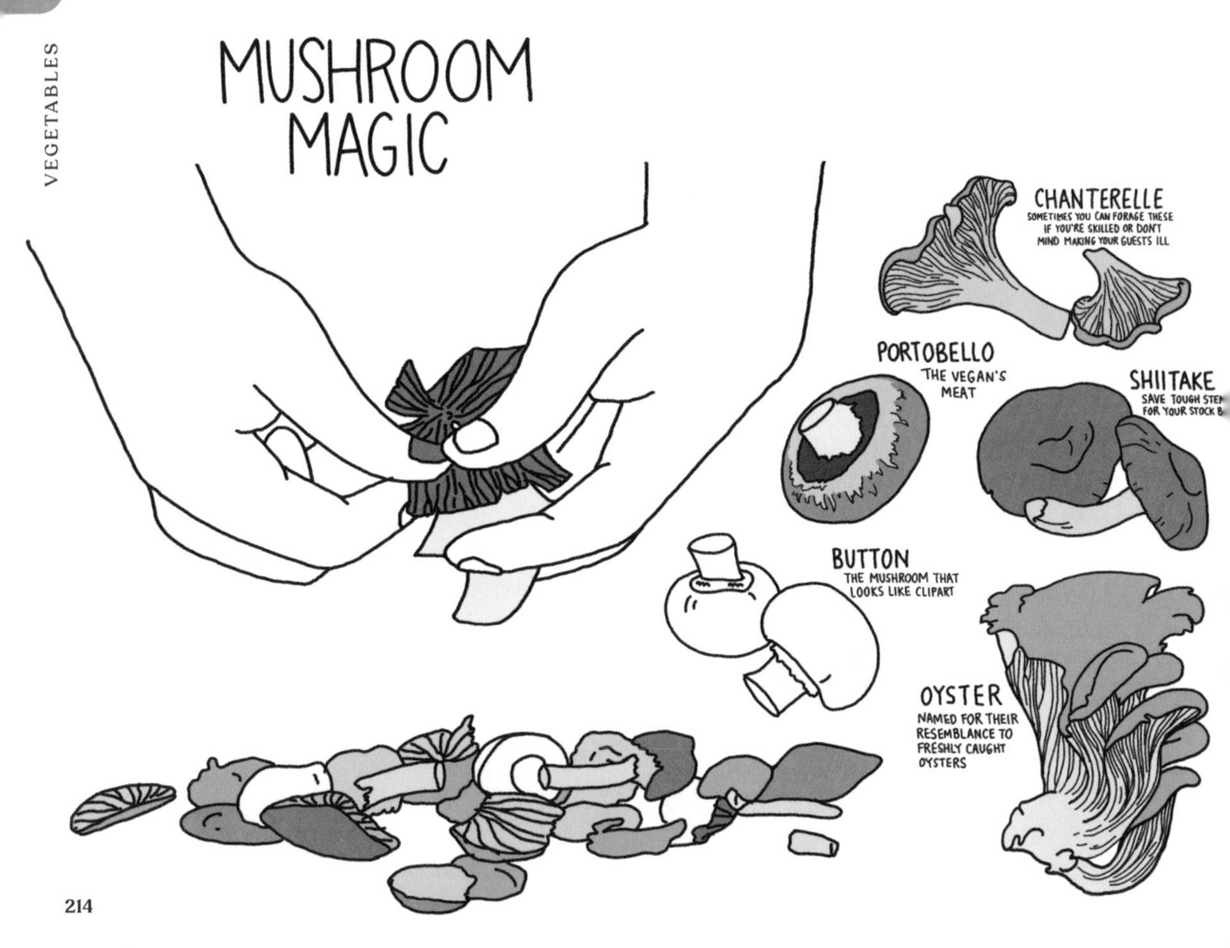

Use-It-Up Ideas

When we've got some mushrooms to use up and no plan in mind, the easiest ways to get them ready to eat are sautéing and roasting. For both methods, keep in mind: (1) you'll need ample fat as they soak up a lot of liquid, so don't be stingy with the oil or butter, and (2) keep them in a single layer so moisture can evaporate, leaving you with more mushroomy flavor and not wet, soggy mushrooms. Once cooked, mushrooms can be eaten straight, mixed into pasta or rice, or worked into any Hero Recipe of your choice.

- **For sautéing**, heat a bit of oil in a skillet over medium heat, add the mushrooms, and cook until they release their liquid, then crank the heat up to medium-high and cook until the liquid evaporates and the mushrooms get deliciously brown and a bit crispy. This could take 7 to 10 minutes or more, depending on the amount and variety. Lower the heat again and stir in a pat of butter, maybe a squeeze of lemon juice and a sprinkling of grated zest, a splash of stock or wine, or chopped fresh herbs (toss sturdy herbs like thyme or rosemary into the pan, sprinkle tender herbs like parsley or basil on at the end), or all of the above before salting to taste.
- **For roasting**, drizzle with extra-virgin olive oil, season with salt and pepper, and roast at 425 degrees for 10 to 25 minutes, depending on the size and style of mushroom. Fun additions include minced garlic, spices like paprika or ground cumin, grated lemon zest, or anything else you like.

- What's a better partnership than **Mushrooms with Garlic and Toasty Bread**? In a large skillet, sauté 6 cups torn mushrooms in the fat of your choice until softened and lightly browned, then stir in a bountiful amount of minced garlic and a few slices of crusty bread, torn into pieces. Mix everything up and let it cook a bit, adding more oil or butter if needed, plus a splash of lemon juice or vinegar. Season with salt and pepper and pile into a bowl, possibly topped with a fried egg or chunks of ripe avocado. Want to throw in some leafy greens? Go for it. Toss in some cured meat or cheese or don't—the mushrooms, bread, and garlic do not need them in attendance to throw a really good party.
- Cooked or raw mushrooms can become a **Mushroom Broth** by adding water or stock and a splash of soy sauce or rice wine and simmering for 15 to 20 minutes, an excellent first step along the path to **Noodle Soup How You Want It** (page 50).
- Make **Marinated Mushrooms** with cooked mushrooms—or even raw ones, for a minimum of prep work and dishwashing—by stirring together ¼ cup low-sodium soy sauce, 2 tablespoons toasted sesame oil, and some minced garlic, ginger, and shallots or scallions. Chopped fresh herbs like basil or mint would be an excellent addition, and a spoonful of chili sauce is never a bad idea. Toss the sauce with a few cups of torn mushrooms and let sit for 15 minutes before eating with rice, noodles, scrambled eggs, you name it.

Wine-Braised Chicken and Mushrooms

Serves 4

Tangy and intense, this is a chicken and mushroom dish for those who like sharp flavors, although you can mellow it out with something creamy at the end if you like. We've made it with 2 cups of mushrooms and we've made it with 6 cups, and all work quite happily, soaking up both butter and the distinctively tart sauce. It's great with red wine, but if you don't have any, you could use stock or water or even more vinegar. Soak up the sauce with rice, buttered noodles, warm whole grains, or thick slices of crusty bread.

2 tablespoons extra-virgin olive oil
2 pounds boneless, skinless chicken thighs or breasts
Kosher salt and freshly ground black pepper
4 garlic cloves, smashed
2 tablespoons butter or more olive oil
4 cups torn mushrooms (or however many mushrooms you have or want)
¾ cup dry red wine, or stock of your choice or water
½ cup balsamic vinegar or another vinegar of your choice
¼ cup cream or another dairy product of your choice, such as sour cream or yogurt, or more to taste (optional)
Chopped fresh parsley, for garnish (optional)

Heat the oil in a Dutch oven over medium-high heat. Pat the chicken dry with paper towels and season with salt and pepper, then add to the pan (in batches if necessary) with the smashed garlic cloves. Lightly brown the chicken parts, 3 to 5 minutes per side, then transfer to a plate. You can let the garlic hang out in the pan while cooking the chicken; transfer the cloves to the plate with the chicken if they start to burn.

(continues)

Add the butter to the pan, let it melt, then add the mushrooms and a good pinch of salt. Cook, stirring often, until lightly browned, about 5 minutes, then add the wine and vinegar. Using a wooden spoon, scrape any browned bits off the bottom of the pan, then let the mixture simmer for a few minutes. Using tongs, return the chicken and any juices (and garlic, if you took it out) to the pot and snuggle the pieces down amongst the mushrooms. Bring the mixture to a boil, then turn the heat to low, partially cover the pan, and let simmer for 15 to 20 minutes, until the chicken is cooked through and the sauce has thickened a bit.

Taste the sauce and season with more salt and pepper as needed, then stir in the cream, if using. Simmer for a few minutes just to let all the flavors meld together before serving, sprinkled with fresh parsley, if you like.

Use-It-Up Mushroom Bolognese

Makes about 7 cups

This meatless Bolognese-type sauce is a rewarding way to fill the kitchen with tantalizing smells *and* clear the whole fridge of random vegetables. If you ever needed a recipe to use up a rutabaga, a cauliflower, and a container of shriveled old mushrooms, this sauce is here for you. If possible, we highly recommend a food processor to save yourself a lot of chopping. Use vegetable stock or water to make it vegan, or add butter, whole milk, or ground meat for a more classic version of Bolognese. And of course while this screams to be spooned straight onto pasta, it can also be layered into lasagna, used as the base for Baked Eggs (page 104), or ladled onto your favorite starch, whether mashed potatoes or polenta or roasted cauliflower.

¼ cup extra-virgin olive oil

1 large onion or another allium, diced

3 carrots, diced

2 portobello mushrooms, chopped, or 2 cups chopped mushrooms (or as many as you like, really)

4 to 6 garlic cloves, chopped

2 tablespoons tomato paste (we substitute ketchup or leave it out altogether if we don't have tomato paste)

2 tablespoons soy sauce

½ cup dry red or white wine

3 cups diced vegetables, such as broccoli, celery, or eggplant (add the stems too!)

4 cups chopped fresh or canned tomatoes, or Easygoing Tomato Sauce (page 104) or store-bought

1 cup stock of your choice, or milk or water

Kosher salt and freshly ground black pepper

1 to 2 teaspoons sugar, if needed

(continues)

Heat the oil in a Dutch oven over medium-high heat. Add the onion, carrots, and mushrooms, cover, and cook for 5 minutes to let the mushrooms release some liquid. Uncover and continue to cook until the vegetables are softened and starting to brown, about 10 minutes. Stir in the garlic, tomato paste, and soy sauce and cook for a few more minutes.

Add the wine and use a wooden spoon to scrape up any browned bits from the bottom of the pan and stir them into the vegetables. Let the mixture cook for a minute or two, then add the remaining vegetables, tomatoes, and stock. Season with salt and pepper, reduce the heat to medium-low, and cover. Cook for at least 20 minutes, until all the vegetables are tender, or leave it to simmer on the stove and make your kitchen smell amazing until it reaches the texture you like, adding more liquid as needed.

Taste again and season with more salt and pepper, and possibly a teaspoon of sugar or two, if you feel the sauce could use a bit more sweetness. Store leftovers in an airtight container in the fridge for up to a week or in the freezer for a few months.

Avocados

IDEAS AND RECIPES

While avocados are technically a fruit, we generally eat them in savory dishes, so we've included them with the vegetables. And, since we mainly eat them raw, instead of recipes you'll find lots of ideas and tips to make sure no expensive avocado ever goes to waste.

Know What You Got

There are many varieties of avocados, but unless you live somewhere warm where avocados grow, like California, Florida, or Hawaii, you may only ever see Hass avocados in the supermarket. They're the dark green, pebbly-skinned kind with buttery yellow and light green flesh, the majority of which are imported from Mexico. If you can find them and can afford it, it's worth springing for sustainably certified avocados, or at least organic. Unfortunately, avocado growing requires large amounts of water and contributes to deforestation, not to mention the environmental impact of shipping hundreds of millions of avocados all over the country.* Even more reason to make sure no avocados end up in the trash.

You'll typically find hard, unripe avocados at the grocery store. Tough if you want to make guacamole right now, but if you can let them ripen on the counter at home, you'll be more likely to catch them at the perfect soft, sliceable texture. If you find ripe avocados at the store (the skin will be a darker greenish-black and the avocado will give slightly when pressed at the stem end—don't buy if they're already very mushy), plan to eat them soon.

Store It Right

Store avocados on the counter to ripen or in the refrigerator if you want to slow the ripening process (conversely, put them in a paper bag if you want to speed it up). Once ripe, avocados usually last a day or two at room temperature, more if you transfer them to the fridge.

Cut avocados should be stored in the fridge with the pit left inside. To avoid browning, cover tightly with a beeswax wrap or another option like plastic wrap or aluminum foil. Other options include squeezing a lemon or lime or brushing some oil on the cut flesh.

*Suzanne O'Connell, "The Avocado in your Super Bowl Guacamole Is Bad for the Environment. You Can Make It Better." *Washington Post*, February 4, 2021 (https://www.washingtonpost.com/climate-solutions/2021/02/04/climate-solutions-avocados/).

Save for Later

In a pinch, avocados can be frozen: Chop or mash, mix in some lemon juice, and seal tightly in a freezer bag. However, keep in mind that the thawed avocado likely won't have the buttery smooth texture of a fresh avocado; consider blending it into a smoothie or a sauce rather than eating it straight on toast or making guacamole.

You Can Still Eat It!

While no one is happy to find a brown avocado, it's good to know that browning is mostly a visual problem; it may not look as appetizing as a pristine green avocado, but you generally can't taste the difference. If it bothers you, use it up in any of the overripe and mushy avocado methods (page 225) so you don't notice the color change.

Extra Bits

Avocado pits and skins generally aren't edible, although some varieties have a very thin skin that you can eat alongside the flesh. However, you can use avocado skins to make a beautiful natural pink dye for coloring anything from fabric to Easter eggs (search online for instructions). The pits can be germinated into adorable little houseplants (that sadly won't grow more avocados): Position a clean, dry avocado pit so the thickest, flattest end of the pit is pointing down and poke four toothpicks evenly around the equator of the pit. Using the toothpicks, suspend the pit over the rim of a small jar full of water so the bottom half (the root end) is submerged. Keep it somewhere warm like a windowsill—Mei likes the window right over her kitchen sink so she remembers to top up and change the water over time. Fingers crossed, the pit should sprout roots within a few weeks and then you can transplant it to soil.

Use-It-Up Ideas

Ripe avocados

You probably have a plan when you have a perfect avocado. Maybe you already have a favorite guacamole (we like ours with onion, cilantro, lime, and salt) or even a particular preference of avocado toast. You may not need help using up good avocados, but here are a few options:

- Put slices on top of **Baked Eggs** (page 104).
- Add chunks to just-cooked **Fried Rice** (page 62).
- Add to a grain bowl or **Grain Salad** (page 162).
- Top any version of **Leafy Green Salad** (page 160) or **Simple Herb Salad** (page 145).
- Serve on top of or wedged inside tacos, burritos, burgers, quesadillas, or **Summer Rolls** (page 44).
- Mix into **Crispy and Crunchy Noodle Salad** (page 46).
- Blend into **Any-Bean Dip** (page 306).
- Lay on top of a **Savory Bread Pudding** (page 78) or a **roasted vegetable tart** (see the note on page 72).

Nonperfect avocados

What you might not have a plan for is all the times you optimistically slice open an avocado hoping for a superbly spreadable toast topping and instead find that the flesh is rock-hard. Or the times when an avocado turns out too mushy, brown, or stringy for true eating enjoyment. Here are a few suggestions for heartbreakingly imperfect avocados to avoid tossing them in the trash.

Underripe and hard:

- **Pickled Avocado:** This genius idea for using up too-firm, underripe avocados comes from *Zaitoun*, the Palestinian cookbook by Yasmin Khan. It's happened to all of us, right? You think you're cracking open perfect guacamole material, and instead you can barely get your teeth through a slice, much less mash it into a paste. Use our starter **Quick Pickle** recipe (page 37) to infuse the avocado slices, ideally with a few peppercorns and maybe some coriander seeds. The brine infuses the avocado slices with a bracing sourness to contrast their natural butteriness, while also softening them into a miraculously satisfying texture in just a few hours. Eat within a day or so, before the avocado starts to fall apart and the flavor gets too intense.
- Lightly fry slices in extra-virgin olive oil until browned, sprinkle with salt, and eat on its own, or atop any of the ripe avocado dishes above.

Overripe and mushy:

- Blend into a dip, like **Any-Bean Dip** (page 306) or **Salsa Fresca** (page 103).
- Mix into a **fritter** (page 64) or **pancake** (page 232).
- Blend into a **Smoothie** (page 228).
- Blend or puree 1 mushy avocado with 3 tablespoons cocoa powder, 1 cup powdered sugar, a pinch of salt, and 1 tablespoon cream or melted coconut oil to make **chocolate avocado frosting** for cupcakes.

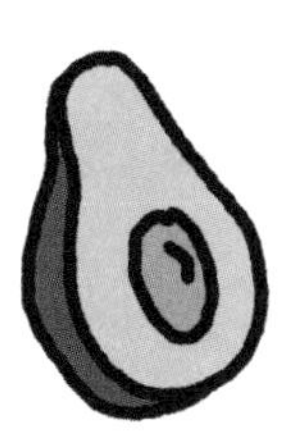

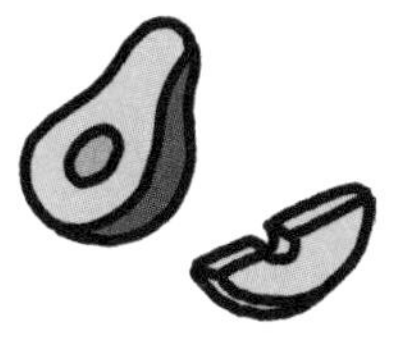

Fruits

Fruits
Fruits
Fruits

Here's where we help you use up your surplus **fruit**, whether you went apple picking, got too excited at the grocery store, or cohabitate with small children, aka fruit consumption machines. Some fruit can last for weeks (**apples** and **oranges**). Some seem to go bad almost immediately, and of course it's always the expensive kinds (**berries**). Luckily, most fruits are incredibly versatile. They can be swapped around in recipes, tossed into smoothies, and, in most cases, frozen easily. Now that we keep a **Smoothie Bag** in the freezer (page 18), rarely does a fruit escape past our clutches into the compost bin. The rest of the **Hero Recipes** (pages 230–42) will also help you mix and match when you've got an assortment of different fruit to use up, in everything from cocktails to cake.

All-the-Fruit Smoothies

Makes about 4 cups

Smoothies are the ultimate fruit use-up trick. Smoothies don't care if your grapes are wrinkly, if your banana was bruised, if your toddler's tooth marks are on the apple slices. (If *you* care, that's another thing; just slice off the offending bits and keep going.) Smoothies welcome your soft fruit, your frozen fruit (stashed in your Smoothie Bag of course!—see page 18), your sweet-leaning vegetables like spinach and roasted beets, even your fibrous kale and the last of your wilting spring mix. Entire cookbooks exist full of specific smoothie recipes, but we generally go by a rough template and improvise from there, using up whatever is available.

2 cups chopped fruit, like an apple and an orange, or mixed berries, fresh or frozen
1 or 2 big handfuls leafy greens or ½ cup chopped vegetables, like cucumber or carrot (optional)
1 frozen banana or very ripe avocado or ½ cup yogurt of any kind
1½ cups any kind of juice, milk, or coconut water, plus more as needed
Honey, maple syrup, agave, or a pitted date

Blend all the ingredients and taste, then adjust the sweetness to your liking. For more ideas and substitutions, see the Smoothie Builder chart on the next page.

- Add flavor with a nut butter, cocoa powder, or fresh ginger.
- Add a scoop of ice cream and make it a milkshake.
- Blend the fruit with yogurt and make Lassi (page 286).

A FLEXIBLE SMOOTHIE BUILDER

	WHAT	AMOUNT	TIPS
THE BASE	CHOPPED FRUIT	2 CUPS	FRESH OR FROZEN OR BOTH!
DO YOU WANT TO ADD VEGGIES?	LEAFY GREENS (GOOD WAY TO SNEAK THEM IN) ROOT VEG MILD-TASTING	½ CUP CHOPPED	FRESH OR FROZEN CHOP INTO SMALL PIECES AS A FAVOR TO YOUR BLENDER MOTOR AND CHOP OFF STEMS AS A FAVOR TO YOUR BREAKFAST (COMPOST OR SAVE!)
ALWAYS GOOD TO MAKE IT CREAMY	BANANA AVOCADO YOGURT NUT BUTTER ICE CREAM (A...MILKSHAKE)	½ CUP YOGURT OR ICE CREAM 1 BANANA FEW TBSPs NUT BUTTER ½ AVOCADO	COMBINE YOGURT + BANANA AVOCADO + ALMOND BUTTER
AND YOU'LL NEED SOME LIQUID	MILK TEA JUICE WATER	1½ CUPS – 2 CUPS	FRUITY → JUICE CREAMY → DAIRY OR ALTERNATIVE MILK MILD → COCONUT WATER OR HERBAL TEA
CHECK FOR SWEETNESS AND ADJUST	MAPLE SYRUP DATES AGAVE HONEY	SQUEEZE 1-2 DATES SCOOP	TASTE BEFORE ADDING ANY SWEETENER FRUIT ONLY MAY BE SWEET ENOUGH VEGGIE MAY NEED SOME EXTRA SWEET
NEED IT CHILLIER?	ICE	HANDFUL (← DON'T HOLD THEM FOR THIS LONG)	ADD ICE IF NONE OF YOUR FRUIT WAS FROZEN

Save-the-Fruit Shrub

Makes about 3 cups

Shrubs are fruity-vinegary drinks ideal for using up any bruised, smooshed, defrosted, or otherwise imperfect or surplus fruits you might have on hand. Combine the fruit with sugar and vinegar and you get a delightfully tart sweet-and-sour beverage to sip on its own or with a splash of something bubbly or something boozy. Shrubs are infinitely versatile, so you can mix fruits and make a blackberry-peach shrub or a cranberry-apple shrub. Add herbs or spices to fashion a blueberry-mint beverage or a plum–pink peppercorn cocktail. Although they require a bit of patience for the flavors to fully develop, shrubs are easy to make and keep in the fridge for months.

NOTE: *You'll notice all the amounts are the same—this "recipe" is essentially a 1:1:1 ratio, so you can adjust the amount according to how much fruit you want to use up. Once you get used to the process, you can alter to taste—super sweet juicy fruits may need less sugar, very tart citrus may need more.*

ANOTHER NOTE: *If you're using a strong vinegar like balsamic, you may want to mix it with another vinegar to mellow it out.*

2 cups roughly chopped fruit, such as berries, stone fruits, apples, or pears
2 cups white or brown sugar
2 cups vinegar of your choice, ideally a wine or cider vinegar

Put the fruit and sugar in a bowl and stir to combine. Leave on your counter for a few hours or overnight, until the fruit is sitting in a pool of juice. If you're busy and don't get to it for even longer, no problem, just move it to the fridge. Once you have a few minutes to get a bit messy, strain out the fruit and refrigerate or freeze it to be blended into smoothies, added to sangria (page 256), spooned onto ice cream, or baked into Any-Fruit Snack Cake (page 236).

Pour the fruity syrup (as well as any remaining sugar—it'll dissolve eventually) into a bottle or jar with a lid, add the vinegar, and shake well to combine. If you're worried about it being too tart, start with a bit less vinegar, but keep in mind that the sourness will mellow over time. Store in the fridge and give it a day or so for the fruit and vinegar to really get to know each other and become best friends. Drink on its own, with gin or vodka or whiskey, or with seltzer, and keep it in the fridge for months.

Use-It-Up Pancakes

Makes 8 small pancakes

We're all about a pancake recipe that does not require the use of any motorized appliances at whatever unfortunate hour your children have chosen to awaken you and demand breakfast. This one accommodates multiple kinds of dairy (who knows whether you'll have buttermilk or yogurt on a given day) and can take any fruit that needs to be used up. Mix in squishy berries, browning apples, the discards from Save-the-Fruit Shrub (page 230), or the remains of your fruit salad, alongside pantry snacks from raisins to chocolate chips.

1 cup all-purpose flour or a gluten-free substitute
2 teaspoons sugar
½ teaspoon kosher salt
½ teaspoon baking powder
¼ teaspoon baking soda
1 egg
½ cup whole milk, cream, half-and-half, or buttermilk
½ cup plain whole-milk yogurt, sour cream, ricotta, or crème fraîche
2 tablespoons butter, melted, plus more for cooking (or neutral oil) and serving
½ to ¾ cup filling of your choice, such as chopped fruit or chocolate chips
Maple syrup or Low-Key Fruit Jam (page 234), for serving

Whisk the flour, sugar, salt, baking powder, and baking soda in a medium bowl. In a large bowl, whisk the egg, milk, yogurt, and melted butter until thoroughly combined. Fold the dry ingredients into the wet ingredients until just combined (you shouldn't be able to see any more flour, but there will still be lumps). Stir in your favorite filling.

Heat a large nonstick skillet over medium heat and add a thin layer of butter or oil. Use a ladle to scoop batter into the pan until you have 4 small pancakes. Cook until bubbles start to appear on the top and the bottoms are golden brown, about 3 minutes. Flip and cook the other side until golden brown, then transfer to a wire rack to cool slightly before eating. Repeat with the remaining batter, adding more butter or oil to the pan if necessary. Serve with butter, syrup, or jam. Leftovers can be kept in the fridge for a few days in an airtight container or frozen in a resealable bag with the air pressed out.

WITH MEI

Low-Key Fruit Jam

Makes 1 to 2 cups

I always get confused about the exact differences between jellies, jams, and butters. Whatever it's called, this extremely low-key, non-shelf-stable, jam/butter/sauce/compote comes in very handy when I go crazy buying fresh local peaches in season and can't possibly eat them all and they start to bruise. Or when I overbuy pears and apples and they start to brown and wrinkle. Toss in a few stray berries or some leftover chunks of mango or whatever else you find in the fruit bowl—as it's not meant to be canned or achieve a certain texture, you can be as gleefully imprecise as you like. Mainly you're aiming to cook the fruit down enough that it becomes a spreadable jammy sauce that can then be eaten in practically infinite ways. Mix it into yogurt, spoon it onto ice cream, stir it into your granola. Put a dollop on your pancakes or waffles or spice up your PB&Js.

1 to 2 pounds fruit (however much you need to use up), chopped

¼ cup water

Juice of ½ lemon, plus more to taste

Sugar to taste, depending on the fruit used

Put the fruit, water, lemon juice, and a pinch of spice, if using, in a heavy-bottomed pot, cover, and cook over medium-low heat for about 20 minutes, or until you like the texture. Check and stir occasionally to prevent sticking; if the mixture gets too dry and threatens to burn, add a few tablespoons more water (or fruit juice or wine). Let the fruit soften and collapse until you can easily mash any large pieces with a fork. Sweeten to taste. Store in an airtight container in the fridge for a few weeks or in the freezer for up to a year.

Spice it up by stirring in a pinch of ground cinnamon or chopped fresh ginger when the jam is almost done.

SURPLUS FRUIT → LOW-KEY JAM

MAKE IT A MEAL

Take the sauce in a savory direction by whisking it into dressings (page 165), swapping it in for the peaches in the Grilled Peach Barbecue Sauce (page 259), or using it as a glaze for pork tenderloin (one of my daughter's favorite dinners): Heat a splash of neutral oil in a large oven-safe skillet and brown a salted and peppered pork tenderloin on all sides over high heat. Roast at 400 degrees for 10 to 15 minutes, until an instant thermometer reads at least 135 degrees in the thickest part. Transfer the pork to a plate to rest and carefully put the skillet back on the stovetop to make the pan sauce. Melt a pat of butter over medium-low heat, then add a splash of vinegar (balsamic pairs nicely with the pork) and scrape up any browned bits. Add about ½ cup jam. Stir and cook for a minute or two to combine the flavors, then spoon over the pork to serve.

Any-Fruit Snack Cake or Muffins

Makes 1 cake or 12 muffins

This simple, easygoing cake is designed for berries or fruit chunks of almost any kind. It's dessert-y enough to be satisfying at the end of a meal, but not so sweet that you can't eat it for breakfast.

1 stick butter, softened

⅓ cup brown or white sugar, plus 1 tablespoon brown sugar for sprinkling

3 eggs

2 teaspoons vanilla extract

2 cups all-purpose flour

1 tablespoon baking powder

½ teaspoon kosher salt

½ cup milk

3 cups chopped fruit of your choice, all one kind or a mix

Heat the oven to 375 degrees. Grease either a 12-inch baking pan or a 12-cup muffin tin.

Combine the butter and sugar in the bowl of a stand mixer fitted with the paddle attachment and cream the two together into a uniform mixture. Scrape down the sides of the bowl with a spatula, then add the eggs and vanilla and stir to combine.

In another bowl, whisk together the flour, baking powder, and salt. Add the flour mixture to the bowl with the creamed butter and sugar, along with the milk, then stir until just combined.

Stir in the fruit and transfer the batter to the prepared pan. Sprinkle with brown sugar and bake until a fork inserted in the center comes out clean, about 20 minutes for muffins, 30 to 40 minutes for a cake. Let cool slightly before slicing and serving; well-wrapped leftovers will keep at room temperature for a few days or in the freezer for a few months.

An Endlessly Riffable Fruit Crisp

Serves 2 to 4

We consider this crisp the perfect use-it-up dessert recipe. Got a bounty of summer berries on your hands? Were you a little overzealous with the apple picking or have a few leftover apple slices from your kids' snack? Note that the butter, flour, oats, and nuts are used in equal amounts, so it's easy to scale up or down depending on whether you need to use up just a few pears or a whole bucket of raspberries. Combine any fruits you like based on what you have in the kitchen—favorites in Mei's house have been plum-mango and pear-apricot, while Irene is a sour cherry die-hard. You can compensate for less-sweet fruit by adding a sweetener like honey or maple syrup and soak up excess liquid with a sprinkle of cornstarch or flour, but we typically leave out both.

3 cups roughly chopped fruit
Maple syrup, agave, or honey (optional)
Cornstarch (optional)
⅓ cup (about 5 tablespoons) cold butter, cubed
⅓ cup all-purpose or whole-wheat flour
⅓ cup old-fashioned oats
⅓ cup chopped nuts, raw or toasted (optional but highly recommended)
¼ cup brown or white sugar
Whipped cream or ice cream, for serving (optional)

(continues)

Heat the oven to 350 degrees. Grease a baking dish that comfortably fits your volume of fruit.

If your fruit is super sweet, place it directly into the baking dish. If it's a little underripe or tart, put the fruit in a bowl, drizzle with a little sweetener, and gently toss to combine. If your fruit is excessively juicy, sprinkle it with a bit of cornstarch and mix thoroughly in a bowl to help thicken the juices. Transfer the fruit to the baking dish.

Put the butter, flour, oats, nuts (if using), and sugar in a bowl and use your fingers to break up the butter cubes and rub them into the flour and sugar until everything is well combined. Scatter over the fruit and bake for 40 to 50 minutes, until the crumbly topping is golden brown and the juices are bubbling up. Serve as is, or with a scoop of something cold and creamy.

Sweet Bread Pudding

Serves 6 to 8

If you happen to find yourself with a surplus of sweetened bread products in the house—even ones that have gone slightly stale—it's the perfect time to make a dessert bread pudding. Leftover chocolate croissants, jammy doughnuts, lightly sweet breads like brioche or challah, or even plain breads can all be rounded up and tossed in the mix. Add fresh or dried or preserved fruit and the spices of your choice and no one will recognize that your sparkling new dessert was magicked up from yesterday's muffins.

NOTE: *This recipe calls for varying amounts of ingredients because bread products range greatly in density and sweetness. We've made this with glazed doughnuts and dried fruit and added no sugar. We've made it with barely sweetened brioche and added ¼ cup sugar. Use your judgment and your taste preferences, and remember you can always serve with a sugary sauce like chocolate syrup or ice cream, but you can't unsweeten once the sugar is mixed in.*

2 to 3 cups milk and/or cream
2 eggs
8 cups sweetened breads of choice, cut into chunks
Up to ½ cup brown or white sugar
1 to 2 cups dried or fresh fruit, cut into chunks
Whipped cream or ice cream, for serving (optional)

Heat the oven to 350 degrees. Grease a 9 x 13-inch baking dish.

Whisk 2 cups milk or cream with the eggs in a large bowl, then add the bread. Press the bread down to submerge it. If there isn't enough liquid to fully submerge the bread, add up to 1 cup more milk until all the bread is wet.

The next step requires a bit of judgment—how much sugar do you want to add? You make the call, depending on what your other ingredients are and

(continues)

how sugary you like your desserts. Unfortunately, you can't taste the dish before cooking thanks to the raw eggs, but we generally err on the side of less sugar. You can always sprinkle sugar on top or drizzle on a sweet sauce if you really undersweeten.

Once all the bread is well soaked, stir in your sugar, if using, and your fruit of choice. Transfer the bread mixture to the prepared baking dish and bake until the bread puffs up and the top is golden brown, about 45 minutes. Serve warm or at room temperature with all the sweet toppings your heart desires.

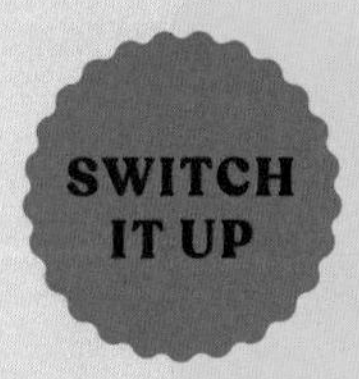

Rifle through your spice drawer when you stir in the fruit and pop in a pinch of cinnamon or cloves, or maybe a teaspoon of vanilla or almond extract. Pantry items like sliced nuts or chocolate chips are also welcome additions.

Mix-and-Match Fruit Galette

Makes 1 galette

This is our lazy version of a pie; spread out the dough, fill with fruit, make a few quick folds, and you've got an impressive-looking dessert with a minimum of fuss. It works with all the popular baking fruits—apples, pears, and stone fruit sliced into wedges, mixed berries piled into a jumble, or some combination of the above. But we've come to love an unexpected new galette fruit: the underappreciated grape, half left whole and half sliced lengthwise for some fun textural variation. Adjust the sugar to the sweetness of your fruit, spoon in some jam or almond filling (page 248) if you like—go ahead and make it your own.

NOTE: *Many store-bought pie crusts are designed for 9-inch pie pans and fit about 2 cups of fruit. If you make your own pie crust, you can often fit in another cup or so, just scale up the sugar, cornstarch, and bake time as needed.*

2 cups fruit of your choice, sliced into small pieces or wedges if needed
¼ cup sugar, plus more as needed
1 tablespoon cornstarch, plus more as needed
Small squeeze of lemon juice and a dusting of grated lemon zest
Tiny pinch kosher salt
1 pie crust, thawed if frozen and unrolled
¼ cup jam or sweet sauce of your choice (optional)
1 egg, lightly beaten with a splash of water or milk, for egg wash
Whipped cream or ice cream, for serving (optional)

(continues)

Heat the oven to 400 degrees. Line a rimmed baking sheet with parchment or a silicone baking mat.

Mix the fruit, sugar, cornstarch, lemon juice and zest, and salt in a bowl and stir to combine. Taste the fruit and add more sugar if the fruit is quite tart, a bit more cornstarch if the fruit is very juicy.

Roll out the pie crust into a rough circle and place on the prepared baking sheet. Spoon the jam onto the crust, if using, and smear it around in a circle, leaving a roughly 2-inch border around the edges. Put the fruit on top of the jam and fold the edges up over the fruit, leaving a border of pastry surrounding an uncovered center (see page 74 if a visual would help). Brush the pastry edges with the egg wash (psst—leftover egg wash makes for an adorable fluffy omelet for a chef's snack). If you're still waiting for the oven to heat or your pastry has started to soften, pop it into the fridge or freezer for a few minutes to help the galette hold its shape. Bake for 25 to 40 minutes, until the pastry is golden brown and the fruit is bubbling. Let cool before slicing and serve warm or at room temperature, plain or with ice cream or whipped cream.

Apples and Pears

IDEAS AND RECIPES

Apples and pears are readily available, relatively affordable, and equally content to be eaten raw or baked up into dessert. Buying bulk bags of either can be handy, but it's not uncommon to find one or two fruits going bad before the rest of the bag. Find a way to quickly use them up—both do very well in any of the Hero Recipes, especially the Any-Fruit Snack Cake (page 236) and Endlessly Riffable Fruit Crisp (page 237)—and you won't have to toss a bad apple ever again.

Store It Right

Apples and pears can be cooked almost interchangeably but differ in optimal storage and timing. Pears typically need to ripen at room temperature before getting stored in the fridge and then last only a few days before softening or going too brown. By contrast, apples can last weeks in the refrigerator. Store both unwashed until right before eating. Once cut, store in the fridge (if you like, try tossing with lemon or honey water to minimize browning).

Save for Later

Sliced apples and pears can be frozen but tend to be soft and brown once defrosted. Rather than eating them straight, we prefer to bake the thawed fruit into a dessert like pie, cake, or any of the Hero Recipes. You can also put raw slices into your Smoothie Bag (page 18), use them to make jam (page 234), or bake them into a dessert before freezing.

You Can Still Eat It!

Wrinkled or lightly soft apples and pears are absolutely fine for cooking and baking. A few bruises are OK too; cut them out before eating. However, if the whole fruit is collapsing, mushy, or moldy, compost it.

Extra Bits

Apple and pear cores and peels can be used to flavor booze and make vinegar. Save all your scraps when you make pie, or slowly accumulate them and store in the freezer until you have enough. To infuse spirits, pour bourbon or scotch over a jar full of apple or pear scraps and let sit for a week. Strain and use in your cocktail of choice, whether a Pear Manhattan or an Apple Bourbon Sour. To make scrap vinegar, fill a glass jar with chopped apple or pear scraps. Pour in sugar water (1 tablespoon sugar to 1 cup water) and cover loosely with a breathable cloth. Let sit in a cupboard or pantry for 2 weeks, stirring every few days and removing any scum that collects on top.

Strain out the scraps, transfer the liquid to another jar with a new cloth, and let sit for another 2 weeks or so, until it starts to taste vinegary. Store in an airtight container in the fridge and use for dressings, soup, and drinking vinegar (page 230)—just don't use it for canning or pickling as it might not be sufficiently acidic.

If you find yourself with lots of peels, Lindsay-Jean Hard suggests making them into chips in her very useful cookbook *Cooking with Scraps*. Toss peels from 5 to 7 apples with 2 teaspoons sugar, a tiny pinch of salt, and small pinches of spices like ground cinnamon and nutmeg, then spread on a rimmed baking sheet and bake at 250 degrees. An hour of baking makes for chewier peels; go longer for crunchier crisps. Snack on them like chips or crumble them onto granola or ice cream; store in a sealed container at room temperature.

Use-It-Up Ideas

- The bright, sweet crunch of apples and pears is particularly welcome in salads like the **Mix-and-Match Slaw Party** (page 42) or **Fruit and Greens Salad** (page 162).
- Make **Baked Apples** by removing most of the core from the top and stuffing the cavity with a mix of butter, sugar or honey, and additions like raisins, nuts, or candied ginger. Bake at 375 degrees until the apples are soft and scoopable, usually about an hour, and serve with whipped cream or ice cream.
- Add apples or pears to **Root Vegetable Soup** (page 200)—they add a lovely subtle sweetness to soups with butternut squash, carrot, and parsnip.
- For more savory uses, try roasting with chicken or sausages, wedging into grilled cheeses, tucking into a pork or lentil stew, or tossing into a Thanksgiving-style stuffing.

Poached Pears or Apples

Serves 6

Poaching is our go-to when we've got an abundance of apples or pears. The spiced soft fruit is so versatile—we eat it for breakfast with yogurt and granola or for dessert with ice cream and a glass of wine. And if you feel ambitious (or need another way to use them up), you can blend them into ice pops with their juice or make the fancy tart on page 248. Flexibility is key—this recipe is our favorite and we always have those ingredients to hand, but make it your own way. Adjust the ingredients and the amount of sweetener based on your taste and your pantry, and scale up or down depending on how much fruit you need to use up.

NOTE: *You can mix and match other fruits as well—stone fruits, tropical fruits, citrus, and dried fruits can all join the fun.*

4 cups wine of your choice (white for subtle color, red for a dramatically jewel-toned dessert; feel free to swap some out for water, cider, tea, and/or fruit juice)

¾ cup sugar or another sweetener of your choice (less if using a sweet juice, more if you like things sweet)

1-inch piece fresh ginger, cut into thick slices

1 cinnamon stick

1 star anise pod

Strips of zest and juice of 1 lemon

6 pears or apples, peeled, halved if you like, or 6 to 8 cups fruit of your choice

---

Put the wine, sugar, ginger, cinnamon, star anise, lemon peel strips, and lemon juice in a not-too-wide pot—you want as much of the fruit covered by the liquid as possible—and bring to a boil. Stir until the sugar dissolves, then add the fruit and lower the heat to a simmer. If the fruit keeps bobbing up and down, you can use a small pot lid or a circle of parchment paper to keep the pieces submerged. Cook for 15 to 20 minutes—firmer varieties and larger or whole fruits may take longer—or until the fruit can easily be poked by a sharp knife but still maintains its shape.

If you'd like to reduce the poaching liquid to a tangy, sweet syrup for drizzling, transfer the fruit to a plate and turn the heat to high. Boil for 5 to 15 minutes, until the liquid reaches a syrupy texture you like.

Eat a bit warm, at room temperature, or straight from the fridge. The fruit is good no matter what, especially with yogurt or whipped cream. Store in the fridge in the juices for a week or so or transfer to the freezer for longer storage.

Poached Fruit and Almond Tart

Makes 1 tart

This is the kind of professional-looking fancy bakery tart that we would typically never make because it seems like an elaborate multistep process. But . . . if we have puff pastry in the freezer and made poached pears last week (page 246), this recipe requires only a bit of mixing, slicing, and spreading before an impressive tart emerges from your oven.

NOTE: *Supermarket puff pastry sheets range in size; this recipe is made with a sheet of Pepperidge Farm, which weighs about 9 ounces. The all-butter Dufour is less widely available and more expensive, but totally worth the splurge; it weighs about 14 ounces, so adjust amounts and cook times as needed.*

1 sheet store-bought puff pastry (about 9 ounces, see Note), thawed if frozen

ALMOND FILLING

½ cup almond flour

3 tablespoons sugar

2 tablespoons butter, softened

1 tablespoon maple syrup

1 tablespoon all-purpose flour

1 egg

2 to 3 poached apples or pears (page 246), cored and thinly sliced, or another poached fruit of your choice

---

Heat the oven to 375 degrees. Line a rimmed baking sheet with parchment or a silicone baking mat.

Unfold the puff pastry onto the prepared baking sheet. Use a sharp knife to score a border about ½ inch from the edge, cutting through just the top layers of pastry. Use a fork to lightly prick holes across the center of the pastry, about one poke per square inch. Put the pastry in the oven to bake for 10 minutes to ensure the base gets cooked.

Meanwhile, make the almond filling by mixing the almond flour, sugar, butter, maple syrup, all-purpose flour, and egg in a medium bowl until smooth. Carefully remove the pastry from the oven and let sit for a few minutes to deflate and cool enough for spreading. Use a silicone spatula to spread the mixture across the puff pastry, trying to stay within the scored border.

Fan the fruit slices across the top of the filling in any pattern you like, then bake for 25 to 35 minutes, until the almond filling and the pastry are both a rich golden brown. Let cool slightly, then serve warm or at room temperature.

Apple Cheddar Muffins

Makes 12 small muffins, but doubles easily

These one-bowl whole wheat muffins hit just the right balance between sweet and salty, healthy and indulgent. The cheddar adds a savory depth without actually tasting cheesy; the apple and maple lend a hint of sweetness without veering into sugar-rush cupcake territory. It's a great way to use up a few apples (especially those a bit too wrinkled to snack on straight), and you can even swap one out for a bendy carrot you found in the back of the crisper drawer. The muffins will last a day or two on the counter, 3 to 5 days in the fridge, or several months in the freezer, tightly wrapped. Whether fresh out of the oven or thawed from frozen, we highly recommend toasting and slathering with an ample amount of good salty butter.

1 cup whole wheat flour (all-purpose works too)
½ teaspoon baking powder
½ teaspoon baking soda
¼ teaspoon kosher salt
2 eggs, lightly beaten
¼ cup plain whole-milk yogurt or sour cream
2 tablespoons maple syrup
2 tablespoons neutral oil
2 medium apples, cored and shredded on a box grater or in a food processor (about 2 packed cups)
1 cup shredded sharp cheddar cheese

Heat the oven to 350 degrees. Grease a 12-cup muffin tin or line with paper or silicone liners.

In a large bowl, whisk together the flour, baking powder, baking soda, and salt. Add the eggs, yogurt, maple syrup, and oil and stir to combine thoroughly. Stir in the shredded apple and cheese until both are well coated with the batter.

Fill the muffin tin with batter—we've found a slightly heaped ¼-cup measure is the perfect size to evenly scoop and fill each cup—and bake for 30 to 35 minutes, until the tops are a medium golden brown and a fork or cake tester inserted into the muffins comes out clean.

Let cool in the tin for 10 to 15 minutes before pulling them out so they hold together a bit better (but if you can't help yourself and want them hot with butter, we get it).

Berries and Figs

IDEAS AND RECIPES

Berries and figs are incredibly versatile and work particularly well in the Hero Recipes—pop them into Use-It-Up Pancakes (page 232) or Any-Fruit Snack Cake (page 236)—as well as the apple, pear, and stone fruit dishes. Like stone fruits, they translate well to otherwise savory dishes like the Fruit and Greens Salad (page 162). Recipes with either sugar or alcohol and some time to marinate, like Save-the-Fruit Shrub (page 230), Macerated Berries (page 254), and A Freewheeling Berry Sangria (page 256), can help dial up the flavor when all you have is out-of-season berries. But when they're in season—ripe, juicy, and bursting with summer sweetness—they're best all on their own, stored on the counter so you can eat them at room temperature, and needing no adornment whatsoever.

Store It Right

Berries and figs should be stored in the refrigerator, unwashed, unless you plan to eat them right away. We find it easiest to keep them in their original container, but if you want to keep softer berries like strawberries and raspberries pristine, lay them out on a plate so they don't smush each other.

Save for Later

To freeze berries or figs, lay them out on a plate or baking sheet and freeze, then transfer to a resealable bag or airtight container.

You Can Still Eat It!

One or two berries in a bunch will often grow mold; pick through the bad ones and discard as soon as possible. The rest will be fine as long as there's no visible mold; just wash them a little more carefully before eating. Mushy berries are excellent in **Save-the-Fruit Shrub** (page 230) and **A Freewheeling Berry Sangria** (page 256), or cooked down into **Low-Key Fruit Jam** (page 234).

Extra Bits

Using a tiny spoon to scoop out strawberry tops saves a lot of the red flesh compared to slicing the tops off with a knife. Even better, leave your strawberry tops on when making smoothies—you won't even notice them. We also like to save the tops and put them in drinking water or sangria for a hint of strawberry flavor.

Use-It-Up Ideas

Macerated Berries, or berries soaked with liquid and sugar, is a great way to use up soft fruit or sweeten up out-of-season berries. It's like a fruit marinade, so adaptable that any halfway-stocked kitchen should be able to cobble something together. Since all they do is sit for hours, these berries are an excellent make-ahead dessert for a dinner party. Mix a quart of berries with ¼ cup sugar or another sweetener and 2 tablespoons citrus juice, vinegar, or wine. If you like, add a tablespoon or two of gin, rum, or bourbon, and anything else that sounds good to you—ground cloves, fresh basil, vanilla beans, the sky's the limit. Let sit for at least 30 minutes or as long as overnight—the longer they sit, the stronger the flavor. Serve with a dollop of whipped cream and some cookie crumbles, layer with yogurt to make a parfait, or spoon on top of cake, ice cream, or pancakes. Keep them in your fridge for a week or so, pulling them out every so often to mix into your favorite spritz cocktail or our **Freewheeling Berry Sangria** (page 256).

FAVORITE COMBOS

Strawberries + brown sugar + rice vinegar + 1 star anise pod + 1 cardamom pod (a favorite from our first cookbook)

Blackberries + white sugar + lime juice + gin + fresh mint

Blueberries + maple syrup + lemon juice + lemon zest + Limoncello (page 272) + 1 cinnamon stick

We consider the British dessert **Eton Mess** to be the perfect use of any macerated berry. Crumble store-bought meringues into large chunks and gently fold into 2 cups soft whipped cream and 3 cups macerated berries (or any chopped fruit you like). Divide into 4 dessert bowls and top with more macerated berries or fresh fruit.

SANGRIA!
RICE
BROWN
GIN
SUGAR
PANCAKES!
ICE CREAM!
CAKE!

A Freewheeling Berry Sangria

Serves 4 to 6

Just about any fruit can be used in sangria, but the beauty of berries is that there's no chopping required. Hooray for fruits that already come bite-size! Letting the berries sit with the sugar and a splash of alcohol for a few hours helps them release lots of juice and soak up the flavors, but we have been known to skip that step when putting together a last-minute party pitcher. And given that the berries are going to be soft anyway, it's an excellent way to enjoy any overly mushy or previously frozen berries. The rest of the recipe is as freewheeling as it comes. We make sangria with whatever beverages we have around—red, white, or rosé wine, plus juice or sparkling water or soda or the rest of that boozy seltzer you bought and decided you didn't like. Tart juice like grapefruit or pomegranate helps avoid a sticky-sweet punch, and a good pour of something sparkling lightens it all up. Unorthodox it may be, but we feel confident that none of the party guests downing your version will voice any complaints.

1 pint mixed berries

1 tablespoon sugar or sweetener of choice, plus more to taste

¼ cup Curaçao, Cointreau, triple sec, Grand Marnier, or another fruit-flavored liqueur of your choice

1 (750-mL) bottle wine of your choice

⅓ cup juice, such as lemonade or grapefruit juice, or more to taste

Splash of something bubbly, like seltzer, sparkling wine, or a not-too-sweet soda

---

Put the berries, sugar, and liqueur in a large pitcher and stir to combine. Let sit for at least 1 hour, or up to overnight in the fridge. Right before serving, add the wine, juice, and seltzer and taste. Do you want it a bit sweeter or less boozy? Add some juice. Do you want it lighter and fizzier? Pour in more sparkling stuff. This is your party—make it how you like it.

Stone Fruits

IDEAS AND RECIPES

Peaches, plums, apricots, cherries, and other stone fruits work in so many of the other fruit recipes that you don't need to worry about finding a way to use them up. Besides, the window for perfectly-in-season stone fruit can be so short, depending on where you live, that Mei eats almost all ripe peaches straight, standing over the sink to keep from dripping peach juice all over the kitchen. Try them in all the Hero Recipes, Apples and Pears recipes, and Berries and Figs recipes, as well as in a Lassi (page 286) or Icebox Cake (page 288). You can also take them in a savory direction by adding them to dishes like Fruit and Greens Salad (page 162) and Salsa Fresca (page 103).

Store It Right

Stone fruit should be stored unwashed on the counter, out of the direct sun, until ripe (cherries are usually ripe already), then moved to the refrigerator. Once cut, store in an airtight container in the fridge. If they're particularly delicate peaches or nectarines, store them in one layer so they don't crush each other and eat soonish to avoid them getting mealy.

Save for Later

To freeze stone fruit, slice and lay the pieces on a plate or baking sheet. Once frozen, transfer to a resealable bag or airtight container. Alternatively, you can cook stone fruit down into Low-Key Fruit Jam (page 234)—a great use for slightly mealy peaches—and keep in the refrigerator for a week or two or freeze for use in pies and cakes.

Extra Bits

Stone fruit pits can be used to infuse liquids like vinegars (for a fruity salad dressing), dairy (heat gently, then strain to make Irene's favorite spin on whipped cream), spirits (for peachy bourbon or cherry vodka), and syrups (for flavored simple syrup). There's also a kernel inside the large stone fruit pits that can be used for flavoring, but it contains a toxic chemical related to cyanide. Heat supposedly renders the compound harmless, but make sure to do some solid research if you feel like giving it a try.

Use-It-Up Ideas

- Mei once impulse-purchased an entire 20-pound case of Bing cherries and managed to preserve them all thanks to a strategically purchased cherry pitter and many gifted jars of **Boozy Cherries**. For roughly 2 cups pitted cherries, simmer ¾ cup sugar or honey with ¾ cup water for 5 minutes with any flavorings you like, such as cardamom pods or whole cloves, a star anise pod, a cinnamon stick, a teaspoon of vanilla extract or a vanilla bean, or strips of citrus zest. Add the cherries and ½ cup brandy or cognac, let cool, then transfer to a jar and store in the refrigerator. Try to let them sit for a few days before eating; they will keep for a few months.

- Use up lightly wrinkled or too-soft peaches in **Grilled Peach Barbecue Sauce**, inspired by chef Bryan Furman of B's Cracklin' BBQ, the best barbecue Mei ate during two years of living in Atlanta. Grill 2 halved ripe peaches, then blend them with ⅓ cup ketchup, 2 tablespoons mustard, 1 teaspoon vinegar, and 1 teaspoon sweetener. Season to taste with salt and pepper and a bit of cayenne or paprika and not a single juicy bite will go to waste.
- Stone fruits make fabulous pies, tarts, cakes, cobblers, the list goes on. Slice them up and use in the **Mix-and-Match Fruit Galette** (page 241), **Sweet Bread Pudding** (page 239), or **Poached Fruit and Almond Tart** (page 248).

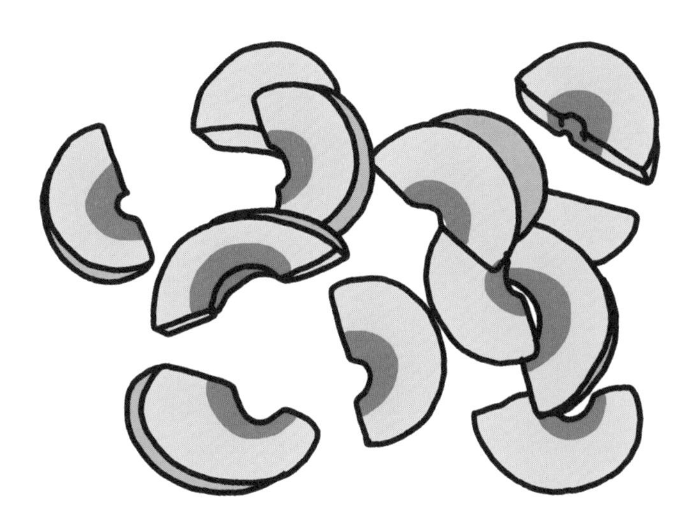

Tagine-Inspired Lamb Stew with Apricots

Serves 6

There's something about stone fruits like peaches and apricots that goes so well with stewed lamb, especially cooked with spices in the style of a North African tagine. *Tagine* refers to the slow-cooked, fragrantly spiced stew of meat and vegetables as well as the pot in which it's often cooked, a wide ceramic dish with a conical lid. In the likely event that you don't own a tagine, a Dutch oven or another pot with a tightly fitting lid also works to hold in the steam and let the condensing moisture drip back over the stew. Tagines are often sweetened with fruit and can be made with dried fruit, fruit preserves, or in this case, softening stone fruit that needs to be used up ASAP.

NOTE: *If you don't have the spice blend ras el hanout, substitute 1 teaspoon each ground cumin, coriander, and turmeric, plus ½ teaspoon each ground black pepper and cinnamon. You're looking for an earthy fragrant mixture that resembles a curry powder, but with stronger notes of cinnamon.*

2 pounds lamb stew meat, cubed
2 teaspoons kosher salt
1½ tablespoons ras el hanout
4 garlic cloves, minced
1-inch piece fresh ginger, minced
2 tablespoons butter or oil
1 medium onion, diced
¼ cup mild vinegar
1 (15-ounce) can chickpeas, drained and rinsed
2 cups stock of your choice
2 to 3 soft apricots or peaches, pitted and cut into chunks, or ½ cup Low-Key Fruit Jam (page 234)

1 slice Preserved Citrus (page 276), rinsed and chopped (optional but highly recommended)

Steamed white rice or couscous, for serving

Chopped fresh parsley, for garnish

Heat the oven to 325 degrees.

Put the lamb in a large bowl and season with the salt, ras el hanout, garlic, and ginger. Stir to coat the lamb, then let sit while you prepare everything else.

Melt the butter in a tagine or Dutch oven over medium heat. Add the lamb, onion, and vinegar. Cook until the onion softens and becomes fragrant, 6 to 8 minutes, then add the chickpeas, stock, fruit, and preserved citrus, if using. Cover, transfer to the oven, and bake for 2 hours or so, until the lamb is falling-apart tender and any fruit chunks are super soft and almost dissolved. Serve spooned over warm bowls of rice or couscous with a sprinkle of fresh parsley.

Peach and Burrata with Fried Prosciutto

WITH IRENE

Serves 2 to 4

I have a philosophy about seasonality in cooking: When something comes into season, eat it with burrata. These massive balls of cream- and curd-filled mozzarella provide a richness that's a bit light and tart, highlighting perfectly ripe produce without totally stealing the spotlight. My burrata partners of choice include new asparagus and snap peas in spring, and here, ripe summer peaches and tomatoes, for a refreshing version of a caprese salad when you're bored of caprese salad. (By the way, my favorite way to spice up this and any other mozzarella-type salad is a heaping spoonful of chili crisp.) It's great for when it's too hot to really cook, but I make an exception for the shattery crispness of fried prosciutto. And as long as you're heating the pan, you might as well fry your basil leaves too.

NOTE: *If your stone fruit is a bit underripe, you can grill them to get some caramelization.*

Neutral or extra-virgin olive oil, for frying

4 to 6 slices prosciutto

Large handful basil leaves, loosely torn

2 ripe peaches or nectarines, pitted and sliced, or 1 cup other sliced stone fruit

2 medium tomatoes, sliced

1 (8-ounce) ball burrata cheese

Extra-virgin olive oil, for drizzling (this is an excellent moment to break out the fancy olive oil)

Kosher salt and freshly ground black pepper

Heat a splash of oil in a large skillet over medium-high heat until shimmering. Add the prosciutto and cook until it shrinks and crisps up like bacon, less than a minute, then flip and cook the other side until browned. Transfer to a paper towel–lined plate, then drop half the basil leaves into the pan and let them crisp up for a minute or two. Once they turn darker green and translucent, use tongs to transfer them to the prosciutto plate.

Arrange the stone fruit wedges and tomatoes in an overlapping pattern on a plate. Tear the burrata into pieces and scatter over the peaches and tomatoes, then drizzle with extra-virgin olive oil and season with salt and pepper. Break the prosciutto into shards and scatter over the salad with both the fried and fresh basil and eat immediately, ideally with a chilled glass of white wine.

Bananas

IDEAS AND RECIPES

We're constantly amazed at the versatility that bananas offer when it comes to cooking. Bananas have a unique texture that bakes up well like other fruits but can also act as a substitute for eggs, sweeteners, or even a certain amount of flour. Once you start using them for everything from pancakes to ice cream and freezing the rest, you will never in your life waste another banana.

Know What You Got

You can help cut down on banana waste before they even reach your kitchen. Most grocery shoppers have an ideal banana purchase in mind: smooth, pristine yellow, quite large, and in a bunch. However, the tendency to buy bananas only in bunches often leads to single bananas rotting and getting thrown out. Next time you go fruit shopping, choose all the solo bananas and save them from the trash.

We also try to buy organic bananas whenever possible, as they usually cost just a few cents more than conventional. Industrially grown bananas are considered "pesticide-intensive" by the Environmental Working Group;* while the peel helps minimize contamination for eaters, the heavy use of pesticides and fungicides harms workers, local communities, and the environment in banana-growing regions. Besides the slightly higher price, consumers often avoid buying sustainably grown or Fair Trade–approved bananas due to their smaller size.† Letting go of our idealized banana visions and buying smaller single organic bananas can both minimize waste and help reduce reliance on harmful chemicals throughout the banana industry.

Store It Right

Store bananas on the counter until ripe. Once ripe, you can store in the refrigerator to extend their life if necessary; although the skin will darken and shrivel, the banana inside will be fine to eat raw for several days.

Save for Later

Bananas freeze extremely well, whether they're perfectly ripe or completely browned and soft. As long as they're not rotten or moldy, they can be saved

*Sonya Lunder, "Banana Cultivation Is Pesticide-Intensive," *Environmental Working Group*, April 28, 2014 (https://www.ewg.org/news-insights/news/banana-cultivation-pesticide-intensive).

†Madison Stewart, "The Deadly Side of America's Banana Obsession," *Pulitzer Center* (https://pulitzercenter.org/stories/deadly-side-americas-banana-obsession).

in the freezer for baked goods, smoothies, and more. In fact, frozen bananas make perfect "ice cream" (page 267) with no other ingredients at all. Peel before freezing to avoid wrestling frozen peels off frozen bananas—we gained this wisdom the hard way and wish to help you avoid the same unpleasant fate. Store frozen peeled bananas in a resealable bag with the air pressed out and use directly in smoothies or thaw briefly before cooking into baked goods.

You Can Still Eat It!

Bruises or brown spots on an otherwise pristine banana can be cut out if desired, and the rest is fine to eat. As the banana starts to age and develop dark spots or turn fully brown, the inside gets sweeter and softer. While they're no longer ideal to eat straight, they're prime for smoothies and baked goods.

Extra Bits

Banana peels are totally edible; just make sure to wash them well before consuming. Make them into a tea by simmering in hot water for 10 to 15 minutes and flavoring with honey or sugar and spices like ground cinnamon or nutmeg. You can also chop the peels and include them in **Banana Bread** (page 268) or **Banana Muffins** (page 267). Mei's kids were skeptical but couldn't identify the peels in a blind banana bread taste test; cut them into tiny pieces and they're barely detectable.

Use-It-Up Ideas

- **Banana Pancakes** are a dream recipe if you have (1) many ripe bananas to use up, (2) eaters with dietary restrictions, and/or (3) children demanding pancakes at a disturbingly early hour of the morning when you are clearly incapable of handling a ten-ingredient pancake recipe. Mash a ripe banana with an egg, a tablespoon of flour (all-purpose or whole wheat, a gluten-free replacement, ground flaxseed or almond flour, or ground oats—all are fair game) and a pinch of baking soda. Fry in a skillet with neutral oil or butter over medium heat until browned on both sides (keep them small so they're easily flippable, as they're more fragile than a typical pancake). Eat as is or with maple syrup, **Low-Key Fruit Jam** (page 234), a dollop of whipped cream, or any combination of the above.

- To make **Banana Fudge Pops**, blend 3 bananas, ⅓ cup peanut butter, 1 tablespoon honey or maple syrup, 1 tablespoon cocoa powder, and ⅓ cup milk of your choice. Pour into 6 ice pop molds and freeze until solid.
- Make flour-free **Banana Muffins** that rise into puffy pillows, then shrink down into a size perfect for chubby little hands, so highly coveted that they get snatched off the counter before they have time to cool. Blend 2 bananas, 2 eggs, 1 cup nut butter, 1 teaspoon vanilla extract, and ½ teaspoon baking soda with a pinch of salt until thoroughly combined, then scrape into a greased muffin tin. Bake at 400 degrees for 12 to 15 minutes, until a fork or cake tester comes out clean.
- **Banana "Ice Cream"** technically isn't ice cream; it's sometimes called "nice cream" or, if your children are also being raised by Daniel Tiger, "banana swirl." Regardless, it's a miraculous dessert with a texture shockingly similar to regular ice cream (and can be steered into soft serve territory if you add a splash of milk of any kind). All you do is put a few frozen bananas in a blender and puree until smooth (if you have a low-powered blender, you may want to briefly zap the bananas in a microwave first). Flavor with cocoa powder, ground cinnamon, crushed Oreos, or any kind of nut butter. Top with fresh or cooked fruit like **Low-Key Fruit Jam** (page 234), the fruit leftovers from **Save-the-Fruit Shrub** (page 230), crushed nuts, chocolate syrup, or your sundae toppings of choice.

The Accidental Best Banana Bread

WITH MEI

Makes 1 loaf

I know what you're thinking: There are 98,345 banana bread recipes out there and they all claim to be the best. I too kept trying supposedly superlative banana bread recipes and never found a clear favorite. Until I decided to try the recipe on a supermarket banana bag on a whim . . . and, haphazardly multitasking the way I often do when cooking, accidentally left out *an entire cup of flour.* Oops. But! Out came the moistest, softest, banana-iest bread, holding together just enough to be sliceable, so rich and rewarding, but somehow actually feeling healthier with a cup of white flour gone and only the cup of whole wheat flour still remaining. I finally feel that banana bread hyperbole is justified, and so do the many skeptics who have tried it and quickly been converted, especially when chocolate chips are involved.

1 stick butter, softened
¾ cup brown or white sugar
2 eggs
1 cup whole wheat or all-purpose flour
1 teaspoon baking soda
½ teaspoon kosher salt
3 ripe bananas, mashed
1 teaspoon vanilla extract
Large handful (or two) chocolate chips (optional but highly recommended)

Heat the oven to 350 degrees. Grease a loaf pan.

Combine the butter and sugar in the bowl of a stand mixer fitted with the paddle attachment and cream the two together into a uniform mixture. Scrape down the sides of the bowl with a spatula, then add the eggs and stir to combine.

Whisk the flour, baking soda, and salt in a medium bowl until thoroughly combined. Add the flour mixture to the bowl of the stand mixer and stir to combine. Scrape down the bowl and add the mashed bananas, vanilla, and chocolate chips (if using) and mix.

Transfer the mixture to the prepared loaf pan and bake for 50 to 60 minutes, until a fork inserted into the center comes out clean. Let cool slightly but eat warm if you can—the gooey chocolate chips take the banana bread to another level. Keep the loaf well wrapped at room temperature for a few days or wrap in aluminum foil and freeze in a resealable bag with the air pressed out for a few months.

Citrus

IDEAS AND RECIPES

Citrus fruits are one of the most useful ingredients in the kitchen, as at home in a savory dish as in a dessert. A squeeze of lemon or lime can't be beat for finishing a dish with a pop of acidity. We often need only a wedge or two at a time though, so it's easy for the remaining fruit to get forgotten until you end up fishing three moldy lemon halves from the back of the fridge. Thankfully, the installation of an Eat-Me-First Box (see page 16) in our refrigerators has saved many a citrus fruit from an ignominious end in the compost bin. And don't forget: While lemons and limes are often favored for savory applications, oranges and grapefruits can add a unique depth of flavor to bright salads, vegetable soups, and meaty braises.

Store It Right

Citrus fruits last the longest in the fridge and can hang out for weeks in the crisper drawer. Since they last for ages, we like to buy lemons, limes, and oranges in bulk to save money. Once cut, citrus can be wrapped in beeswax paper or placed in an airtight container to slow down the drying-out process.

Save for Later

If you have a lot of citrus to rescue, we recommend freezing the peel and the juice separately as the pith and membranes only get in the way once defrosted. Use a vegetable peeler or a Microplane to peel or zest the outer layer and freeze in a resealable bag with the air pressed out. Halve the lemon and juice into a glass jar with a lid for freezing, then compost the spent rinds. If you have room in your freezer, you can even freeze lemons and limes whole! Zest them while still frozen and thaw in the microwave to get the juice flowing.

You Can Still Eat It!

If you've got a lemon or lime with one wedge cut out, just slice off the dried-out portion and you're good to go. If you've got halved lemons or limes that have dried out, try tossing them into a soup or stew. Small brown spots or specks of mold on the outside may not affect the juice on the inside, especially if the fruit has a thick rind, but once the whole fruit starts to mold or collapse, it's time for the compost bin.

Extra Bits

Citrus zest is as flavorful as the juice, so don't let your peels go to waste. Just make sure to wash your citrus well first. If you have a recipe that uses only the juice, remove the peel in large strips with a peeler before squeezing. Stash the peels in a small bag in the freezer and pop them into cocktails, soups, stews, and bottles of booze.

Use-It-Up Ideas

- Make a nontoxic multipurpose cleaner by mixing equal parts white vinegar and water with a handful of citrus peels. Let sit for a week on the counter, then strain, compost the peels, and transfer the solution to a spray bottle.
- Add thin slices of lemon when you're roasting vegetables, poultry, or fish, as well as **roasted grapes** (page 282) or **Slow-Poached Vegetables in Olive Oil** (page 40).
- Put a small handful of citrus peels in bottles of clear spirits like vodka, gin, and white rum. Infuse for a week or so, then strain and compost the peels and use the spirits in any citrusy cocktail.
- Make **Limoncello** by infusing peels from 8 to 10 lemons in a bottle of high-proof vodka. Let sit for a few weeks, then strain and mix with 1 to 3 cups **Simple Syrup** (page 142) to taste. Refrigerate for up to a month or freeze for up to a year. Experiment by using different kinds of citrus or **Herb-Infused Simple Syrup** (page 142).
- Candy any kind of citrus peel by simmering the peels in water for 20 minutes. Drain and set aside (or repeat as many times as you like to minimize bitterness). Make a syrup in the same pan with equal parts sugar and water, simmer the peels for an hour or so until they become translucent, then drain and toss in sugar to coat. Let air-dry overnight to minimize moisture, then store in an airtight container in a cool, dry place for up to a month or in the freezer for even longer.
- Of course, there's always tangy, delicious citrus juice!

Citrus Curd

Makes about 1½ cups

Citrus curd, made with any combination of citrus fruits you have around, feels like a blast of sunshine with its pure pastel color and bright, tangy flavor. We have been known to eat it straight from the pan with a spoon, but more socially acceptable options include stirring into yogurt and granola, spreading onto pancakes, muffins, or scones, or dolloping onto ice cream.

NOTE: *If you don't have a heat-proof bowl that can double as a double boiler, you can mix everything in a small heavy-bottomed pan over medium-low heat.*

½ cup fresh citrus juice of any kind, one fruit or mixed
¼ to ⅓ cup sugar, depending on how sweet you want it
1 tablespoon grated citrus zest
2 eggs
3 egg yolks
1 stick butter, softened

Fill a medium pot with an inch or two of water and bring to a boil over medium heat. Whisk the juice, sugar, zest, eggs, and egg yolks together in a heatproof metal or glass bowl. Place the bowl over the pot (you're basically making a DIY double boiler setup—make sure the bowl doesn't touch the boiling water below) and gently heat, whisking constantly, until the mixture thickens to a pudding-like consistency, 3 to 5 minutes. Remove from the heat and whisk in the butter. If there are any bits of cooked egg, or you don't want the zest in the final curd, strain the mixture before letting it cool, then store in an airtight container in the refrigerator for at least a week.

This recipe is very flexible with regard to using up stray egg yolks—Mei has made it with 5 egg yolks and no whole eggs and also with 3 eggs and 2 egg yolks and all versions were excellent.

What's-in-Your-Fridge Citrus Cake

WITH MEI

Makes 1 cake

This is one of the easiest cakes out there (dump, stir, pour, bake) and oh-so-very flexible. When I first sent this recipe to my friends, we all went on a frenzy of citrus cake baking from North Carolina to Rhode Island to the Alpine village of Klosters, Switzerland. Over the weekend, we churned out about a dozen variations (and *not* because I made them do it, but because the cake is that good, I swear). Everyone made their own version based on the citrus and dairy in their home at that moment, from lemon-yogurt to orange-ricotta to grapefruit–crème fraîche, and raves flew in from all locations. Whether you need to use up citrus, clear out some dairy products, or just bake a beautifully simple cake, this is the one for you.

1¾ cups all-purpose flour

1 cup brown or white sugar

2 teaspoons baking powder

½ teaspoon kosher salt

¾ cup sour cream, plain whole-milk yogurt, ricotta, or a similarly thick dairy combination (see chart on page 331)

3 eggs

½ cup oil (neutral oil if you don't want it to stand out, coconut oil for flavor)

¼ cup citrus juice

1 tablespoon grated citrus zest (about 2 lemons or 1 grapefruit)

Heat the oven to 350 degrees. Grease a 9-inch round cake pan or loaf pan.

In a medium bowl, whisk together the flour, sugar, baking powder, and salt. In a large bowl, whisk together the dairy, eggs, oil, juice, and zest. Slowly mix the dry ingredients into the wet ingredients until everything is just combined and no floury bits remain (lumps are fine, though).

Pour the batter into the prepared pan and bake until a tester or fork poked into the cake comes out clean, 40 to 50 minutes for a cake pan, 50 to 60 minutes for a loaf pan. Let the cake cool for 10 minutes or so, then run a knife around the edges to help release the cake before removing it from the pan. Glaze or soak the cake if desired (see Note) and store in an airtight container at room temperature for up to 3 days—if it lasts that long.

GOT EXTRA JUICE?

If you have a bit of extra citrus juice to use up, combine it with a small amount of sugar to soak the cake or a large amount of sugar to glaze the top. To soak the cake, heat ¼ cup juice with 1 tablespoon sugar until the sugar dissolves, then pour over the cake while still warm. To glaze the cake, whisk 2 to 3 tablespoons juice with 1 cup powdered sugar and drizzle over the cake once cool.

Preserved Citrus

WITH IRENE

I hate running out of fresh lemons and limes. Not having a burst of fresh citrus when you want it for a dish (or a drink, if you have a dedicated cocktail maker in the house) feels like an easily preventable tragedy, so I buy large bags of lemons and limes to save money and shopping time. Sometimes, though, they start to pile up and I start to regret my bulk-buying habits and wish for a way to remove all the citrus from my fridge at once and start over. Luckily, there are these fantastic flavor-boosting, tart-and-citrusy, sweet-and-savory bits of magic called preserved lemons, a staple of North African cuisine, and you can work this particular alchemy on any citrus taking up space in your fridge.

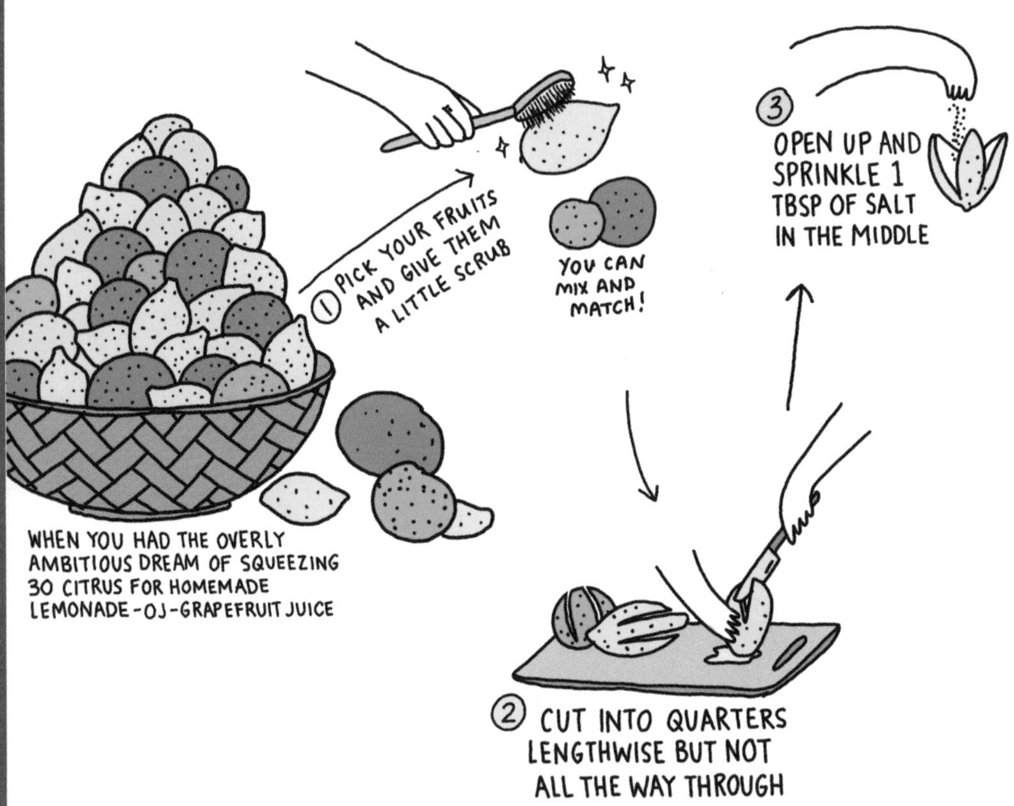

After 15 minutes of work and a few weeks of hanging around, you'll have spectacularly bright and tangy cured citrus fruits for adding to salads, making sauces, mixing into pasta, tossing onto fried things, and putting in my favorite tagine (page 260). There are plenty of different methods and flavor combinations with spices like black peppercorns, bay leaves, cinnamon, and cardamom. I like to keep it simple, but go for any variation you like. And for those of you who haven't preserved citrus before, don't worry—it's honestly pretty hard to get this "wrong." There isn't an exact ratio of lemon to salt, so don't fret about amounts. If yours are extra salty when you take them out, you can rinse them before eating, but I rarely do.

(continues)

At least ½ cup kosher salt, or more as needed

At least 4 lemons or citrus fruits of any kind, but you can use as many as you have, as long as they fit in your jar

An additional 1 to 3 lemons, for juice (peel or zest first and save for infusing booze or flavoring stews), or more as needed to cover your citrus

---

Find a wide-mouth glass jar that has a lid and will hold all your fruit. Bring some water to a boil and pour it into the jar to sterilize (or use your cleaning/sterilizing method of choice—Vivian Howard suggests running your jar through the dishwasher in *This Will Make It Taste Good*), then empty it out again. Pour a thin layer of kosher salt into the bottom of the jar.

Wash and lightly scrub your lemons. One by one, stand each lemon on its end and cut it into quarters lengthwise, but don't cut all the way down. The idea is for the lemon quarters to open up like the petals of a flower with the stem end still attached. Sprinkle a tablespoon of kosher salt in the center (a bit less for tiny limes, a bit more for gargantuan grapefruits) and rub it all over the inside, then close the lemon back up and put it in the jar, pressing down with a spoon to release the juice and squash the citrus down. The more you can squish the lemons down, the less juice you'll need at the end to cover. Top the lemon with another spoonful or two of salt, then repeat the process until the jar is full. Add any spices you like, then squeeze the additional lemons over the jar until the juice covers everything (a bit of peel sticking up is OK—it'll collapse over time). Seal the jar up and swish it a few times to distribute the liquid.

Place the jar somewhere relatively cool and dark, but prominent enough that you'll walk by every few days and turn the jar upside down (place it in a larger jar or bucket if you're worried about it leaking) and then back the next time you see it. You can let the lemons continue to cure at room temperature, but I usually move it to the fridge after a few weeks.

The preserved lemons are ready once the rinds are tender and lightly translucent, but the longer you leave them, the better the flavor. Typically, you'll want at least a month to get to the best texture. When using, you can rinse to remove some salt and scrape away the bitter pith, or just use as is.

Add the minced rind to savory recipes like Anything-in-the-Kitchen Pasta (page 68) or Any-Bean Dip (page 306), make dressing (see the box below), and put the pulp in broths or braises. They'll keep basically indefinitely in the fridge.

NO-WASTE TIPS

Make a **Preserved Citrus Dressing** by blending half a preserved lemon (or the equivalent of a different citrus fruit) with a minced garlic clove, a pinch of salt, and roughly ⅓ cup extra-virgin olive oil. Taste and adjust the oil and salt as needed and drizzle onto Mix-and-Match Slaw Party (page 42) or Fancy-Looking Roasted Vegetables (page 201). Stir some into Green Sauce (page 138) and drizzle on Pick-Your-Protein Salad (page 297), or use to dress just about anything you make with the Leafy Greens Salad Builder (page 160), especially a Grain Salad (page 162) or Pasta Salad (page 162).

Grapes

IDEAS AND RECIPES

For some reason, we almost always have a half-eaten bag of grapes sitting in our fridges. Actually, we can drill that down to a specific reason: Grapes come packaged in very large bags, often containing 2 to 3 pounds of grapes. Grapes do have a reasonably long shelf life, but we think you can do more than snack on surplus grapes.

Store It Right

Store grapes unwashed in the fridge and keep them on the stem as long as possible.

Save for Later

Put whole grapes straight in the freezer for icy cold grape snacks or tiny ice cubes that won't melt in your wine or Berry Sangria (page 256).

You Can Still Eat It!

Rogue wrinkled, collapsed, or moldy grapes can be removed before they contaminate their neighbors. Wrinkled grapes can be added to your Smoothie Bag (page 18) or cooked into any of the Hero Recipes, but once they mold and collapse, it's time for the compost.

Use-It-Up Ideas

If the clock starts ticking on a bag of grapes, consider incorporating some of these tips and recipes into your routine:

- Puree a bunch of grapes with a bit of sugar and a squeeze of lemon juice, freeze, then blend again to make a grape slushie.
- Cook the grapes down into **Low-Key Fruit Jam** (page 234)—grape jam works particularly well with simple meat dishes like pork chops or grilled chicken.
- Add to salads, of both the **leafy green** variety (page 160) and the **chicken** variety (page 297).
- Throw some grapes into the pan underneath your pork shoulder or whole roast chicken—Irene's favorite!
- Grapes bake up surprisingly well in desserts—**grape galettes** (page 241) are a beloved treat in Mei's house.

WITH MEI

Roasted Grape, Olive, and Blue Cheese Toasts

Serves 6 to 8 as a snack

Whenever I think of cooked grapes, I think of a roasted grape crostini I ate at my friend Lex's house years ago, based on a Smitten Kitchen recipe by Deb Perelman. It's perfect for already wrinkly grapes, since they'll shrivel up further in the oven, as well as slightly stale bread. The original recipe suggests a mild ricotta, but I'd argue that a smear of creamy, funky blue cheese takes this combination to another level. Use any kind of grapes and olives you have but choose different colors, unless you want to play the fun but disorienting "is this a grape or an olive" mind game with every bite. As this is a superb dinner party snack (preppable in advance + scales easily + impresses your friends), I've given amounts for a crowd, but you can scale it back down if it's just for you.

2 cups grapes of any kind
2 cups pitted olives of any kind
Olive oil
Kosher salt and black pepper
A good-sized wedge of spreadable blue cheese
1 baguette (or any good bread you like, slightly stale works great)

Heat the oven to 400 degrees. Put the grapes and olives in a roasting pan, drizzle with enough olive oil to coat, and toss to combine. Sprinkle with a good pinch of salt and a few grinds of black pepper, then cook for about 45 minutes, or until the grapes and olives have shriveled up a bit and released their juices into the pan.

During those 45 minutes, cut the baguette into thin slices (about ¼ inch thick) and pop them into the oven on a baking tray. Toast for about 5 minutes, then flip and toast the other side for 5 minutes, or until golden.

Smear blue cheese onto each crostini and top with a spoonful of olives and grapes and a drizzle of the juices left in the pan.

Skillet Roasted Chicken with Grape Gravy

WITH MEI

Serves 4 to 6

Once you come around to cooked grapes, you might also consider roasting them with your next chicken. The burst caramelized grapes infuse a mellow sweetness into what I feel comfortable declaring the best gravy I've ever made. Roasting a chicken goes surprisingly quickly when you spatchcock or butterfly the chicken (that is, cut out the backbone) for faster, more even cooking. If you've never spatchcocked a chicken before, it can seem intimidating; when I actually did it, I realized it takes about 3 minutes. All you need is a sharp pair of scissors and some bone-cutting determination, and easier roast chicken—with the best gravy ever—is yours.

NOTE: *To spatchcock a chicken, lay the chicken breast-side down on a stable cutting board. Position a pair of sharp scissors at the tail end next to the backbone and cut directly through the chicken from the tail to the neck, staying close to the backbone as you go. Repeat on the opposite side. There you go—your chicken is butterflied! Save the backbone and neck for your Kitchen Scrap Stock Bag (page 18)—I even roast them along with the rest of the chicken before stashing in the bag. And if this whole idea fills you with horror, ask someone at the butcher counter to do it for you.*

3½- to 4-pound whole chicken, spatchcocked (see Note)
2 tablespoons extra-virgin olive oil, divided
Kosher salt and freshly ground black pepper
2 shallots or 1 medium onion, sliced
2 cups grapes of any color (wrinkled grapes are totally fine)
Several woodsy herb sprigs, such as rosemary, sage, or thyme, if you have them
1 heaping tablespoon all-purpose flour
½ cup dry red or white wine
1½ to 2 cups chicken stock

(continues)

Heat the oven to 450 degrees.

Pat the chicken dry with paper towels and rub it all over with 1 tablespoon of the oil. Generously salt and pepper the chicken all over.

Put the remaining 1 tablespoon oil in a large cast-iron or other oven-safe skillet. Add the shallots and grapes and lightly toss in the oil, then sprinkle with salt and pepper. Lay the herbs around the edge of the pan. Place the chicken on top of it all, skin-side up, and flatten it out so it cooks a bit more evenly. Roast for 35 to 45 minutes, until the chicken is fully cooked (I use a digital thermometer and make sure the joint between the thighs and breast is 165 degrees or higher).

Carefully move the skillet to the stovetop and transfer the chicken to a cutting board to rest, loosely covered with aluminum foil, while you make the gravy. Sprinkle the shallots and grapes with the flour and heat over high heat, using a wooden spoon to combine everything and smash it down a bit. Add the wine and bring to a boil for 2 minutes, then add 1½ cups stock. Stir to incorporate and scrape all the bits off the bottom of the skillet, then lower the heat and simmer for 10 minutes, or longer if you want a thicker gravy; add up to ½ cup more stock if you like a thinner gravy. Remove and discard any herb stems. Carve the chicken and serve with the gravy.

Leftover chicken and gravy can both be incorporated into Eat-Your-Leftovers Pot Pie (page 76); extra gravy can be frozen in an airtight container.

Tropical Fruits and Melons

IDEAS AND RECIPES

Tropical fruit and melons differ from most other fruits in their use and structure; as they tend to be waterier, they're less likely to be cooked or baked in pies or cakes. However, this texture makes them easily blendable and thus ideal in smoothies and cocktails as well as a refreshingly sweet addition to salad or slaw.

Store It Right

Tropical fruit, including mangos, papayas, and pineapple, should be stored on the counter until ripe, then moved to the refrigerator. Melons should also be stored at room temperature, but put them in the fridge if your house is particularly hot. Once cut, store in an airtight container in the fridge.

Save for Later

To freeze any of the tropical fruits, peel and cut into chunks and freeze on a plate or baking sheet. Once frozen, transfer to a resealable bag or airtight container. Frozen melon works best in cocktails and smoothies, so we like to puree before freezing to get that step out of the way, plus it takes up less space.

Extra Bits

Subtly sweet, crisp-crunchy watermelon rinds make a classic Southern pickle, but also share similarities with the unripe green papayas used in Thai salads. Toss together a sauce with lime juice, fish sauce, sugar, a diced chile, and a minced garlic clove and drizzle it over julienned watermelon rinds (with the outer green layer removed). We like to mix in other crunchy raw vegetables like sliced celery or halved grape tomatoes and never say no to a hefty sprinkle of crushed peanuts.

Use-It-Up Ideas

- Tropical fruits are prime for making **Lassi**, the yogurt-based drink made across the Indian subcontinent that can be salted or sweet, spiced or fruity. In the US, we most commonly see mango lassi on restaurant menus, but you can use any soft ripe fruit and additional flavorings (ground cardamom! rose water!) you like. Blend 1 cup diced fruit with 1 cup plain whole-milk yogurt, ¼ cup milk, water, or whey, and 1 tablespoon honey or sugar, or more to taste. Drink it right away or pop it into the fridge to chill.

- Try chunks of watermelon, honeydew, and cantaloupe in salads—we like pairing them with mild lettuces and ingredients that help bridge the sweet-savory gap, like ginger and lime juice.
- Given that melons don't cook well and freeze best when pureed, it's good to have an array of melon drinks in your arsenal. Feel free to swap for the melon of your choice as well as pureed mango or pineapple.

HOW TO DRINK YOUR MELONS

	CANTALOUPE DAIQUIRI (1 SERVING)	HONEYDEW JALAPEÑO MARGARITA (4 SERVINGS)	WATERMELON SPRITZ (DEPENDS ON HOW DRUNK YOU WANT TO GET)
WHICH MELON?	4 OZ PUREED CANTALOUPE (FROZEN IF YOU WANT IT ICY!)	2 CUPS PUREED HONEYDEW (FROZEN IF YOU WANT IT ICY!)	1 CUP PUREED WATERMELON (STRAINED IF YOU LIKE)
WHAT BOOZE ARE WE TALKING?	WHITE RUM 2 OZ	TEQUILA* 8 OZ CURAÇAO 3 OZ	APEROL 8 OZ PROSECCO/CAVA OR SPARKLING WINE 2 CUPS
MAKE IT POP	LIME ½ OZ	LIME 3 OZ	APEROL HAS BITTERNESS
ARE WE SWEETENING?	HONEY OR SIMPLE SYRUP ½ TSP.	SIMPLE SYRUP 2 OZ	SWEETNESS FROM WATERMELON
HOW DO I SERVE THIS?	SHAKE WITH ICE AND STRAIN	PITCHER FOR SHARING	PITCHER SERVE OVER ICE

* PUT A SLICED JALAPEÑO IN THE TEQUILA AND LET SIT FOR 20 MIN–2 HOURS THEN REMOVE

Mango Icebox Cake

Makes 1 cake

Mei has been known to purchase entire cases of her favorite fruits when in season (see Boozy Cherries, page 258), and it's so helpful to have a community of Internet friends to ask how to use them up. Once when she needed ideas for surplus mangos, our buddy Trish suggested making a riff on a Filipino dessert called Mango Royale, or Mango Icebox Cake. We're all for no-bake desserts, the fewer ingredients the better, and quite often have the ingredients for this simple version in the pantry (if you don't, this is as good a reason as any to start). Once the icebox cake idea has been introduced to your repertoire, you can improvise as you like by swapping in other cookies, substituting coconut cream and sweetened condensed coconut milk for a vegan version, and using any other fruit, like kiwis, papayas, peaches, plums, or strawberries. All you need to do is assemble the ingredients and wait until it's cold, which is unquestionably the hardest part.

2 cups heavy whipping cream

½ to ¾ cup sweetened condensed milk, depending on how sweet you want it

2 sleeves graham crackers, or more as needed

3 or 4 ripe or overripe large mangos, or 6 to 8 small mangos, peeled, pitted, and sliced

---

Using a stand mixer or handheld mixer, whip the heavy cream on medium speed until it forms soft peaks (when you lift the whisk attachment out of the cream, it creates a small rounded hill that quickly flops over). Turn the speed down and slowly pour ½ cup condensed milk into the cream while continuing to whip. Taste and add up to another ¼ cup if desired. Once all the condensed milk has been added, return the mixer to medium speed until the cream is thick and scoopable (some cream should cling to the whisk when lifted out).

Line a 9-inch square baking dish with a layer of graham crackers, breaking as needed to fit. (If all you have is a round pan, use your best puzzle-assembling skills to cover the bottom.) Dollop on a layer of the sweetened whipped cream (about a cup), then lay down a layer of mango slices to cover all the whipped cream. Repeat twice more (graham, cream, mango) so you have three full layers of deliciousness. Spread the remaining whipped cream on top. If you have any other remaining ingredients, you can fan out slices of mango in a pretty pattern or sprinkle crushed graham crackers on top.

Freeze for a few hours if you want a softer texture, or overnight, before serving. The cake can live in your freezer, wrapped, for several weeks at least; just let it thaw slightly before serving.

oteins an
Dairy Pro
ry Protei
ns and Da
y Protein
oteins an

Proteins and dairy products play more of a supporting role in the world of minimizing food waste. We tend to buy them in small amounts, know that they go in the fridge, and often know how to use them up or freeze for later. And many of us are used to creating meals around proteins or tossing a bit of **cheese or meat** into any number of dishes—flip over to the Vegetable Hero Recipes (page 34) if you need some more inspiration! However, it's always helpful to have a few specific ideas or recipes on hand to transform **cooked meat** leftovers or use up a surplus of **eggs or beans**. In addition, we'll cover proper storage and evaluation of **raw proteins** as well as ways to swap, substitute, and save every last bite.

Meat and Seafood

People tend to waste meat and seafood less often than other foods, given their typical status as the centerpiece of the meal. Across many cuisines, cooks build dishes around these expensive proteins, so we don't shove them to the back of the fridge as regularly. Plus, we can easily buy the parts we want and find a multitude of recipes based on exactly what we have, whether it's chicken thighs, pork chops, or salmon fillets. Lastly, most people are more familiar with freezing meats than freezing produce, so it's a natural move to transfer proteins to the freezer when a best-by date approaches. For all these reasons, we focus here on ways to use up leftovers, add protein to assorted dishes, and store meat and seafood properly.

Store It Right

You already know this (because you're still alive): **Raw meat and seafood** should be stored in the refrigerator. Ideally, keep raw meat in its original container or rewrapped in airtight packaging and store it at the bottom of your fridge so it's impossible for any juices to drip onto other foods and contaminate them. Keep an eye on sell-by dates—they're much more useful on raw animal proteins than on packaged goods—but you don't have to adhere to them over your own common sense. If the meat looks fine and smells fine, it should be fine to eat even if the expiration date was a few days ago. Keep in mind that discoloration is common with raw meat, especially beef—it hasn't gone bad; it just changed color due to exposure to oxygen and/or light. However, if meat or seafood smells weird or rotten, is slimy or oddly soft, or has visible mold or rot, it should definitely be thrown out.

Cured meats and deli meats should be refrigerated and kept airtight. While some cured meats like hard salamis may be sold at room temperature, they should be refrigerated once opened and cut. Unopened, some cured deli meats like prosciutto or salami can last several weeks. Sliced cooked meat like turkey has a shorter shelf life, typically 3 to 5 days. If you're ever unsure about cold deli meats, you can always cook them to kill off any bacteria, especially after a use-by or best-by date. Similarly to how pregnant people may choose to cook deli meats, you can pan-fry prosciutto bits to scatter on salads, heat sliced turkey for a sandwich, top pizza with salami, or dice any cured meat and put it in an omelet.

Fresh fish and shellfish require a bit of extra care. If you want to be extra safe, make the seafood counter the last stop of your shopping trip and bring a cooler or ask for a bag of ice. Conventional wisdom has you store fish on ice in the refrigerator (without actually touching the ice), but that can be a pain. Even seafood expert Barton Seaver finds this method too inconvenient; in his book *The Joy of Seafood*, he suggests placing wrapped fish in a dish in the coldest part of the refrigerator and refraining from opening the fridge too much. For shellfish, put it in a shallow pan and cover with a wet cloth or paper towel and cook within 1 to 2 days, draining any excess liquid periodically. Live lobsters and crabs should ideally be cooked the day you bring them home.

NO-WASTE TIPS

We typically buy fresh seafood only when we have a specific recipe and occasion in mind. Otherwise, we prefer the flexibility of frozen fish and shellfish, which is generally both more affordable and more widely available. In addition, it's easier than ever to access sustainable seafood, frozen at the peak of freshness, which is a great option if you don't have access to a good fishmonger.

Save for Later

All fresh, cooked, and cured meats can be frozen following the Freezer Basics instructions on page 21, as can fish and shellfish such as shrimp or scallops. Remember to minimize air and moisture, wrap tightly, and thaw safely in the refrigerator (or in cold water, if fully sealed in plastic).

If you find yourself forgetting about meat and seafood often, try one of these tricks:

- Try to buy it only when you have a plan for it, like a specific recipe or a special occasion. If you want to stock up but don't have a plan for it, put it into the freezer right away instead of letting it slowly age in the fridge.
- Set a reminder for yourself to cook it a few days before its best-by date, like "Roast the chicken on Friday!" using your phone, a wall calendar, a whiteboard on your fridge, or whatever works best for you. If life gets in the way and Friday roast chicken doesn't happen, use your reminder to take 30 seconds to move the raw chicken into the freezer instead.

Extra Bits

Many typically discarded bits of meat and seafood can be saved for other uses. Chefs will never let bacon fat, chicken skin, fish heads, or meat bones go to waste, and neither should you.

- Cook chicken or fish skin in a well-oiled pan until crispy, then dust with salt. Eat straight like potato chips, use as a crunchy garnish for soup or salad, or wedge into a sandwich.
- Save bacon or chicken fat by straining it through a paper coffee filter, then storing in the refrigerator for use as a cooking fat. We're particular fans of bacon or chicken fat fried rice with **Ginger-Scallion Lettuce Sauce** (page 92).
- All meat bones and skin—raw or cooked—can go into your **Kitchen Scrap Stock Bag** (page 18).
- Keep a separate bag in the freezer for shrimp or lobster shells and fish bones. Once you've accumulated a few cups' worth, you can make **Seafood Stock** by sautéing the shells and/or bones in extra-virgin olive oil or butter along with a diced onion or two and a few diced carrots and celery stalks. Cook until the vegetables are soft and lightly browned, then add about 6 cups water, maybe a generous splash of white wine, and bay leaves and/or herb sprigs like thyme or parsley. Bring to a boil, lower the heat, and simmer for about an hour, then season with salt and pepper to taste. Once strained, this stock makes an excellent base for **Noodle Soup How You Want It** (page 50) or **Corn Chowder** (page 126).

Use-It-Up Ideas

Repurposing cooked proteins keeps dinner interesting and ensures none of your pricey meat goes to waste. Roast a chicken and put the leftovers into quesadillas, salads, and noodles. Scatter sausage crumbles on top of a savory tart or mix pulled pork into your baked pasta. The following recipes in this book welcome many types of leftover cooked meat:

- Bubble and Squeak (page 207)
- Any-Root-Vegetable Hash (page 203)
- Easygoing Tomato Sauce (page 104)
- Savory Bread Pudding (page 78)
- Leafy Greens Salad Builder (page 155)
- Fridge-Forage Baked Pasta (page 70)
- Rice Fritters (page 64)
- Grain Salad (page 162)

Try any of the following for your leftover cooked fish:

- Gently heat in a skillet and then make fish tacos or burritos.
- Add flakes of cooked fish to **Corn Chowder** (page 126).
- Add to **Fried Rice** (page 62) just at the end to rewarm.
- Stir into **Anything-in-the-Kitchen Pasta** (page 68) right before serving.
- Eat cold or room temperature on top of a salad or a grain bowl.

Pick-Your-Protein Salad

Serves 2

It's easy to make chicken salad, egg salad, or tuna (or another fish) salad with your leftovers and a few items foraged from the fridge. An ample spoonful on crusty buttered bread scores highly on both the deliciousness scale and ease factor, while ensuring none of your proteins go to waste. Feel free to experiment with other dairy products like sour cream or yogurt or a combination; swap the capers for olives or pickles; use up any fresh herb in the house.

NOTE: *This recipe can easily be scaled up or down depending on your taste and the amount of leftovers you need to use up.*

2 cups cooked chicken, eggs, or fish, chopped or flaked into small pieces
¼ cup mayonnaise, or more to taste
2 tablespoons minced allium of your choice, such as red onion, shallot, scallions, or chives
1 tablespoon capers, roughly chopped
1 tablespoon chopped fresh dill or parsley, or another tender herb of choice
Kosher salt and freshly ground black pepper
Several dashes mustard or hot sauce, or a squeeze of lemon (optional)

(continues)

Mix the protein of your choice, mayonnaise, minced allium, capers, and herbs in a medium bowl until thoroughly combined. Taste and add salt and pepper as needed, along with any other flavorings of your choice.

For an excellent way to use up the leftovers of a flavorful fish like salmon or a smoked fish like trout or mackerel, make a **Fish Pâté**. Simply swap the mayonnaise for double the amount of cream cheese. It makes for a luxurious breakfast, an impressive homemade appetizer, or a fancy-schmancy riff on a tuna fish sandwich lunch.

PROTEIN: PICK ONE
EGGS:
A GOOD CHOICE TO ASSURE NO ONE SITS NEXT TO YOU ON PUBLIC TRANSPORT
CHICKEN
FISH
DRESSING: PICK ONE (OR TWO)
YOGURT
PLAIN
(UNLESS YOU'RE GOING EXTREME ON THE USE IT UP MISSION AND ARE VENTURING INTO THE UNCHARTED AND NOT RECOMMEND TERRITORY OF SWEET EGG SALAD)
CREAM CHEESE
MAYO
FEAR NOT OUR LACTOSE INTOLERANT SALAD MAKERS
SOUR CREAM
PIZZAZZ!
AS MANY AS YOU WANT!
CAPERS
PICKLES
OLIVES
ONION
IF YOU NEED A GOOD CRY
SHALLOT
SCALLION
CHIVES
HERBS
TOASTED BUT NOT SO CRUNCHY THAT THEY'RE SCRAPING WEAPONS

Fish (or Shrimp, or Crab, or any Leftover Seafood) Cakes

Makes 6 fish cakes

Leftover fish or shellfish often stymies people. It doesn't reheat as well as cooked meat, so we often get questions about how to use it up. Thankfully, there are fish cakes (or crab cakes or shrimp cakes or insert-water-dwelling-protein-of-choice cakes), which don't try to emulate last night's dinner at all. Instead, they go for crunch and dippability, two qualities we adore, and make it way more fun to eat leftovers. This ingredient list is merely a starting point; from here, we like to poke around in the fridge door and add a squirt of mustard or spoonful of capers as the mood strikes. Almond flour or leftover mashed potatoes can serve as a stand-in for the breadcrumbs.

1 pound simply cooked fish or shellfish (about 2 cups, broken into flakes or chopped into pieces)

½ cup Toasted Breadcrumbs (page 80) or panko

2 eggs

¼ cup thinly sliced or diced allium of your choice (we like scallions or chives, but shallots or onions are an easy alternative)

¼ cup mayonnaise or sour cream

Kosher salt and freshly ground black pepper

Neutral oil, for frying

Lemon wedges, for serving

Herby Ranch (page 141) or Creamy Green Dip (page 140), for serving

In a medium bowl, combine the fish, breadcrumbs, eggs, allium, mayo, and any add-ins of your choice and gently fold all the ingredients together with a generous pinch of salt and a few grinds of pepper. Form into 6 small patties, about the size of your palm; if you find them too wet, add some more breadcrumbs or a teaspoon of flour. If they seem dry, add a spoonful more mayonnaise.

Heat a thin layer of oil in a large skillet over medium heat and fry the patties until browned, 3 to 5 minutes on each side. Sprinkle with salt right after frying and serve with lemon wedges and lots of dip. Store leftovers in the fridge in an airtight container—they reheat well and make an easy protein-rich topping for a simple salad or rice bowl.

There are so many ways to dress up these fishcakes. Forage in the crisper drawer for some diced celery or bell peppers, wade through the spice cabinet for a sprinkle of paprika or Old Bay seasoning, check your condiments section for something unconventional like kimchi or sauerkraut, and you can never go wrong with any chopped fresh tender herb.

Four-Ingredient Meatballls

WITH MEI

Serves 4

We're big meatball eaters in my house. Meatballs are beloved by my children, they're an easy source of protein, and they're an excellent last-minute dish when you have random jars of use-it-up sauces in the fridge. If you've made any savory sauces from odds and ends, especially anything with herbs or alliums, congratulations! You now have instant homemade flavor to add to your meatballs and can be 10 minutes away from eating. (If you don't have any sauces made, just add some salt, which you may want anyway depending on how strongly your sauce is seasoned.) Of course, you can always add extra herbs, spices, or flavorings from black pepper to ground cumin to grated Parmesan. Serve with rice or pasta, add to a stew or soup, and freeze any leftovers for future meals.

1 pound ground meat of any kind (we like pork or beef, but chicken or turkey will work, as will fish or shrimp)

½ cup Toasted Breadcrumbs (page 80) or panko

1 egg

¼ cup Green Sauce (page 138), Ginger-Scallion Lettuce Sauce (page 92), or Sofrito (page 89)

Kosher salt (optional)

Turn your broiler on high with the top oven rack about 6 inches away. (If you prefer not to broil, you can pan-fry the meatballs in oil until browned on all sides, maybe with some Easygoing Tomato Sauce, page 104.)

Combine the meat, breadcrumbs, egg, and sauce of choice in a medium bowl. Fry or microwave a tiny piece to check for seasoning and salt to taste. Roll into roughly 1-inch balls and place on a rimmed baking sheet. Broil for 6 to 8 minutes, until lightly browned and cooked through, flipping them with tongs or shaking the sheet every so often so they cook evenly.

Eggs, Beans, and Tofu

IDEAS AND RECIPES

Vegetarian proteins have a relatively long shelf life, so they're particularly useful to have on hand to help round out a meal. Beans and tofu can add heft to nearly any dish in the Vegetables section, and we are firm believers in the widespread applicability of the mantra "put an egg on it," whether poached, scrambled, or fried. Then, when you've got just a bit left to use up, you could make Any-Bean Dip (page 306) with that open can of beans, or whip up a Soy-Garlic Tofu Sauce (page 304) with the half-consumed tofu package sitting in the fridge. And if you ever have a full container of eggs right before you go on vacation for two weeks, use them all up in one tasty swoop with a big Sheet Pan Frittata (page 308), then pop individual portions into the freezer to await your return.

Store It Right

Eggs have a longer shelf life than you might think, and given their unbeatable versatility, they're always easy to use up (name us another ingredient that goes well with every single vegetable *and* chocolate cake!). Store eggs in the main part of the refrigerator where it's coldest and they will generally stay fresh for a month past the sell-by date on the carton, if not more.

Dried beans will last indefinitely in an airtight container in a cool, dark place. The only issue with years-old beans is they can take longer to soften, so consider using a pressure cooker or be prepared to wait. Canned beans also have an extremely long shelf life, lasting years in the pantry. Once opened, transfer the beans and their liquid to an airtight container in the refrigerator (if you don't have enough liquid, you can cover them with water) and keep for up to 5 days, if not longer.

Keep tofu in its original package and store in the refrigerator, unless you purchased a shelf-stable carton, which can be kept in the pantry. Once opened, store any remaining tofu in a new airtight container, submerged in water. Change the water daily, and it should last for up to 5 days, if not more. Need something to do with a small amount of leftover tofu? Check out pages 303–4.

Save for Later

Did you know you can freeze tofu? Interestingly, freezing does more than just save it for later; the water inside expands as it freezes so it flows out easily once thawed, leaving your tofu firmer and ready to soak up more flavor. Freeze it straight in its original package or drain, slice, and store in an airtight container for quicker defrosting.

Cooked or canned beans can be frozen in their liquid in an airtight container, but remember to leave room for the liquid to expand. Bean dishes with lots of moisture, like chili and soup, freeze well.

To freeze whole eggs, remove them from the shell, beat lightly, and store in an airtight container. Egg whites can be frozen as is; yolks need to be beaten with a pinch of salt or simple syrup to stay smooth when they return to room temperature.

You Can Still Eat It!

If you're not sure about tofu or beans that have been in the fridge for a while, and there's no visible mold or strong discoloration, give it a smell. Discard if you get a whiff of sour or rotten odors; if you're not sure, taste a bit and see. And if you don't think you'll get to it in time, freeze it.

Extra Bits

Did you know that the liquid in a can of chickpeas, known as aquafaba, can be whipped into a foam to make a vegan meringue or an egg-free binder for baked goods? Our favorite use is in a **Garlicky Vegan Mayo**—combine ¼ cup aquafaba, 1 teaspoon vinegar, 1 teaspoon lemon juice, 1 teaspoon miso, ½ teaspoon garlic powder, and a large pinch of salt in a tall jar. Blend with an immersion blender, then keep the blender running with one hand while slowly drizzling in ¾ cup neutral oil with the other hand. Don't rush; just move the blender up and down every so often to incorporate the oil so it thickens up; the whole drizzling process should take a minute or two. Taste, adjust with salt and lemon, and smear on sandwiches and roasted vegetables and anything else you can think of—it's so good you may have trouble not just spooning it out of the jar.

Use-It-Up Ideas

- **Crispy Baked Tofu Bites** are a great way to use up a block of tofu and make an easy protein add-on for any number of meals. Wrap a 14- to-16-ounce block of tofu in a clean kitchen cloth or paper towel and put something heavy on top (we use a cast-iron skillet) for 10 minutes to press out the water, then cut the block into bite-size cubes. Whisk 1 tablespoon each neutral oil and soy sauce in a large bowl, then add the tofu cubes and toss gently to coat. Sprinkle with salt and 2 tablespoons cornstarch, plus any spices you like, and toss again until the cubes are lightly coated. Spread out on a rimmed baking sheet and bake at 450 degrees for 20 to 25 minutes, until lightly browned and crisp. Pop them onto a grain or rice bowl, toss them in a salad, mix them into noodles, or just eat them straight. They'll keep well in an airtight container for tomorrow's lunch, and a few days after that.

- If you ever need to use up a bit of extra tofu in the fridge, mix it into a sauce or dressing. It's perfect for vegan eaters or anyone looking for a protein alternative, or if you just want simple new sauce options in your life. Silken tofu blends smoothly, whereas firm tofu will give you a thicker, grainier version, so add more liquid if you want a lighter sauce.
    - Make a **Soy-Garlic Tofu Sauce** by blending ½ (14- to-16-ounce) block tofu, 1 garlic clove, 1 tablespoon soy sauce, 2 teaspoons toasted sesame oil, 1 teaspoon vinegar, and a pinch each sugar and salt. Taste and tinker until you find the right balance of flavors, then drizzle on noodles or roasted vegetables.
    - Use silken tofu in place of the mayonnaise or dairy in **Herby Ranch** (page 141), **Caper-Mayo Dressing** (page 167), or **Creamy Green Dip** (page 140).
    - Blitz a bit of silken tofu with **Ginger-Scallion Lettuce Sauce** (page 92) for a smooth dip.
    - Swap out half the beans in **Any-Bean Dip** (see below) for firm tofu.
    - Blend a little silken tofu into **Nut Butter Sauce** (page 318).
- If you ever find yourself with half a can of beans in the fridge, make **Any-Bean Dip**. You can make a deliciously savory spread whether you have chickpeas, black beans, or white beans, aiming for a texture similar to hummus. (As our friend Reem Assil writes in her beautiful cookbook *Arabiyya, hummus* means "chickpea" in Arabic so "if it don't got chickpeas, it ain't hummus.") Break out your blender or food processor and put in the half can of beans (drained and rinsed), a small garlic clove, 2 tablespoons

ice-cold water, 2 tablespoons tahini, 1 tablespoon lemon juice, and a pinch of kosher salt. Blitz to a smooth puree, then adjust to taste with more salt and lemon and serve drizzled with good extra-virgin olive oil and sprinkled with chopped fresh herbs or toasted nuts. Double the recipe if you want to make it with a full can of beans, quadruple if you want enough dip for a crowd.

SWITCH IT UP

- You can never go wrong with a **Garlicky Bean Dip**. Use ½ cup Garlic Confit (page 90) in place of the raw clove, and Garlic Oil (page 90) in place of the olive oil.
- Get rid of your leftovers by pureeing them into a **Roasted Veggie Dip**! Add ½ to 1 cup sliced or diced roasted vegetables, such as broccoli, sweet potatoes, or beets with the beans, then increase the olive oil and salt as desired to taste.

- **Leftover Bean Soup** might be the fastest soup of all time, whether made from the heirloom beans you cooked yesterday or the half bag of frozen peas that's been sitting at the back of your freezer for months. Sauté a small diced onion in butter or oil in a medium pot over medium heat until softened, then add 1 cup cooked beans or frozen peas and 2 cups any kind of stock. Bring to a boil, then let simmer until the legumes are tender and cooked through, about 5 minutes. Puree using your choice of blender (remember to let the steam escape if using a regular blender), then add salt to taste. Garnish with your choice of toppings—perhaps a swirl of something creamy like plain yogurt or sour cream, maybe something crunchy like **Toasted Breadcrumbs** (page 80) or crushed tortilla chips, or what about a squeeze of lemon or a splash of fancy vinegar? This soup freezes very well in an airtight container (don't forget to leave enough room for the liquid to expand).

Sheet Pan Frittata

Serves 4

Frittatas love all your cheese ends and random condiments, from olive tapenade to herby Green Sauce (page 138) to that jar of artichoke hearts you opened and then pushed to the back of the fridge. And unlike stovetop frittatas, which require careful monitoring, this one gets popped into the oven and ignored. Using a sheet pan also allows for a lot of surface area, meaning that you can customize different sections for different members of the family. As long as you've got enough eggs, the rest of the meal is up to you.

8 eggs (or more, if you'd like to scale up)

Milk, cream, or another dairy product of your choice (optional)

Kosher salt and freshly ground pepper

2 cups filling of your choice, cut into bite-size pieces, such as cooked vegetables, leftover meat, bits of cheese, etc.

¼ cup chopped fresh tender herbs (optional)

Heat the oven to 400 degrees. Lightly spray a rimmed baking sheet or 9 x 13-inch baking dish with nonstick spray or lightly grease with neutral oil. If you have parchment paper, spread a piece over the pan and lightly grease again to make it even easier to lift the frittata out after baking.

Crack the eggs into a large bowl and add a splash of dairy if you like and a large pinch of salt, then whisk to combine.

Scatter your filling across the prepared baking sheet along with half the herbs, if using, then pour the eggs on top. If your eggs don't completely cover the pan, whisk another egg and add it to the mix. Bake until the frittata is just set in the middle, usually 12 to 15 minutes, but it depends on the size and depth of your frittata. Slice and serve hot with the remaining herbs sprinkled on top. Leftovers can be stored in an airtight container in the fridge for up to 4 days and make fabulous frittata sandwiches.

Baked Beans with Whatever You Have

Serves 4 to 6

In our family this is called Hammy Baked Beans since it's perfect to use up the remnants of a big holiday ham, but please feel free to change "hammy" to "cheesy" or even to "vegan." The garlicky oil, infused with as many cloves as you like, more than makes up for the omission of meat or cheese, and you can always add flavor boosters like olives or nutritional yeast. Stir in chopped hearty greens like kale or spinach to get your greens in or use up some chopped alliums or leftover cooked vegetables. Our preference here is a white bean like cannellini or great northern, but you can substitute any bean you want. And while a good melty cheese like mozzarella makes this dish acceptably pizza-like to Mei's kids, use whatever you have in the fridge. We also greatly enjoy scattering the remnants of a cheese board across the top and broiling it to a toasty brown cheese celebration.

¼ cup extra-virgin olive oil or Garlic Oil (page 90)

4 to 6 garlic cloves, thinly sliced

1½ cups chopped ham, cooked bacon, or another meat of your choice (optional)

2 (15-ounce) cans white beans, rinsed and drained

1 (14-ounce) can diced or crushed tomatoes and juice (or whole, and crush them yourself)

Kosher salt and freshly ground black pepper

1 cup shredded or crumbled cheese of your choice

(continues)

Heat the oven to 400 degrees.

Heat the oil in a large oven-safe skillet over medium heat. Add the garlic and ham (if using) and cook for a few minutes, letting the garlic soften and the ham fry a bit, then add the beans, tomatoes, a good pinch of salt, and a few grinds of black pepper. Stir to combine, then transfer to the oven and bake for about 40 minutes. Switch the oven over to the broiler setting, sprinkle the top of the beans with the cheese, and return to the oven for a few minutes, until the top is bubbling and golden brown. (If you're crunched for time, you can sprinkle on the cheese before baking, crank the oven up to 475, and bake for about 15 minutes total, but we like the way the beans soften up during a longer bake.) Leftovers keep in an airtight container for up to 5 days—we like them warmed in a pan with a bit of oil, then served over eggs or folded into a taco.

Braised Tofu with Mushrooms and Leftover Greens

WITH MEI

Serves 4

This dish reimagines our mom's favorite restaurant tofu dish, hongshao doufu, in which I always want to eat the bouncy, fragrant, umami-rich tofu wedges and rarely want to eat any of the less exciting vegetables. Since I'm in charge here, I like to add mushrooms and clear the fridge of leftover vegetables, whether that's roasted broccoli or charred cabbage or Braised Greens (page 173). Include all the bits *you* want, so you're not the one picking out all the good parts and hoping your mom won't notice.

1 (14- to 16-ounce) block firm tofu
1½ cups stock of your choice
2 tablespoons soy sauce
1 tablespoon oyster sauce or vegetarian stir-fry sauce
1 tablespoon Shaoxing wine (or dry sherry, in a pinch)
½ teaspoon sugar
Kosher salt
2 tablespoons neutral oil (or something flavorful, like bacon fat)
½ cup torn mushrooms of your choice
2 garlic cloves, minced
1 to 2 cups mixed cooked or raw greens or other vegetables, cut into bite-size pieces
1 tablespoon cornstarch whisked with 1 tablespoon water (optional)
Steamed white rice, cooked noodles, or other grain, for serving

---

(continues)

Wrap the tofu in a clean kitchen towel or paper towels and place a large skillet on top (ideally one that you can then use for cooking). Let the water drain out for at least 10 minutes or up to an hour.

Meanwhile, mix together the stock, soy sauce, oyster sauce, Shaoxing wine, sugar, and a small pinch of salt in a medium bowl and set aside.

Cut the drained tofu lengthwise into slices about the thickness of your finger, then crosswise into bite-size pieces. Heat the oil in the skillet over medium-high heat until it starts to shimmer. Add the tofu in a single layer and sprinkle with a layer of salt. Fry until the bottoms are lightly brown, about 2 minutes, then flip, sprinkle again with salt, and lightly brown the other side, another 2 minutes. Gently push the tofu to the side and add the mushrooms. Stir-fry for 2 to 3 minutes, until the mushrooms are lightly oiled and softened, then add the garlic and stir-fry for 30 seconds or so.

Add the sauce mixture and bring to a boil, then lower the heat to medium and let the mixture simmer for 5 minutes before adding the vegetables. If you're using cooked leftovers from the fridge, they need only a minute or two to warm up. If you're using raw vegetables, give them an extra few minutes to cook.

At this point, you may be happy with the dish, or you may want a thicker sauce like the way the dish is often made in restaurants. If you want to thicken it, slowly drizzle in the cornstarch mixture while stirring until the sauce reaches the texture you're looking for. Serve with rice, noodles, or other grains.

If you don't have leftover vegetables that would go well here, substitute the quick-cooking vegetables of your choice, such as thinly sliced sugar snap peas and chopped kale.

Nuts and Seeds

IDEAS AND RECIPES

Tree nuts, peanuts, and seeds offer flavor, crunch, and a generous boost of protein, all in one easy sprinkle. Whether raw or toasted, salted or candied, they can be used in all types of sweet and savory dishes. With their relatively long shelf life, nuts and seeds typically play a valuable supporting role in helping you use up other food rather than being something you need to use up. But every so often we'll go overboard in the bulk bin aisle or forget about a container in the back of the pantry, so it's good to have some flexible recipes on hand for using up nuts and seeds.

NUT OR NOT A NUT?

Know What You Got

- **Common tree nuts** include almonds, cashews, hazelnuts, pecans, pistachios, walnuts, Brazil nuts, and macadamia nuts.
- **Peanuts** are generally considered a nut, but are actually part of the legume family. (This is why some people are allergic to peanuts but not tree nuts, and vice versa.)
- **Seeds** used in cooking and eating include flax seeds, sesame seeds, pine nuts (technically a seed, sometimes considered a tree nut), pumpkin seeds, sunflower seeds, hemp seeds, and chia seeds.

Store It Right

Store nuts and seeds in airtight containers in a dark pantry if you think you'll use them up within a few months. Stick on a piece of tape labeled with the date you opened the container as a reminder. For an even longer shelf life, store in the refrigerator or even the freezer. All nuts and seeds will keep the longest when whole, so hold off on grinding, chopping, or shelling until right before using.

Use-It-Up Ideas

- If you need to use up a bunch of nuts or seeds, try sprinkling on top of any **Leafy Greens Salad** (page 160) or **Simple (Yet Infinitely Adaptable) Herb Salad** (page 145), garnishing any soup or stew for extra flavor or crunch, or blitzing into **Green Sauce** (page 138) for a variation on pesto.
- Use up random nuts in place of breadcrumbs to make extra-crunchy gluten-free **Nut-Crusted Chicken Tenders**. Finely crush 1 cup nuts of your choice and scatter them on a shallow plate or tray. Put 1 pound boneless, skinless chicken tenders (or breasts, cut lengthwise into strips) in a bowl, sprinkle with kosher

salt, and add a large spoonful of mayonnaise, stirring to evenly coat the tenders. Coat each tender with the nuts, pressing lightly so they stick, then transfer the tenders to a foil- or parchment-lined baking sheet. Bake at 450 degrees until golden brown on one side, 6 to 8 minutes, then carefully flip over all the tenders and continue to cook until the other side is browned, another 6 to 8 minutes. Serve with the dipping sauce of your choice, like **Herby Ranch** (page 141).

- Transform plain nuts and seeds into **Spiced Candied Nuts and Seeds** and they'll become the first thing you pluck off the pantry shelf at snacktime. Mix 2 cups assorted nuts and seeds with ¼ cup maple or agave syrup, 1 tablespoon extra-virgin olive oil or melted butter, and a pinch of salt (if you don't have any sweet syrup but you do have an egg white to use up, whisk it until frothy and mix with ¼ cup sugar for an equally sticky nut coating). From there, spice it up according to your taste buds and the contents of your cabinet—we like 1 or 2 teaspoons of something spicy like cayenne, chili flakes, or chili powder and ½ teaspoon of something more flavorful such as ground allspice, cumin, ginger, or garlic powder. Toss so the nuts are evenly coated, transfer to a rimmed baking sheet lined with parchment or a silicone baking mat (scraping candied sugar off your bakeware is no fun), and bake at 350 degrees for 15 minutes. Give the nuts a stir, using a spatula to recoat the nuts in any syrup that has pooled at the bottom. Return to the oven for 2 to 10 minutes, until the nuts are nicely toasted and the syrup has hardened to a candy coating. Set them out for cocktail hour, let cool and package them up for gifts, add them to your breakfast yogurt, or snatch them straight off the baking sheet still warm from the oven.

Nut Butter

For each cup of nuts, you get about ½ cup nut butter

I'm generally more of a nut butter buyer than a nut butter maker, but every so often I end up with a surplus of nuts in the pantry (I say this as if I wasn't the one to put all the ginormous containers in the Costco cart myself) and it's time to get down to business. Nut butter is a glorious way to transform just about any nut into an irresistible and easily consumable snack, whether smeared onto apple slices for kids or whisked into a noodle sauce for dinner (see below). Toast them up beforehand to add richness and complexity (even already roasted nuts benefit from a few minutes in the oven, a great tip from chef and food writer Sohla El-Waylly), add whatever sweeteners or flavorings as you like, and you might find yourself eating it out of the jar with a spoon.

At least 1 cup nuts, but ideally 2 or 3
Pinch kosher salt
Flavorings of your choice, including sweeteners such as honey or maple syrup and add-ins such as coconut flakes or chocolate chips

---

Heat the oven to 350 degrees.

Spread the nuts on a rimmed baking sheet. If you're working with raw nuts, bake for 15 to 20 minutes, tossing halfway through. You want the nuts to be golden brown and toasted all over—the toastiness should waft out of the oven when you open the door to check—but don't overdo it. It's better to undertoast than burn! If you have already roasted nuts, bake for 5 to 10 minutes to warm them up and make blending easier. Remove from the oven and let cool until they're just the slightest bit warm. If the nuts have skins, which can be bitter, put the nuts on a clean kitchen towel, gather up the corners, and shake/rub the towel to dislodge some of the skins.

(continues)

Transfer the nuts to a food processor and puree until smooth, which can vary quite a bit depending on the type and amount of nuts as well as the strength of your food processor. Softer cashews and walnuts might take 5 minutes, while almonds could require 10 or more, so let the processor take its time. Scrape down the sides with a spatula when needed, pause the motor for a few minutes if it gets too hot, and allow the lovely smooth nut butter to emerge from the crumbs. Season to taste with a pinch of salt and the sweeteners or add-ins of your choice. Store in an airtight container in the fridge for a few months or in the pantry for a few weeks.

MAKE IT A MEAL

Make **Nut Butter Sauce** by whisking 3 tablespoons nut butter with 2 tablespoons soy sauce, 1½ tablespoons vinegar or lime juice, 1 tablespoon water, and 1 teaspoon toasted sesame oil. Tinker with the saltiness and acidity as different brands and taste preferences make a big difference here. You can always whisk in more water if it gets too strong. I like to eyeball the amounts and pour everything into a near-empty peanut butter jar, then give it a good shake to clear out the last bits of peanut butter. The sauce is great on noodles, rice, eggs, and roasted veggies, and particularly perfect with Freestyle Vegetable Summer Rolls (page 44).

NUT BUTTER
1 CUP NUTS = 1/2 CUP BUTTER
BAKE UNTIL TOASTY
SHAKE IN A CLEAN TOWEL TO REMOVE SKINS
YOU WILL INEVITABLY FIND SKINS ON YOU THE REST OF THE DAY
FOR THE TOUGH NUTS: 10+ MINUTES ALMONDS
FOR THE SOFTIES: QUICK+EASY 5 MINUTES CASHEWS WALNUTS
BLEND 'TIL YOUR CRUNCHY ↔ CREAMY SWEET SPOT
BE SURE TO LET YOUR FOOD PROCESSOR COOL DOWN IF IT GETS SUPER HOT BECAUSE WE ALL DESERVE REST SOMETIMES!
NOODLE SAUCE
APPLE SNACK
ON TOAST

Clear-Out-the-Pantry Granola

WITH MEI

Makes about 8 cups

My son's first food obsession was granola, which he referred to as "nut" and requested with milk every morning for a solid year of his life. Specifically, he loves Nekisia Davis's phenomenal Olive Oil and Maple Granola from *Food52 Genius Recipes* cookbook, a widely popular and dearly beloved recipe across the Food52 community. It's the only granola I make, but it's slightly different every time because I use it as an opportunity to clear the pantry of all the random nuts, seeds, and dried fruits that I regularly buy and forget about. I've tweaked it to accommodate for this improvisation, in case you have extra sunflower seeds or you really love walnuts. The only essentials are the oats, olive oil, maple syrup, and brown sugar, plus a pinch of salt, although you're welcome to try a different oil or sweetener like agave or honey. I usually double the recipe because everyone in my house loves it so much, but if you don't have daily granola eaters in your house, it makes a great gift.

NOTE: *I've included weights so you can easily add everything in one bowl, if you have a digital scale. Save yourself from washing all your measuring cups!*

3 cups (300g) old-fashioned oats

1½ to 2 cups (130 to 210g) larger seeds, grains, or kernels, like sunflower kernels or pumpkin seeds

1½ to 2 cups (150 to 200g) chopped or whole nuts of any kind, or a mix

¼ cup (35g) smaller seeds or grains like flax, chia, or sesame (optional)

¾ cup (180g) good maple syrup

½ cup (80g) extra-virgin olive oil

½ cup (110g) packed brown sugar

1 teaspoon (5 g) kosher salt

1 cup dried fruit of any kind and/or 1 cup chocolate chips or cacao nibs (optional)

Heat the oven to 300 degrees. Line a rimmed baking sheet with parchment or a silicone baking mat.

Mix all the ingredients together in a large bowl, saving any dried fruit or chocolate chips for the end. Spread onto the prepared baking sheet and bake for 40 to 50 minutes, until the granola is toasty brown and your whole kitchen smells amazing. If you want, you can stir every 15 minutes, but I don't usually bother because (1) I like the way it clumps together when I leave it alone and (2) it's kind of a pain and I end up knocking granola all over the inside of my oven.

Let cool slightly before stirring in any additional ingredients. Store in an airtight container for up to a month.

Whatever-You've-Got Nut Sauce

Makes about 1 cup

One of our favorite uses for raw nuts is this smooth and almost creamy sauce—it's fantastic spooned onto pasta, swirled into soup, or even put straight into your mouth via a cracker or carrot stick. Cashews are especially popular in this type of vegan sauce, but raw almonds and walnuts also make for a rich, savory, protein-forward option. This recipe scales up easily if you have lots of nuts to use up and acts as a blank canvas to play with your seasonings of choice. Keep it vegan with nutritional yeast or miso, stir in some grated Parmesan, or add any spices you like. We like to toss in a packed cup of whatever tender fresh herbs need to be cleared out of the fridge.

NOTE: *Nut skins can add bitterness, so either use blanched nuts or add extra fat or flavorings to balance out any harshness.*

1 cup raw nuts, such as cashews or walnuts
1 cup boiling water
1 garlic clove, peeled
1 tablespoon extra-virgin olive oil
1 teaspoon vinegar or a squeeze of lemon juice, or more to taste
½ teaspoon salt
1 cup packed fresh tender herbs (optional)

Put the nuts in a heatproof bowl. Pour the boiling water over the nuts, cover with a plate, and let sit for 10 to 15 minutes. Strain the nuts, reserving the soaking liquid to blend into the sauce.

Transfer the nuts and half the soaking liquid to a blender or food processor and add the garlic, olive oil, vinegar, salt, and fresh herbs, if using. Blend until smooth, adding more liquid as desired to reach the consistency of your choice. Keep it thick if you want something scoopable with a potato chip; add more liquid if you want it to coat strands of pasta. Taste and season as desired, sprinkling in more salt or blending in more olive oil for richness or vinegar for brightness.

SWITCH IT UP

- Use stock in place of water, or add in place of the reserved boiling water.
- Stir in Green Sauce (page 138) to make an extra nutty pesto-type sauce.
- Use as a dairy-free substitute for cream.
- Spice it up with chipotle, harissa, chili crisp, or the hot sauce of your choice.
- Thin with more water, oil, and/or vinegar, and drizzle onto roasted vegetables or use as a salad dressing.

Dairy

Dairy products like milk and cheese can sometimes seem challenging from a food waste perspective. It can be hard to find recipes that use up large amounts of yogurt or cottage cheese, and we suspect we're not the only ones to discover a forgotten container of cream cheese hidden in the back of the fridge. But once you get into the use-it-up mindset, you'll find lots of ways to cut down on the number of sour cream tubs and moldy cheese bits in the trash. From freezing and preserving (yes, you can freeze milk and cheese!) to swapping and substituting, we've got tons of ideas and recipes to use up every bit of dairy in your fridge.

Cheese

We love cheese and rarely waste it, based mostly on the following theory: Most dishes will allow you to substitute an entirely different cheese than the one intended and still create a fabulous meal. You can clear your whole cheese drawer with the right Vegetable Hero Recipe! Plus, with a little bit of planning, many cheeses can be cooked, frozen, or otherwise preserved before going off. We also view nearly any cheese measurement with a grain of salt; Parmesan amounts, for example, skew wildly depending on how tightly a cup is packed. What really matters is how much cheese *you* want in the recipe. Leave it out altogether, or double the amounts we suggest—it's all up to you.

Store It Right

Blocks or wedges of cheese will stay fresh longest when wrapped in a breathable material such as cheese paper, beeswax wrap, or parchment paper. Yes, most cheese at the supermarket is wrapped in plastic, but that's so you can see and touch them safely when shopping. Plastic can trap moisture and bacteria inside, so if you're hoping to maximize the life of a fancy cheese you splurged on at the cheese counter, rewrap in paper and use your trusty permanent marker and painter's tape to seal and label with the name and date. You can then stash it inside a resealable bag or wrap it in foil and store in the crisper or deli drawer of your fridge. To keep it the longest, wrap in new paper each time you take it out (we rarely do this, but we also don't let cheese hang around too long).

Shredded or sliced cheeses can generally be kept in their original wrapping (press the air out before resealing) in the fridge, as can wet cheeses like fresh mozzarella or ricotta.

Put **very stinky cheeses** in their own airtight container in the fridge to avoid smells getting picked up by other foods.

Save for Later

Despite what some people say, you can freeze cheese, but you should plan to cook the cheese once thawed as it may change texture or dry out. And freezing works best for average cheese, not your favorite fancy cheese, so splurge only on small amounts. Shredded cheese can be frozen as is, in a freezer bag with the air pressed out. Blocks or wedges of cheese should be chopped or grated first. Save the rinds of hard cheeses and pop them into your Kitchen Scrap Stock Bag (page 18) or straight into a soup, stew, or pot of beans to add more flavor.

You Can Still Eat It!

Hard cheeses can last for ages, sometimes months, depending on the type. A bit of mold isn't an immediate death sentence; cut off the mold and at least ½ inch beyond and save the rest.

Soft cheeses have shorter shelf lives; if you get mold on a soft cheese, it's generally wiser to discard (unless of course it's deliberately moldy, like a blue cheese, in which case mold should be celebrated and consumed with abandon).

Use-It-Up Ideas

- If we ever notice cheese hanging out in the fridge for too long, it's time to put together a dish that can take a flexible amount of mixed cheeses. Beyond the classics such as grilled cheese sandwiches, quesadillas, and omelets, consider any of the following cheese use-up recipes:
    - Fridge-Forage Baked Pasta (page 70)
    - Savory Bread Pudding (page 78)
    - Sheet Pan Frittata (page 308)
    - Baked Beans with Whatever You Have (page 309)
    - Anything-You-Like Galette (page 72)

- Use up soft spreadable cheeses like ricotta, feta, and cream cheese by whizzing them into **Cheese Dip**. Put the cheese in a food processor or large bowl (it may help to let it soften at room temperature for a while, especially with cream cheese). Add a spoonful of a thick dairy product such as sour cream or yogurt to help thin it out, or a splash of extra-virgin olive oil. Pulse to process or use a wooden spoon to break up the cheese and mix. From there, season as you like with chopped fresh herbs or a sprinkle of spices, plus a squeeze of lime or lemon. Salt and pepper to taste and use as a dip for raw vegetables or crackers, a schmear for sandwiches, or a base for an **Anything-You-Like Galette** (page 72).
- **Marinating** is a great way to extend the life of a medium–firm cheese or punch up the flavor of a mild cheese. Logs of goat cheese, balls of mozzarella, and blocks of feta are all perfectly primed for a new home in a jar of flavored oil. Slice the cheese into blocks or rounds and place in a clean jar. Pour over enough extra-virgin olive oil to cover, then add the flavorings of your choice, such as spices, seeds, sturdy herb sprigs, or sliced onions or shallots and store in the fridge.

Any-Cheese Fondue

WITH MEI

Serves 4 to 6

I've been lucky enough to get personalized fondue coaching from my friend Jessica, who lives in Switzerland, along with her Swiss fondue-making partner-in-crime, Roger. While Roger has many opinions on preferred cheeses for fondue (namely Gruyère, Appenzeller, and raclette—Vacherin Fribourgeois being difficult to find at American supermarkets and Emmentaler a bit too soft), he also says that you can add just about any cheese, noting that blue cheese fondue and other seemingly non-traditional options can be found all over Switzerland. Use something hard and flavorful as the base—as Jessica points out, you don't want it to taste like melted plastic—but otherwise feel free to mix in whatever you find in the cheese drawer. As for liquids, a dry white wine is classic, but you could swap for beer, a dry red, an old-school classic like kirsch, or another spirit of your choice. Anything you've found in the fridge and think would be good to eat in hot cheese, such as chunks of crusty bread, boiled potatoes, mushrooms, tomatoes, cubed apple or pear, cold fried chicken . . . it'll work.

1 garlic clove, cut in half, plus more sliced garlic if desired

½ to 1 cup dry white wine (or substitute beer, cider, or another spirit of your choice)

1 tablespoon cornstarch

1 pound hard cheese, grated, such as Gruyère, raclette, or Appenzeller

8 ounces other grated cheese(s) of your choice (optional)

Freshly ground black pepper

Rub the halved garlic clove all over the inside of a medium, heavy-bottomed pot. Add the wine and bring to a simmer over medium heat. (I use a bit more than ½ cup wine to 1 pound cheese, and closer to 1 cup with 1½ pounds cheese.) Most recipes have you discard the cut garlic, but obviously I would never instruct you to waste good garlic—slice it thinly and add it to the wine, plus a few extra sliced cloves if you like.

Meanwhile, sprinkle the cornstarch over the cheese in a large bowl and toss to combine. Add the cheese to the pot, stirring as you go with a wooden spoon or whisk, until all the cheese has been added. Continue to heat and stir constantly, taking the fondue from lumpy and stringy to velvety smooth and bubbling, adjusting with a splash more wine if it's too thick or if your cheese is threatening to curdle. Season with a few grinds of black pepper and eat right away while it's hot and melty, returning it to the stove to heat if it starts to get cold or congeal (or transfer to a fondue pot or burner setup if you want it to last longer). Dip in all the things you like!

NO-WASTE TIPS

Tejal Rao's "Fondue Party" essay in the *New York Times Magazine* offers the brilliant idea of cracking an egg directly into the fondue pot as the fondue is on its last legs, then swiping crusty bread through the browned bits of egg and cheese. Inspired by this glorious combination, I put any leftover fondue in the fridge, reheat it the next day over high heat until browned, then crack an egg over it and lower the heat. Cook until the whites are just set and the yolk is still oozy, and sprinkle with chopped fresh herbs, chili flakes, and some flaky salt and black pepper.

Milk, Cream, Yogurt, and More

Dairy products have an unfortunate habit of going bad fairly quickly, causing great disappointment when you pry open the lid of your artisanal yogurt to find a colorful mold explosion. When dealing with ingredients of shorter shelf life, it's all about finding ways to use them up before they need to be tossed. So our best advice on reducing dairy waste focuses on swaps and substitutes, allowing the new you to freely dollop on yogurt or stir in mascarpone when the old you would have run to the store to buy more sour cream. Get used to adjusting between milk and cream or subbing dairy for coconut milk, for example, and you're more likely to finish off a carton before your grocery money gets poured down the drain.

To get you more comfortable with substituting dairy products, we've put together a (totally nonexhaustive) visual representation showing the lightest to heaviest consistencies, keeping in mind that texture often differs depending on the producer or the style. Consider it a rough guide for the moments when you need to use up a small amount of one dairy product or run out of another in the middle of a recipe. For example, if a recipe requires cream but all you have is milk and sour cream, you could whisk the two (one thin, one very thick) to approximate the texture of the medium-weight cream. Note that many dairy products, including buttermilk, yogurt, sour cream, and crème fraîche, are cultured or soured with acid or bacteria. They can be substituted for the others as long as you don't mind a little tang. Conversely, you can approximate their taste with a squeeze of lemon juice or vinegar into a noncultured product—see more on page 330. Cultured dairy has a tendency to curdle when heated too quickly or at too high a temperature, so heat gently. Dairy with a higher fat content is less likely to curdle.

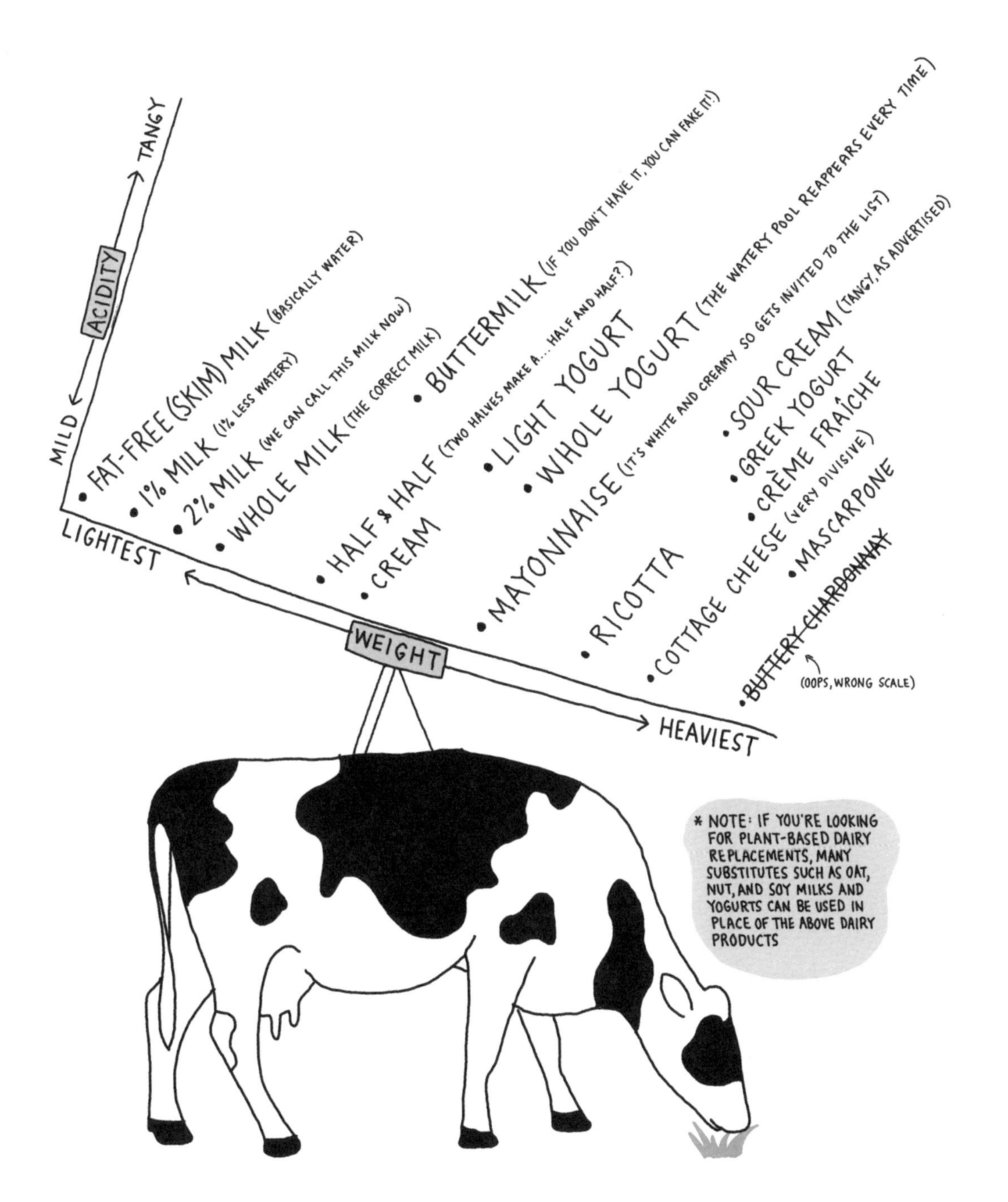

TANGY
ACIDITY
MILD
LIGHTEST
WEIGHT
HEAVIEST
• FAT-FREE (SKIM) MILK (BASICALLY WATER)
• 1% MILK (1% LESS WATERY)
• 2% MILK (WE CAN CALL THIS MILK NOW)
• WHOLE MILK (THE CORRECT MILK)
• BUTTERMILK (IF YOU DON'T HAVE IT, YOU CAN FAKE IT!)
• HALF & HALF (TWO HALVES MAKE A... HALF AND HALF?)
• CREAM
• LIGHT YOGURT
• WHOLE YOGURT (THE WATERY POOL REAPPEARS EVERY TIME)
• MAYONNAISE (IT'S WHITE AND CREAMY SO GETS INVITED TO THE LIST)
• RICOTTA
• SOUR CREAM (TANGY, AS ADVERTISED)
• GREEK YOGURT
• CRÈME FRAÎCHE
• COTTAGE CHEESE (VERY DIVISIVE)
• MASCARPONE
• ~~BUTTERY CHARDONNAY~~
(OOPS, WRONG SCALE)
* NOTE: IF YOU'RE LOOKING FOR PLANT-BASED DAIRY REPLACEMENTS, MANY SUBSTITUTES SUCH AS OAT, NUT, AND SOY MILKS AND YOGURTS CAN BE USED IN PLACE OF THE ABOVE DAIRY PRODUCTS

Store It Right and Save for Later

We view **butter** as nearly indestructible. It isn't, of course, but with a constant rotation of butter from the freezer to the fridge to the counter, we've never had butter go bad yet. We always keep a stick of salted butter at room temperature so it's warm enough to spread on toast; just make sure to use it relatively quickly. Butter in the fridge will keep for several months, and butter in the freezer will last basically forever. Ghee or clarified butter can be stored in the refrigerator or sometimes a cool dark pantry; read the package for instructions.

Milk lasts longer these days than ever before and even comes in shelf-stable cartons, although these should be moved to the refrigerator once opened. Pasteurized milk can be used up to a week after the sell-by date on the package. Try to keep it inside the fridge and not in the door, which is warmer than the rest of the refrigerator. The smell test works well to let you know when milk is past its prime, as does weird clumping when you pour it into coffee. Milk can be frozen for several months (use an airtight container or freeze in ice cube trays and transfer to a resealable bag; we also put cartons straight into the freezer) but may separate if frozen for longer than a few months. You can either blend it to re-emulsify or use it in a cooked dish.

Breaking news: Sour pasteurized milk can be consumed safely! If you're ever on the fence about milk—let's say the smell test is inconclusive—Dana Gunders suggests cooking it into pancakes in *The Waste-Free Kitchen Handbook*. But if it smells terrible or has separated into big clumps or you'd prefer not to for any reason at all (particularly a health sensitivity), discard it.

Half-and-half and cream can both be treated similarly to milk; just keep in mind that cream will often naturally clump due to its high fat content. We personally have no problem with a glob of cream in our coffee—it's like drinking coffee ice cream—but pour it down the drain once it starts to smell funky. Frozen then thawed cream will still whip, but perhaps into less voluminous peaks.

We've just recently found ourselves in a comfortable relationship with **buttermilk**. If you don't have it, you can fake it (see the box below). If you have too much, use up the surplus in lots of different dishes, from baked goods to tonight's dinner. The basic idea: Buttermilk is regular milk with a bit of extra acid. It's typically made these days by culturing milk with bacteria that thickens and sours, helping tenderize both the biscuits and the chicken on your Sunday dinner table. The acidity also activates baking soda, making it a useful ingredient for anything you want leavened, like pancakes.

Thick dairy products such as sour cream, yogurt, cream cheese, and cottage cheese usually last at least a week or more after being opened, and often much longer than the best-by date indicates. Streamlining your shopping can help if you often have too much dairy: Mei used to buy fruity yogurt for the kids as well as plain yogurt for cooking, and never managed to eat it all before it went bad. Now she buys just plain yogurt and mixes it with maple syrup whenever anyone wants sweetened yogurt. Using a clean spoon every time you scoop keeps bad bacteria from being introduced to the carton (and also helps avoid playing the is-that-jam-or-mold game that we always seem to set up for ourselves). All these items can be frozen, although be prepared for some separation into lumps and liquid. You can try to blend them to re-emulsify or use in cooked dishes or baked goods.

(continues)

NO-WASTE TIPS

In the middle of a recipe and realized you don't have any buttermilk? Don't run out to the store! To make a substitute buttermilk, you can either acidify milk or thin down a dairy product that is already cultured, a list that includes yogurt, sour cream, and crème fraîche. To make it with milk, add 1 tablespoon lemon juice or white vinegar to 1 cup milk, half-and-half, or cream, or a combination, depending on how thick you want it. To thin it down, we typically start by whisking equal parts thick cultured dairy product with milk, then adjust as needed.

Given, then, that a bit of acid is welcome in just about any dish, replacing milk with buttermilk just makes for a slightly zingier version of whatever you had before. Here are a few ways to use up buttermilk:

- Buy Samin Nosrat's spectacular cookbook *Salt, Fat, Acid, Heat* and make her buttermilk roast chicken.
- Swap buttermilk for regular milk in Corn Chowder (page 126) or any other soup you like.
- Swap buttermilk for regular milk in Use-It-Up Pancakes (page 232).
- Add it to Herby Ranch (page 141), Green Sauce (page 138), or Fridge-Door Dressing (page 165) to make a creamy and tangy salad dressing.
- Use it as the liquid in your next Smoothie (page 228).
- Whisk it into mayonnaise for a slaw (page 42) or tuna or chicken salad (page 297).
- Use in a baked dish like Fridge-Forage Baked Pasta (page 70) or bread pudding, sweet (page 239) or savory (page 78).

Use-It-Up Ideas

The following dishes can help you use up varied dairy products:

- Use-It-Up Pancakes (page 232)
- Creamy Green Dip (page 140)
- Herby Ranch (page 141)
- Savory Bread Pudding (page 78) or Sweet Bread Pudding (page 239)
- Cream-of-Anything Soup (page 48)
- Cucumber Yogurt Dip (page 112)
- Wine-Braised Chicken and Mushrooms (page 217)
- Fridge-Forage Baked Pasta (page 70)

And the following dishes always welcome a swirl of sour cream or a spoonful of yogurt, as do most soups and stews:

- Anything-in-the-Kitchen Pasta (page 68)
- A Very Flexible Curried Lentil Stew (page 58)
- Toss-in-Any-Vegetable Stew (page 55)
- All-the-Greens Saag Paneer (page 178)
- Mushrooms with Garlic and Toasty Bread (page 216)

Further Reading

Waste and Scraps Ideas

Cooking with Scraps: Turn Your Peels, Cores, Rinds, and Stems into Delicious Meals
Lindsay-Jean Hard

The Waste-Free Kitchen Handbook: A Guide to Eating Well and Saving Money by Wasting Less Food
Dana Gunders

The Zero-Waste Chef: Plant-Forward Recipes and Tips for a Sustainable Kitchen and Planet
Anne-Marie Bonneau

Food and Science Know-How

On Food and Cooking: The Science and Lore of the Kitchen
Keys to Good Cooking: A Guide to Making The Best of Foods and Recipes
Harold McGee

The Food Lab: Better Home Cooking Through Science
The Wok: Recipes and Techniques
J. Kenji López-Alt

Fruit and Vegetable Inspiration

Martha Stewart's Fruit Desserts: 100+ Delicious Ways to Savor the Best of Every Season
Martha Stewart

Ruffage: A Practical Guide to Vegetables
Abra Berens

Six Seasons: A New Way With Vegetables
Joshua McFadden with Martha Holmberg

Vegetable Kingdom: The Abundant World of Vegan Recipes
Bryant Terry

Vegetables Unleashed: A Cookbook
José Andrés and Matt Goulding

Other Cookbooks We Mention, Were Inspired by, or Just Generally Love

Arabiyya: Recipes from the Life of an Arab in Diaspora
Reem Assil

Black Girl Baking: Wholesome Recipes Inspired by a Soulful Upbringing
Jerrelle Guy

Cooking At Home: Or, How I Learned to Stop Worrying about Recipes (and Love My Microwave)
David Chang and Priya Krishna

Dinner for Everyone: 100 Iconic Dishes Made 3 Ways—Easy, Vegan, or Perfect for Company
Mark Bittman

Eating Out Loud: Bold Middle Eastern Flavors for All Day, Every Day
Eden Grinshpan

Food52 Genius Recipes: 100 Recipes That Will Change the Way You Cook
Kristen Miglore

Indian(-ish): Recipes and Antics from a Modern American Family
Priya Krishna with Ritu Krishna

In Pursuit of Flavor: The Beloved Classic Cookbook from the Acclaimed Author of The Taste of Country Cooking
Edna Lewis

The Joy of Seafood: The All-Purpose Seafood Cookbook with More Than 900 Recipes
Barton Seaver

Jubilee: Recipes from Two Centuries of African American Cooking
Toni Tipton-Martin

Madhur Jaffrey's Ultimate Curry Bible
Madhur Jaffrey

My Shanghai: Recipes and Stories from a City on the Water
Betty Liu

Ottolenghi Flavor
Yotam Ottolenghi and Ixta Belfrage

Paella
Alberto Herraiz

Salt, Fat, Acid, Heat: Mastering the Elements of Good Cooking
Samin Nosrat

This Will Make It Taste Good: A New Path to Simple Cooking
Vivian Howard

Zaitoun: Recipes from the Palestinian Kitchen
Yasmin Khan

Acknowledgments

We're endlessly grateful to all the people who helped make this book happen, including all our family and friends who were ready and willing recipe guinea pigs, the many supporters of Mei Mei and *Double Awesome Chinese Food*, the authors and chefs behind so many of our favorite books and restaurants, and all the committed, passionate folks working to improve our food system and take care of our planet.

Thank you to our wonderful agent, Lori Galvin, who believed in us and this message from the very beginning. We're so happy you helped this book find its rightful home.

To Melanie Tortoroli, thank you for your constant support and enthusiasm, and your graciousness and guidance throughout this very very long, even-more-pandemic-elongated process. We could not be more grateful for your sure and knowledgeable hand behind this book.

To Iris Gottlieb, thank you for your incredible artwork and all the belly laughs your commentary has brought to the table. It's an honor to go from fangirls to collaborators. We're so glad to be part of the wonder and beauty and insight that your books and illustrations have brought to the universe.

To Allison Chi, thank you for bringing this book to life in such vibrant and colorful form. Your art direction brings us such joy!

To Karen Wise, thank you for your detailed, thoughtful copyediting and generally making this book so much better (especially the life-changing lemon tip!).

To Annabel Brazaitis, Lauren Abbate, Susan Sanfrey, and everyone else at Norton, thank you all for your hard work in making this book happen!

To Mel Schultz, chief recipe tester and fellow food obsessive, thank you for all the fantastic food you've made, both from this book and from your own mind. Thanks also for the coparenting and compound life—this couldn't have been done without you.

To everyone who tried and tested a recipe, especially Jessica Coughlin and Andrea Weigl, thank you for your incredibly helpful commentary and for helping us clear out our fridges again and again.

Mei

To Leo, thank you for all the extra support at crunch time, washing so many dishes, and helping to make my career and our life happen. Love you all of it.

To my favorite Kira, thank you for eating all the red of the strawberries, yelling "Food Waste Feast" when you finish your plate, and being the best dessert helper and the best dessert eater ever.

To my favorite Lewis, for your love of all smoothies, for always asking "is dis tompost?," for loving the food you love and (ever so slowly) learning to try the food you don't.

To my crew since forever—Jessica, Kellin, Lauren, Lex, and Rachel—thanks for keeping me highly entertained (see Happy Happy Fun Time) and somewhat sane (via The Vibes Are Garbage) from afar. Love you all.

Irene

To my sister Mei, who did basically all the work on this book. To my business partners, Alyssa, Annie, Dylan, and Carla, who do basically all the other work.

To my roommates—husband Chris, who does the laundry and always eats whatever I cook, and cousin Devin, who cooks when I don't feel like it.

Recipe Index

Page numbers in *italics* refer to illustrations.

T

U

V

W

Y

Z

Index

Page numbers in *italics* refer to illustrations.

C

D

E

F

G

H

N

O

P

W

Y

Z